Monty Waldin's
Best Biodynamic Wines

Monty Waldin's
Best Biodynamic Wines

10·v·14

To Victoria,

Best wishes,

Monty Waldin

Floris Books

Published in 2013 by Floris Books

 This book is also available
as an eBook

British Library CIP data available
ISBN 978-086315-960-2

Printed in Poland

To the wine-growers

CONTENTS

PINK OR ROSÉ WINES 120

RED WINES 130

CHAMPAGNE AND OTHER SPARKLING WINES

Preface

When asked how I got into this business, my honest answer is a big nose and lazy temperament make me well suited to a life sniffing wine.

Around age ten I made my first wine at home from tap water, supermarket oranges, supermarket sugar and yeast from the chemist. It was wonderfully unpalatable. I'd been interested in wine before I could drink it, and at secondary school, despite the suggestions of my teachers, I already knew my path wasn't academic. My mind was made up: wine.

Also at a young age I recognised that nature is smarter than humans, and that smart humans who work with nature understand this. My father was one of those humans. He was a teacher and headmaster who grew up during the Great Depression of the 1930s. He told me that when the horse-drawn milk dray arrived in his street, the boys would all try to be first filling their pails with milk. My dad, meanwhile, would run to collect any manure the horse had left and use it to grow tomatoes for the family.

When I was young, he would take me to collect leaf mould for the garden. Leaf mould is just fallen leaves left to decompose over time: a dark, crumbly wild compost if you like. We'd go to a coppice in a field behind our house to find it. We'd fork it into a wheelbarrow, and its earthy, forest-floor smell was even better than fresh-baked bread to me. We'd use leaf mould to feed the soil as compost or as a mulch around plants. Mulching stopped weeds growing and made watering our vegetables and strawberries more efficient, especially in the famously hot British summer of 1976 when I was nine.

I was an enthusiast in the garden, willingly collecting leaf mould and also cow manure. I was not such an enthusiastic student in school, however, and risked failing a crucial French examination. So I was packed off to France for a summer.

11

St-Émilion in Bordeaux, France.

I chose to work for a small château near St-Émilion in Bordeaux, the world's biggest and most prestigious wine region. Instead of studying French, I spent most of my time there reading wine books and examining the local vineyards.

I'd assumed that all wine was grown like our family vegetables. We always had weeds in our home vegetable garden and managed them by leaf-mould mulching. I was surprised to find so few weeds growing around the Bordeaux vines, and stunned to hear they were routinely sprayed off with weedkillers. Yet people were still prepared to pay huge sums for bottles of wine because supposedly the liquid inside spoke of its unique 'terroir' or sense of place. How could you have wines tasting of their place while removing the whole eco-system from the vineyard using herbicides so hazardous you had to wear a mask to spray them?

A few years later in the early 1990s, I began selling wine in London. Our shop listed as many organic wines as possible. It helped that the first rules legally defining organic farming had just been enacted in Europe (in 1992).

Although welcome, these rules implied organics was more about what farmers were *not* allowed to do than what they should or could be doing. Organic farmers could not use chemical herbicides, organophosphate pesticides, soluble fertilizers and plant-penetrating fungicides.

Then in 1993 I returned to work in Bordeaux. Marc Quertinier, a sixty-something oenologist, used to lunch at the chateau where I'd continued to odd-job since my first visit as a schoolboy. Based in Bordeaux, Quertinier had worked with or informally advised almost every top Bordeaux château, winemaker, professor and consultant I'd ever heard of, but in a truly under-the-radar, self-effacing way. He suggested I go and meet Paul Barre in Fronsac (see p. 193). Paul was a biodynamic grower, the first I'd ever met. Marc had heard my ranting about my belief that the more soluble fertilizers and chemical sprays were applied to the grapes, the more additives and other corrective treatments were needed subsequently in the winery.

The winery where I worked was typical of this highly interventionist approach. This did, though, make it a great place to learn, because I got to use almost every 'modern' wine-growing and winemaking tool available. My conclusion was that many of these modern tools were expensive, unnecessary and were not working. Our vines were clearly getting weaker, and the wines were becoming more boring to drink. The chateau was on its way to bankruptcy.

Quertinier knew this. I sensed he agreed with my perhaps rather simplistic notion of letting vines express themselves by working with nature rather than making war on the vines with a different chemical every morning. Our chateau's storeroom was literally overflowing with dilute wines we'd had to pump up artificially yet legally with sugar and colour, but which we still couldn't sell. Despite this, we continued using really expensive soluble fertilizers to boost yields. It was a vicious circle that made no sense.

Quertinier gave me Paul Barre's name and address in Fronsac but without mentioning biodynamics. 'Barre is doing something that might interest someone like you,' was all he said, adding, 'Fronsac is not a zone that suffers mediocrity easily and its red wines can be flat, and lacking in aroma,' as a warning. But I found Barre's wines the complete opposite. They were aromatically uplifting and texturally expressive, and had an inner vibrancy I'd never previously encountered. They were the first real Bordeaux reds I had ever tasted. I'd already visited most of Bordeaux's top chateaux, the ones with the very best soils. So I asked Barre how his vines, which had only moderately interesting soils, made such diverting wine?

He was reticent at first, shrugging his shoulders (he *was* French...) and saying that he just made his red wines in the same way as everyone else. But I trusted my nose and my nose said his wine smelt different. I didn't believe him.

I grabbed Barre's arm and dragged him out into his vineyard. His vines visibly radiated health, and the vineyard soil smelt as earthy as a forest floor. Unlike the compact, hard, bleached soils of the vineyard I'd been working in, Barre's soils were so soft I could dig my hands in.

Then Barre said his vineyard was 'biodynamic'. When I asked him what this meant he said biodynamics was a bit like organics but with some vital differences. First, biodynamic vineyards try to be as self-sufficient and biodiverse as possible. Second, vineyards become biodynamic only if regularly treated with specially prepared sprays and composts using cow manure, quartz (an abundant, sand-like mineral) and seven medicinal plants including chamomile, stinging nettle, dandelion and oak bark. Third, biodynamics makes both the vineyard and the wine-growers more aware of and sensitive to lunar and other celestial rhythms.

All of this made immediate sense to me, but I gathered from Barre's initial defensiveness he'd been worried I'd take him for a wacko.

Over the next few weeks I visited every biodynamic wine-grower in Bordeaux. This was easy. Bordeaux had 10,000 wine-growers, but only half a dozen were biodynamic. I started tracking down biodynamic wineries in other parts of France, finding small but growing clusters in Alsace, the Loire and Burgundy. I went to work in an organic German vineyard, then in a biodynamic Californian vineyard. I knew I learnt things best when doing them first-hand.

Biodynamics is the oldest 'green' farming movement, pre-dating organics by a generation. Largely people agree that biodynamic wines taste different from mainstream wines, but sceptics say this 'differentness' is nothing to do with biodynamic practices, it occurs because biodynamic wine-growers merely 'pay more attention' to the vineyard when pruning, ploughing or picking. Yet such dismissal of biodynamic techniques cannot explain why both conventionally and organically reared cows have been hit by BSE ('mad cow disease'), but biodynamic cows have never succumbed to the infection.

When I began writing about wine, I specialised in biodynamics. I knew many established wine critics would find this odd, but also that if my tastebuds were correct in telling me biodynamic wines actually tasted rather good and were really individual, then this movement had a chance of catching on.

The number of biodynamic vineyards worldwide has been consistently growing every year since about 1989. Every major wine region worldwide has at least one biodynamic vineyard. In this book, I have profiled wines from some of my favourite biodynamic wine producers, but because the movement is growing so fast there were many I could not cover.

Before listing the wine profiles, my Introduction contains a short history of biodynamics and describes biodynamic processes for making wine.

Introduction: Biodynamic Wine

Although our generation enjoys drinking wine regularly, and we have become breezily familiar with the names of grape varieties our grandparents had never heard of, few of us would claim we have a really confident understanding of wine. There are so many different – and often very confusing – labels to choose from, and the wines inside are often described in flowery language few of us speak. Unlike beer or vodka, two identical bottles of wine from the same grape grown in the same place and made by the same person will taste different every year, or every 'vintage' in wine-speak. For wine buffs these complexities bring tears of joy and wonder. For the rest of us, wine remains an unnecessarily overcomplicated puzzle.

But we like drinking wine, and are drinking more of it than ever before, instead of our historic favourites, beer, spirits, and even cider. Perhaps this is partly because wine makes us feel less bloated than beer, so we can enjoy eating and drinking at the same time. 'Wine and food culture' is an appealing phrase.

We also seem to sense there is something special about wine, something deep-seated within us that makes drinking and appreciating wine significant, even meaningful. This may be because humans started drinking wine about the same time we swapped our original patterns as hunter-gatherers for a more settled agricultural life. About 12,000 years ago humans settled into communities and started farming. We grew what we wanted to eat rather than just letting nature decide. We started trading food, we learnt to write, and we also began wine-growing, or viticulture.

Wild vines used tree trunks to climb up towards the sun, so grapes grew on the edge of forests. Vines needed sunlight and heat to sweeten and ripen their grapes. Humans soon realised the sugary pulp in grapes would, if left alone, bubble and turn into a drier-tasting but more strongly flavoured drink, which gave us feelings of boldness and other-worldliness.

We still depend on nature for light, heat, food and fresh water, yet most of our daily lives have become rather divorced from the world's natural rhythms and processes. Modern hunter-gatherers armed with credit cards can find fresh strawberries 365 days a year, 24 hours a day, when we should really only be able to buy them fresh once a year in early summer. We have constant availability because we can now transport anything rapidly around the world, and because we have learnt how to manipulate the elements our crops need to grow. We can eat food grown using heat and light made in factories called power stations, and fed using soil and water to which laboratory-developed, factory-made liquid food or fertilizers have been added. We can grow almost any food, anywhere.

Artificial fertilizers allow us to produce more food, more cheaply, from less land. They boost yields because they contain the three main nutrients crops need to grow: nitrogen (N), phosphorus (P) and potassium (K) (they are often called 'NPK' fertilizers). But as well as boosting farm crops, fertilizers make weeds grow more aggressively too. And artificially fertilised farm crops, including grapevines, seem to lose some of their in-built resistance to pests or fungal diseases like mildew and rot. The question remains as to whether we, who eat artificially fertilised crops, are also becoming weaker to infections.

Although all wine grapes are still grown with the natural light of the sun, their diet has fundamentally changed. Around nine out of ten bottles of wine are grown using fertilizers, plus weedkillers (herbicides), fungicides and pesticides. But recently, there has been a surge of interest from wine producers in choosing 'alternative' methods: sustainable, natural, organic and biodynamic. Advocates of biodynamic methods now include a rapidly increasing number of wine producers, both big and small, famous and unknown, worldwide.

Biodynamics offers effective, creative and sustainable solutions to common problems with grapes and wines: compacted vineyard soils lacking life and fertility, vines that struggle to resist common pests and diseases, and grapes that are increasingly complicated to ferment into wine and produce wines lacking flavour and vitality. It offers positive solutions to the problems posed by modern farming processes.

Rudolf Steiner: the founder of biodynamics

The issues surrounding the costs and benefits of modern farming techniques have troubled farmers and consumers alike since the first artificial fertilizers were developed by a German chemist called Justus von Liebig in the mid-nineteenth century. In the spring of 1924 around 130 farmer-landowners organised a cry-for-help conference at Koberwitz in eastern Germany (now part of Poland). They asked Rudolf Steiner, an Austrian, to be the main speaker. Steiner was in his late fifties and already well known for his unusual views about medicine, social reform and even children's education. He is the same Steiner who created the curriculum for the Steiner school movement (Waldorf schools in America).

Rudolf Steiner gave his advice to these farmers in a week-long series of lectures called *Spiritual Foundations for the Renewal of Agriculture (Agriculture)*.

Steiner said what we need is to find a way of growing food and drink that does three things. First, food production should leave the farm in a better, more vital, state than it was before. Second, the food itself must be tasty and nutritionally wholesome for our bodies. Finally, food should also be good for our spirits.

Manure from their Highland cows keeps the vines strong and healthy at Burn Cottage Vineyard, New Zealand.
Burn Cottage Vineyard

Self-Sufficient Farms or Vineyards

To achieve these three aims, Steiner prescribed a general philosophy for farming, which was that each individual farm or vineyard should be as self-sufficient as possible. Farmers and wine-growers need to stop buying in fertilizer pellets to boost crops. They should avoid a system in which produce is trucked out of the vineyard each year and the nutrients it contained are then replaced with fertilizer manufactured in some far-off place. Instead of fertilizer, all green waste – the prunings, leaves, grapeskins and seeds – need to be returned to the soil through composting, and thus retained on the farm. Cycles of growth, use and replenishment should be local. The particular advantage of self-sufficiency for vineyards is it contributes to the grapes retaining their unique flavour of place – their *terroir*. That is, it helps produce wine with a 'could only come from there' taste, rather than with a 'could come from anywhere' taste.

Increasing numbers of biodynamic vineyards have horses for ploughing and manure, like these ones enjoying the view over the vines at Seresin Estate in New Zealand.
Seresin Estate

Biodynamic wine-growers must keep their vineyards fertile by making their own compost, not buying in fertilizers. All of the green waste is mixed in with animal manure. Steiner said cow manure was the best one to use, although manure from horses and even sheep can work well too. Good compost needs to be made from materials rich in both nitrogen and carbon. Fresh animal manure is nitrogen rich, while hay and straw from cow barns are carbon rich, as are shredded vine prunings. Both contain a much wider range of nutrients than factory fertilizers. And, crucially, animal manure is also absolutely teeming with life. It gives finished compost all of the microbes, like bacteria, and fungi and worms, which soil and plants need to stay healthy.

As part of the shift towards self-sufficiency, biodynamic wine-growers are encouraged to get some cows or horses as a manure source. Although most biodynamic wine-growers do still use tractors, biodynamics has sparked a growing trend in vineyards worldwide to use horses when ploughing and spraying their vines. Many vineyard workers describe being able to get closer to the vines and be more conscious of all the natural processes in the vineyard when working with a horse rather than a tractor. Horses also compact the soil less than machinery.

Tractors are still widely used on biodynamic vineyards, like this one at Sedlescombe Vineyard in southern England.
Sedlescombe Vineyard

21

Biodynamic Preparations

As well as recommending a general philosophy of self-sufficiency, Steiner described nine remedies for farms. Known as the biodynamic preparations, these are unique to the biodynamic method and constitute a toolbox for the biodynamic farmer or vine-grower. They are made from plants, animal manure and a mineral, so from the three so-called 'kingdoms' of nature. Steiner suggested adding six biodynamic preparations to compost piles, and to spray the other three directly on the farm and its crops. Farms and vineyards that describe themselves as biodynamic must use these preparations.

HORN MANURE 500 AND HORN SILICA 501

Rudolf Steiner was so keen on cow manure because it has an incredible fertilising power. A cow can live off the grass in one field, but, when used carefully, her manure can keep both her own field and the neighbouring field fertile. Steiner said that when we eat, two things are released into our bodies: substances like vitamins, which help our bodies grow physically, and 'life forces', which our brains need to keep us alive as sentient beings. This sounds a bit odd, but it arises from Steiner's conviction that there is more to life and the processes of life than the physical elements science can measure. Analysing living things in terms of numbers – weight, density, size and so on – gives us only half an answer, he said.

Steiner believed that cow manure is such a powerful fertilizer because it is especially abundant in life forces; that cows don't use most of the life forces in the food they eat; and that cow horns are vital to the circulation of life forces in a cow. Cows on biodynamic farms never have their horns removed. De-horning is permitted on organic and conventional farms, however.

Scientists would say Steiner's theory about the power of cow horns is complete bunkum. But no biodynamic cow has ever contracted 'mad cow disease' or 'BSE'. During his 1924 *Agriculture* conference Steiner warned of the dangers of turning vegetarian cows into meat-eaters, a practice which contributed directly to the BSE epidemic. Blood flows around the base of the horns. De-horning cows so they can be put in enclosures is a bloody business, and one that weakens the cow and changes her nature. Cows with no horns will look at you only with their eyes. Cows with horns will perceive you by first lowering their heads and pointing their horns at you. The horns are sense organs: antennae.

Two of Steiner's preparations for assisting plants involve filling cow horns with manure or with silica (quartz), and burying them for a specific season. To make Steiner's horn manure '500' soil spray, we fill horns with manure then bury them between autumn and spring, when the earth is digesting the fallen leaves that had filled with the sun's energy during the summer. When the filled cow horns are dug up in spring, the manure inside has changed. It turns into a very dark soil-like substance, which smells of super-charged earth. This so-called 'horn manure' is teeming with all the good micro-organisms soils need to stay healthy

Mike Brown at Gemtree Vineyards in South Australia, with his biodynamic preparation 500 (horn manure).

and rich in humus. The manure from inside the horns is stirred into water in a rhythmical way. This is called dynamising, and turns the manure into a liquid, which will regenerate soil when sprayed over it.

In contrast, horn silica '501' atmosphere spray is for the shoots, leaves and fruits of the plants rather than the soil. Silica, or quartz, is a hard, sand-like substance, which is the most abundant mineral on earth. It has a strong relationship with the heat and light of the sun. The most silica-rich parts of our bodies are our skin and our eyes, which react to the sun's light and heat. The silica-filled horns stay buried between spring and autumn, when the sun is high in the sky and plants are pushing their shoots and leaves up to the sun.

Dynamised horn silica is sprayed over the crops when the sun is rising, meaning early in the morning, and in spring and early summer. It encourages plants to stretch up: you should be able to identify vineyards sprayed regularly with horn manure and horn silica, because the shoot tips of the vines will point up to the sky, as if they are really stretching themselves. In a conventional vineyard shoot tips appear more floppy. A vine can only have pointy shoots above ground if the roots underground are doing the same thing, pushing outwards and downwards, to give the vine a solid foundation.

We want wines to taste of two things: the soil or the place the vines grew in, and the individual fruit flavours different grape varieties contain. Horn manure helps vine roots to transmit a sense of place to the grapes, while horn silica ensures the grapes taste ripe enough for the wine to be enjoyable and age-able. They both also assist vines' disease resistance.

THE OTHER PREPARATIONS

Biodynamic wine-growers stimulate the vines' immune systems and deter pests and diseases by making teas and other sprays from plants growing wild in and around the vineyard. While biodynamic (and organic) growers can use sulphur- and copper-based sprays, like Bordeaux mixture, to control mildew, on biodynamic vineyards these are increasingly being replaced by plant and compost teas.

Dynamising at Sedlescombe Vineyard in southern England. Sedlescombe Vineyard

Steiner's preparations use the medicinal properties of particular common plants: yarrow flowers are used in preparation 502, chamomile flowers in 503, stinging nettle in 504, oak bark in 505, dandelion flowers in 506 and valerian flowers in 507. Yarrow is naturally rich in sulphur to prevent powdery mildew; chamomile stops vines stressing in extreme heat; stinging nettle is full of nutrients vines need, like iron; oak bark acts like an antiseptic; dandelion brightens vines to make them less disease-susceptible; valerian seals in the vitality brought to the compost pile by the other preparations; and common horsetail grows in swampy places but does not suffer swampy fungus diseases.

Steiner learnt about plants' healing powers from an old peasant called Kogutski who sold wild medicinal herbs. He met Kogutski regularly on the train when travelling to science lectures in Vienna. Steiner sensed that the intimate spiritual connection to plants that men like Kogutski had would soon be lost because science alone thought it had all the answers.

Reducing Additives in Winemaking

If grapes are naturally healthy and vital at harvest it means winemakers can make wines with a minimum of intervention and additives. The main permitted additive in all wines (organic, biodynamic, conventional) is sulphur dioxide. This helps grape juice that has fermented into wine survive in bottle rather than doing what nature intends, which is turn into vinegar. Some wine drinkers says sulphur dioxide in wine (and beer, salad dressing, fruit juice) gives them headaches or allergic reactions. If you are worried about sulphites look for wine labelled 'no added sulphites' or 'no detectable sulphites'. Sulphite-free wines are gaining in popularity among wine drinkers and winemakers, if not yet among mainstream wine critics.

Vegans should look for wines made without recourse to things like egg white and milk protein. These are added to make some wines taste smoother and look brighter. They don't stay in the wine, but drop out before the wine is bottled.

The moon rises over Avondale Wines, South Africa.

Lunar and Other Celestial Cycles

As well as a philosophy of self-sufficiency for farms, and the nine biodynamic preparations, Steiner recommended that farmers be aware of lunar and other celestial cycles. He told the audience for the *Agriculture* lectures that life on earth was a reflection of what was going on in the wider universe around us, and that we should grow our food with this in mind. Most of us have lost our connection to lunar and other celestial cycles. In 2007 the balance tipped for the first time in human history: now more of us live in cities than in the countryside. Urban light pollution means we cannot see the stars, which we feel have little relevance to our daily lives, certainly less than our twinkly iPhones and iPads. Yet everything around and inside us was once part of a star.

Both organic and biodynamic farmers and wine-growers care for the soil, but only biodynamic growers try to time farm work – pruning, ploughing, picking – to celestial cycles. For example, the full moon is seen as a time of fertility, so it is a good time to spray horn manure, and sow seeds for cover crops ('green manures') between the vine rows. The extra light and moisture the full moon generates seems to help seeds germinate better.

Most biodynamic wine-growers use celestial calendars to help them decide when best to time their work to celestial cycles, with Mathias Thun's annual *Sowing and Planting Calendar* the most popular choice. There is even a calendar *When Wine Tastes Best: A Biodynamic Calendar for Wine Drinkers* to help you decide the best day to uncork a particular wine.

The Biodynamic Movement

Steiner died less than a year after first describing his nine biodynamic preparations. Soon after his death an organisation named after the Greek goddess of the fruits of the earth, Demeter, was formed by some of those who attended his *Agriculture* course. Demeter still promotes, regulates and certifies biodynamic farming worldwide today.

Biodynamics is the first 'organic' farming movement: the organic movement we are now familiar with began in England only after the Second World War. My experience of working in conventional ('chemical'), organic and biodynamic vineyards is that organics is a big and positive step away from conventional wine-growing, but that organics got me into a 'don't do this, you mustn't spray that' mindset. I found it restricting. It left me feeling that although I had moved beyond 'chemical' sprays I wasn't really moving forward in my farming. Biodynamics, on the other hand, gave me both some new tools and a new way of thinking.

Demeter and Biodyvin

Demeter International (www.demeter.net) is a non-profit body. It regulates and promotes biodynamic farming and food worldwide. Food and wine carrying either of Demeter's two logos is officially recognised as biodynamic as long as they comply with the relevant Demeter Standards. All biodynamic farms and vineyards must also comply with the international rules laid down for organics. These can be summarised as: no weedkillers (herbicides), no synthetic pesticides or fungicides, and no genetically modified organisms (GMOs). There are Demeter-certified farms in nearly fifty countries worldwide.

France's Syndicat International des Vignerons en Biodinamie (www.biodyvin.com), or the international biodynamic winegower's syndicate, only allows biodynamic wine-growers as members rather than biodynamic farmers in general. It is known as 'Biodyvin'.

In Australia, vineyards and farms can be certified biodynamic by either Demeter Australia or by government-appointed agencies.

The vast majority of the wines in this book are from certified biodynamic vines, or certified organic vineyards in which biodynamic practices are used. I have given details in each profile.

BIODYVIN

THE NINE BIODYNAMIC PREPARATIONS

Each of the nine biodynamic preparations can be referred to by name or by number. They are:

THREE SPRAYS

Horn manure '500' soil spray

Horn silica '501' atmosphere spray

Common horsetail tea or liquid manure
'508' soil or crop spray

SIX COMPOST PREPARATIONS

Yarrow '502'
from the flowers of *Achillea millefolium*

Chamomile '503'
from the flowers of *Matricaria chamomilla*

Stinging nettle '504'
from *Urtica dioica*

Oak bark '505'
from *Quercus robur*

Dandelion '506'
from the flowers of *Taraxacum officinale*

Valerian '507'
from the flowers of *Valeriana officinalis*

Conclusions

Wine is a luxury item in our diets, not a necessity, so there is an extra onus for wine to be grown in a way that puts something back into the earth it comes from. Leaving the earth poorer and our neighbours to clean up pollution from controlling weeds and diseases is unfair. The public rather than farmers pay to clean this mess up. Cheap wine comes at a price, after all.

> More and more wine-growers are switching to greener methods. Nearly 5 per cent of the world's vineyards are now organic or biodynamic.

We want wines to have a sense of place. In other words a chardonnay from the cool limestone soil of Chablis in northern France should taste different to a chardonnay from warmer, sandier soils along France's Mediterranean coast. Steiner's biodynamic method is a highly effective way for wine-growers and their vines to reconnect with their soil and thus with place.

Farming with biodynamic compost and the spray preparations plus plant teas is cheap, effective, safe and low-tech. Anyone, even kids, can make the nine biodynamic preparations.

As shown in the experiences recounted through the wine listings that make up this book, biodynamics is better for the environment, better for wine-growers and workers, can help create a sense of local community around a vineyard, and can provide wines with rich individual character.

Biodynamic wine is something we should all raise a glass to.

WHITE WINES

White wines are made by squeezing the juice from the grapes –
usually those with green or yellow skins rather than red ones – and
fermenting this juice on its own without the grapeskins. (On the
whole, red grapes are not used in white wines though they are
used in champagne.) White wines are a bit more fragile than reds;
their aromas are easily lost if they are allowed to ferment too hot.
So white wines ferment at cooler temperatures: about 15–20°C
(60–70°F). To squeeze the juice out, most winemakers put the
grapes in a wine press. Slow gentle pressing yields the best juice,
meaning juice with clear and fruity flavours rather than murky or
bitter ones. The juice will usually be allowed to settle overnight in
a clean tank so impurities fall to the bottom. The clear juice is then
racked, meaning run off, and then fermented in either a tank or an
oak barrel. Barrel-fermented white wines will pick up oak flavours,
which add complexity to the wine. Some grapes are more suited
to barrel fermentation than others, chardonnay being a good
example. To avoid excessive oaky flavour in, say, a chardonnay, the

winemaker may ferment some of the juice in barrels and the rest in a tank made of a neutral material, like steel, fibreglass or cement.

Another decision for makers of white wines is whether to allow the wine to undergo a second 'fermentation' naturally. Bacteria (rather than yeasts) change apple-tasting, or 'malic', acid in freshly fermented wine to softer, creamy-tasting 'lactic' acid. This acid softening conversion is rather confusingly called the 'malo-lactic fermentation', even though no alcohol is produced by it. In hot climates, such as Australia, makers of white wines will stop this process from happening, because the sun burns most of the acid out of the grapes while they are still on the vine. Low-acid wines don't age well and their fruit flavours soon turn bitter in the bottle. In cooler climates, such as Burgundy, the grapes may have so much appley acid it might make sense to let the bacteria chew some of it out of the wine before it gets bottled.

Finally, makers of white wines must decide whether the wine will be dry, off dry or fully sweet (most red wines are bottled dry or near dry). Some grapes, like chardonnay and sauvignon blanc, are best suited to dry styles, meaning the grapes are picked with ripe-tasting flavours and enough sugar to make a balanced wine between roughly 12 and 14.5 per cent alcohol. Others, like riesling, can be anything from bone dry to very sweet, depending on the region where the grapes are grown, whether the grapes are picked early, or very late and thus super-high in sugar, and whether the winemaker ferments all the sugar into alcohol or leaves some of it unfermented. Experience allows winemakers to seek the right balance of freshness (acidity), alcohol and sweetness for their particular grapes in any particular year.

WHITE WINES FROM SINGLE GRAPE VARIETIES (VARIETAL)

CHARDONNAY

Chardonnay is the world's most popular grape variety, making dry, agreeably fullish, classically flavoured, often slightly oaky white wines, which are as easy to drink as they are to pronounce. Chardonnay is the white grape of Burgundy, so is responsible for the steely dry white wines from Chablis, Mâcon, Meursault, Puligny-Montrachet and other sub-regions in this area of eastern France.

If you have become so bored with this ubiquitous grape that you have joined the ABC (anything but chardonnay) crew, then try a pinot blanc (see p. 75) instead.

There is some overlap between **chablis** wine and **chardonnay** wine. All chablis wine is made wholly from chardonnay grapes, but the term 'chablis', though it has in the past been used generically for 'white wine', should properly only apply to chardonnay from the region of Chablis.

Californian and Australian chardonnays are rounder, and used to be stereotyped as too oaky and too heavy in alcohol. But styles have become more elegant, with growers planting in cooler sub-regions for slower ripening grapes. These make chardonnays with fresher fruit flavours, often pretty enough to need little or no oaky disguise.

Domaine de la Boissoneuse, Chablis (Burgundy, France)

Route de Chablis, F-89800 Préhy (Yonne), France
T:+33 (0)3.86.41.49.05 www.brocard.fr

Jean-Marc Brocard started making chablis (chardonnay from Chablis in France) only in 1973, but soon became one of the region's biggest producers. From 1998 his son Julien began converting one of the family's vineyards, the 11-hectare (27-acre) Domaine de la Boissonneuse, to biodynamic methods (Demeter certified). Chablis is Burgundy's most northerly wine-growing area, and its climate can at times be bracing. This helps make its dry chardonnays characteristically lean and nervy, but, on the downside, it can also make it hard to control vine diseases. Julien says,

> *Our vines have become more disease resistant since we started using biodynamic compost, and teas made from a mix of willow, stinging nettle and common horsetail. They feed the vines in the right way while stimulating their self-defence mechanisms.*

Now more of the family's vineyards are being converted to organic and biodynamic methods. Julien makes up to 60,000 bottles of biodynamic chablis from Boissoneuse each year. The wine ferments in tanks rather than barrels, and is viscous greeny-gold in colour. It shows steely, fresh, lemony fruit with an underlying richness of grilled nuts. Julien has also started experimenting with adding no sulphur during winemaking to a small per centage of his chablis.

Terroir means that the wines gain a sense of the place where the grapes are grown.

Domaine Emmanuel Giboulot, Côte de Beaune Blanc La Combe d'Eve (Burgundy, France)

4 rue de Seurre, F-21200 Beaune (Côte d'Or), France
T:+33 (0)3.80.22.90.07

When Emmanuel Giboulot took over his father's vines around Burgundy's prettiest town of Beaune, they were already organic. 'My father's mixed farm had fruit, vines and cows. Then in the late 1950s he became the first here to use weedkillers, fertilizers and pesticides. They didn't work, so in 1970 he became one of Burgundy's organic pioneers.' Emmanuel took over in 1985 aged 24, converting the 10-hectare (24-acre) vineyard to biodynamics (with organic certification). He says,

> Biodynamics provides physical tools like compost and spray preparations for wines to have more terroir character. But biodynamics, uniquely, also makes the spirit of the wine-grower become part of his or her terroir too. [Modern farming techniques, like] propagating vine cuttings in petri dishes rather than with seeds, have divorced vines from their origins. Vines have lost their sense of self.

To correct this, Giboulot sprays all his vines with essences made from vine shoots, leaves and grape pips taken from his chardonnay vines in a 3-hectare (7-acre) plot called 'La Combe d'Eve'. These vines are naturally isolated from other wine-growers by trees and scrub, so there is no risk of chemical spray drift. They are also well protected from the cold north wind, lying in a mini-valley or 'combe'. Combe d'Eve produces ripe-tasting, dry white wines of real tension and precision. Fermenting the juice relatively warm and in old barrels gives the wine's lean, chalky, citrus character a roundness, adding depth to its inspiring levity. Giboulot makes around 5,000 bottles each year. Try with snails in garlic butter, a Beaune speciality.

Domaine des Comtes Lafon, Meursault 1er Cru Charmes (Burgundy, France)

Clos de la Barre, F-21190 Meursault (Côte d'Or), France
T:+33 (0)3.80.21.22.17 www.comtes-lafon.fr

Dominique Lafon cemented this estate's reputation as one of Burgundy's finest for white wines, having taken over from his father in the early 1980s. There are around 14 hectares (35 acres) of vines: a third for fine pinot noir reds from Volnay (see p. 156) and Monthélie (see p. 157), and the rest for chardonnay in Meursault and in the grand cru – or vineyard nominated as of the highest quality – of Le Montrachet (see also p. 39). His diligence and common sense in the vines, rigour and flair in the winery, and enviably rugged good looks have led one Burgundy trade buyer to describe Dominique as 'being on the side of the angels'. Nevertheless Dominique's approach to biodynamics is more practical than spiritual, seeing the biodynamic preparations (which he uses in mainly spray form) as being the best tool to revitalise ageing, flagging vines. And while Dominique says he tries to time biodynamic sprays to celestial cycles, see p. 28, he says the main thing is to get the influence of the biodynamic preparations onto the vines effectively, rather than worrying about the perfect moon:

> *If the moon is favourable but your soils are wet from rain you will do more harm than good by driving all over the vineyard with your spray rig.*

In the early 1990s, Dominique's Meursault premier cru wines from Genevrières, Goutte d'Or, Perrières and Charmes were rich, dense, viscous and sinewy examples of Burgundian chardonnay. Charmes used to be especially overloaded with nut, vanilla, acacia and honeycomb flavours. Now it is tighter, crisper, more citrussy and longer lasting: a result, says Dominique, of the biodynamic regime producing grapes that ripen earlier but with more balanced flavours.

Grand cru is an official French term for vineyards producing potentially the highest quality grapes in terms of their ripeness, complexity and flavour. Only 32 vineyard plots in Burgundy are designated as grand cru, or 'great growth'. *Premier cru* or *1er cru* ('first growth') is the second-highest classification level in Burgundy.

Domaine d'Auvenay, Auxey-Duresses Blanc (Burgundy, France)

St Romain, F-21190 Meursault (Côte d'Or), France
T:+33 (0)3.80.21.23.27

Domaine d'Auvenay, a manor with twelfth-century origins, lies in the hills above St Romain in south-central Burgundy. Its owner, Lalou Bize-Leroy, also owns Domaine Leroy (see p. 152) and is a shareholder at Domaine de la Romanée-Conti (see p. 148). Lalou inherited d'Auvenay in 1960, but has run it only since 1988, when she converted it to biodynamics (Demeter certified). Grape yields are so low, one of France's top wine critics suggested Lalou was starving her vines by giving them only miniscule doses of biodynamic compost. Lalou marched him around every plot she owned, after which she says he was exhausted, 'but graceful. He realised our vines were well cared for.' Lalou's 4 hectares (10 acres) of pinot noir and chardonnay vines comprise a patchwork of tiny plots across five far-flung villages. Her Auxey Duresses Blanc comes from half a hectare (1.5 acres) of chardonnay grapevines planted in 1972. Fermented and aged in old barrels, this wine has intensely edgy stonefruit flavours that unfurl slowly. Decant two hours before drinking. 2,000 bottles are made each year.

Domaine Leflaive, Puligny-Montrachet 1er Cru Les Pucelles (Burgundy, France)

F-21190 Puligny-Montrachet (Côte d'Or), France
T:+33 (0)3.80.21.30.13 www.leflaive.fr

Most wine critics agree that the world's best chardonnay comes from Burgundy, and that Burgundy's best chardon-nay comes from the village of Puligny-Montrachet. Its Jurassic lime-stone soils produce bone dry and initially nervy white wines, which need five or more years of bottle ageing for their fabulous richness and density to be revealed. Domaine Leflaive has more Puligny vines than anyone else. Under its visionary and shrewd matriarch, Anne-Claude Leflaive, the estate helped pioneer biodynamics in modern Burgundy. Anne-Claude felt her father's adoption of soluble fertilizers and weedkillers in the 1970s and 1980s had made the family's wines rather simple, uniform and lumbering, even if the famous Leflaive name meant they remained easy to sell. She decided the best way to convince the estate's thirty-plus family shareholders to go biodynamic was to farm one trial vine plot in three different ways: using conventional, organic and biodynamic methods. Biodynamics produced the most interesting bottles: wines that were taut, graceful, yet built for the long haul. It took ten years, from 1993 to 2002, to convert Domaine Leflaive's entire patchwork of vine plots across several villages to biodynamics (Biodyvin certified), but it was worth it because, as Anne-Claude says,

> We found that not only do the wines now age and develop much better in bottle, but the vines are living much longer because the soil they grow in has more life.

Domaine Leflaive produces around 16,000 bottles from its 3-hectare (7-acre) Les Pucelles plot each year. The grapes are hand picked and their juice is fermented in oak barrels. Leflaive's Les Pucelles is archetypal Puligny-Montrachet, with a delicious, lacy creaminess and a delicate touch of tropical fruit.

Domaine Guillemot-Michel, Viré Clessé Quintaine (Burgundy, France)

Quintaine, F-71260 Clessé (Sâone et Loire), France
T:+33 (0)3.85.36.95.88   www.domaineguillemotmichel.com

Marc and Pierrette Guillemot-Michel are tall and wiry. Their extremely long hair convinces you they visit their local hairdresser in the Mâconnais hamlet of Viré in south Burgundy once a decade at most. In short, they look slightly odd. Turn up uninvited at sunrise and you risk seeing Marc loping through the vines spraying horn silica 501 via two long antennae that poke skywards from his backpack-sprayer. He resembles a human TV aerial or the fearsome outrider of a recently-landed UFO. Yet practicality is what counts here. Horn silica 501 needs to be sprayed right over the tops of the vines to help them connect with the sun's heat and light forces. Marc and Pierrette have surrounded their vines with hedges and habitat breaks for biodiversity. The vineyard is a carpet of stumpy green clovers and spindly wildflowers, providing food for the vines and encouragement for beneficial insects respectively. The soil is friable and worm-rich: Marc's foot-slogging efforts at being a human tractor pay dividends, for they avoid the soil compaction that comes with heavy machinery.

Domaine Guillemot-Michel's 6 hectares (15 acres) of chardonnay vines (Demeter certified) produce ripe, golden and healthily thick-skinned grapes. Every berry is sugar-rich, luminous and packed with mineral and fruit flavours. Both Marc and Pierrette are in fact qualified winemakers, not hippy hobbyists. You'd be hard pressed to find a deeper, clearer, riper, more precise and satisfyingly uplifting, authentic south-Burgundy chardonnay than theirs. Around 35,000 bottles are made each year.

Domaine des Vignes du Maynes, Mâcon Blanc Cruzillé Aragonite (Burgundy, France)

Sagy-le-Bas, F-71260 Cruzillé (Sâone et Loire), France
T:+33 (0)3.85.33.20.15   www.vignes-du-maynes.com

This domaine's name, 'vignes du maynes', means 'the monks' vine-yards'. Cistercian monks first made wine here, in Mâcon, south Burgundy, in AD 922. The vineyards are now owned by the Guillot family, who first arrived here in 1940, escaping the German occupa-tion of their native Paris. Although they were intellectuals rather than horny-handed men of the soil, the Guillot family played a key role in kick-starting France's embryonic organic movement in the 1950s. They felt farms were likely to produce healthier crops if treated with living composts and mineral-rich seaweed extracts, rather than with nitrogen fertilizers made by former munitions factories whose stockpiles of (potentially explosive) ammonium nitrate were being converted for use in farming. Under Julien Guillot, the third

41

generation of his family to farm here, Les Vignes du Maynes converted to biodynamics (Demeter certified). There are 7 hectares (18 acres) of vines: gamay for punchy red wines and chardonnay for dry whites. All the domaine's vines lie on limestone, but the oldest chardonnay vines, planted in two stages the early 1900s and in the 1950s, lie on aragonite, a unique, manganese-rich limestone, which gives the wine its name. Bone dry, but with soft, insistent, honeyed ripeness and a wet, stone savouriness, Aragonite needs at least five years in bottle to start to open up. 2,500–3,000 bottles of Aragonite are made each year.

Domaine La Soufrandière, Pouilly-Vinzelles (Burgundy, France)

Bret Brothers, Aux Bourgeois, F-71680 Vinzelles (Saône et Loire), France
T:+33 (0)3.8535.67.72   www.bretbrothers.com

The Bret brothers, Jean-Philippe, Jean-Guillaume and Marc-Antoine were all under thirty in 2001 when they made their first wines – chardonnay whites from Pouilly-Vinzelles and Mâcon-Vinzelles in southern Burgundy, and Beaujolais reds from Leynes. Their Domaine La Soufrandière comprises 9 hectares (22 acres) of biodynamic vines (Demeter certified). To pay for their own winery they started a side activity called Bret Brothers, making wine from other local growers' grapes – all from old vines. As part of this exchange, Bret Brothers advise the vineyard owners on working towards certified organic or biodynamic methods (most of their grape suppliers are in fact certified). They also send in their own picking crews (which is unusual), so the grapes are picked at exactly the right moment.

Their top Domaine La Soufrandière dry white wines from their own grapes include the greengage-fresh Mâcon-Vinzelles 'Le Clos de Grand-Père' (up to 5,000 bottles from a walled vineyard or *clos* planted with chardonnay in the 1950s by their maternal grandfather), and the richer, more multi-layered Pouilly-Vinzelles 'Les Quarts' from a sunny slope of sandy limestone, where the oldest chardonnay vines date from the 1940s (up to 5,000 bottles). They also make a basic Pouilly-Vinzelles called simply 'La Soufrandière' from the younger vines (planted in the 1960s and 1980s) in Les Quarts (up to 10,000 bottles). Part-aged in older barrels, this is a beautifully polished, rich, ripe chardonnay. Drink within 3–5 years of the harvest.

OTHER CHARDONNAY SPECIALISTS IN BURGUNDY

...include Domaine Pierre Morey (www.morey-meursault.fr) in St-Aubin for Meursault and Bâtard-Montrachet grand cru (Biodyvin). Morey was for many years the winemaker at Domaine Leflaive (see p. 39).

Guy Bussière of Domaine de la Vouivre (www.guybussiere. fr) in the Saône valley and Dominique Derain in St-Aubin add no sulphites (sulphur-dioxide preservative) to their chardonnays during winemaking. The trend of wines being made with no added sulphites is growing worldwide.

Domaine André et Mireille Tissot, Arbois Chardonnay Les Bruyères (Jura, France)

F-39600 Montigny-les-Arsures (Jura), France
www.stephane-tissot.com

André and Mireille Tissot founded this 30-hectare (75-acre) vineyard in 1962 in Arbois, in the mountainous Jura region of eastern France. Their livewire son, Stéphane, and his wife, Benédicte, now run it. Stéphane converted the vines to biodynamics (Demeter certified) and reintroduced horses to work the smallest, steepest plots like Clos de la Tour de Curon and Les Bruyères, where vines have often been planted deliberately close together. This makes each vine fight harder for its food and water, so producing fewer grapes with deeper, more interesting flavours.

Tissot's chardonnay from Les Bruyères comes from vines mainly planted in 1938 on south-facing (sunny) slopes. The slightly blue-coloured, limey clay soils here are typical of the Jura region, and warm very slowly in spring. Tissot ferments the juice in used rather than new barrels. He is confident enough in the quality of his soils and the health of his grapes to let it ferment with minimal intervention. The result is a chardonnay with an unusual amberish colour and breathtaking, sappy-fresh lime and ginger flavours. What I love about this wine is it has a really strong sense of place, with the kind of fullness but frankness one would expect in chardonnay from cool-but-sun-kissed soils, washed occasionally by summer rains, and clothed nightly by the Jura's cool mountain air. Tissot's hands-off winemaking allows these pure, rich chardonnay flavours to develop an invigorating sherried savouriness with four to five years of bottle age. No more than 6,000 bottles are made each year. Try with the Jura's signature dish of *coq au vin*.

Pignier, Côtes du Jura Chardonnay Cuvée à la Percenette (Jura, France)

Pignier Père and Fils, 11 Place Rouget-de-Lisle, F-39570 Montaigu (Jura), France

T:+33 (0)3.84.43.18.10 (Antoine) www.domaine-pignier.com

The Pignier family's cavernous Jura wine cellar was first used by Carthusian monks in the thirteenth century. It passed to the Pignier family when religious land was secularised after the French Revolution. Current winemaker Antoine Pignier runs the 15-hectare (40-acre) vineyard and converted it to biodynamics (Demeter certified) from 2004. He says,

Organics appeared to me as something all wine-growers can and should be doing. But when I heard about biodynamics, I felt it was a much broader way of looking at farming, going further than organics by looking at living forces, and by really making you understand the need to make your farm, your vineyard, your little patch of land into something self-sustaining. Biodynamics has really helped me to evolve as a wine-grower.

The Pignier family is lucky in that they have the only vineyards in Montaigu 'so there is no risk of any drift from neighbours spraying chemicals,' says Antoine. 'In fact, all our vines are surrounded by fields in which cows are grazing or by meadows.' Antoine sprays the vines with whey from local cows' milk (used to produce the local Comté cheese) to help disinfect them of fungus disease organisms. Wild plants like meadowsweet, chamomile, dandelion and stinging nettle are gathered from the surrounding fields to make teas to stimulate the vine's immune system. Rainwater is used for spraying.

Over the last decade the Pignier's huge range of Jura wines (red, white, pink and sparkling) has become clearer, more vibrant and more focussed. And the wines last longer in bottle, too. Their chardonnay La Percenette (which is named after the plot it comes from) has a bone-dry, almost austere, mineral feel when you smell it, typical of what one might expect from chardonnay grown on cool, hard, clay-rich limestones, but then on drinking, it has a satisfying, creamy, rich fullness.

Grgich Hills Estate, Chardonnay Carneros Selection, Napa Valley (California, USA)

1829 St Helena Highway, Rutherford, CA 94573, USA
T:+1 707.963.2784 www.grgich.com

Grgich Hills produces what many consider are the Rolls Royces of Californian chardonnays: strong, elegant wines stuffed as full of history as they are of technical excellence. Croatian-born Miljenko 'Mike' Grgich pitted a 1973 chardonnay he had made against the best of France at a blind tasting held in Paris in 1976, and won. The so-called 'Judgement of Paris' was a seminal moment in California's wine history, granting it self-belief as a world-class wine region. It gave Grgich and his business partner, Austin Hills of Hill Bros coffee fame, the confidence to open their Grgich Hills winery the following year. There are 150 hectares (370 acres) of vines across five separate vineyard sites in Napa Valley.

If you want a full-bodied, blockbuster chardonnay then try Grgich Hills' Napa Valley Chardonnay. If you want something with more crispness yet almost as much power, try their Carneros

Chardonnay. It's from a sub-region of Napa, which is especially chilly, as it is closer to the Pacific and gets cool, ocean-driven fogs. Carneros produces some of California's top pinot noir reds and chardonnay whites and, having helped make Carneros chardonnay for another winery there, I think Grgich Hills produces an absolute beauty in terms of its smoothness, richness of texture, precision and lift.

The Carneros vines are relatively young, and have a long life ahead, but it was the realisation that Grgich Hills' older vineyards (planted in 1959) were succumbing to pests and diseases ahead of their time that led Grgich to trial biodynamics and then adopt it across the entire estate in 2006. As well as being America's largest Demeter-certified biodynamic wine-grower, Grgich Hills is also fully solar powered, from a network of panels installed on the winery roof. This is a winery with a strong identity and sense of its past, but with a very definite view of its future, too.

Cobaw Ridge, L'Altra Chardonnay, Macedon Ranges (Victoria, Australia)

31 Perc Boyers Lane, East Pastoria, Victoria 3444, Australia
T:+61 03.5423.5227 www.cobawridge.com.au

In the 1990s, Australia cemented its place as a serious player on the world wine stage with its big, buttery, alcohol-rich chardonnays. As tastes changed, Australian chardonnay repositioned itself, becoming zippier and fresher but still with amazing levels of fruit intensity. Currently nowhere outside France produces chardonnay of such range, interest and quality as Australia, both for everyday drinking and for special occasions. Joshua Cooper of Cobaw Ridge is a prime example of a younger generation of Australian winemakers who see biodynamics as a key tool in creating wines with stronger, fresher flavours but lower alcohol levels. Joshua's parents, Alan and Nelly, founded Cobaw Ridge in 1985 in the Macedon Ranges north of Melbourne. There are 5 hectares (12 acres) of biodynamic (certified organic) vines, including shiraz and the rare lagrein for reds, and

Opposite: The American Canyon Vineyard where Grgich Hills Estate grows their chardonnay grapes. Rocco Ceselin

chardonnay for whites. The sandy granite soils at Cobaw Ridge, allied to the vineyard's high altitude of over 600 metres (2,000 feet), combine to produce chardonnay with incredible lightness and elegance given the intensity of its tightly layered, lime flavours. For his 'L'Altra' chardonnay, Joshua ferments the juice in oak barrels and bottles it unfined and unfiltered to preserve its mealy wholesomeness. A wine that is a meal in itself.

TOP SOURCES OF BIODYNAMIC CHARDONNAY OUTSIDE FRANCE
...include Günther Schönberger (www.weingut-schoenberger.com) in Austria (Demeter certified), Bergström in Oregon (see p. 162) and two Australian wineries: Sorrenberg (www.sorrenberg.com) in Beechworth, Victoria (Demeter certified) and Cullen in Western Australia (see p. 205).

CHASSELAS (GUTEDEL)

Chasselas is an uncomplicated white wine grape grown mainly in Alsace, Germany, and Switzerland. The German name for it is *Gutedel* and the Swiss call it *fendant*. Chasselas is one of the few wine grapes also used as a table grape. Some of you may even grow it up pergolas in your back gardens for eating.

Weingut Wilhelm Zähringer, Heitersheimer Maltesergarten Gutedel (Baden, Germany)
Johanniterstraße 61, D-79423 Heitersheim, Germany
T:+49 (0)7234.50 4890 www.weingut-zaehringer.de

The Zähringer family's 9-hectare (21-acre) vineyard is in the Markgräflerland sub-region of Baden, southern Germany. It has been organic since 1987 and biodynamic since 2010 (Demeter certified). This is as green a vineyard as you could wish to find, not least because its manager, Paulin Köpfer, is mad about sowing cover crops or green manures. He even co-wrote a book on the subject. Paulin sows alfalfa (lucerne) because its deep taproot gets air into soil compacted by tractors and provides vertical shafts for earthworms to move along. Mustard is sown because the smell of its roots discourages potentially poisonous worms. Flowering clovers, salad burnet, mallows and calendula attract beneficial insects, and their red, purple, pink, yellow and white flowers also seem to attract just as many tourists to the winery's tasting room.

One of the most popular wines here is a dry white made from chasselas grapes, here called gutedel. Zähringer makes around 80,000 bottles of gutedel from the Maltsergarten vineyard in Heitersheim. This is a dry white wine with fairly neutral almond flavours – perfect for glugging at lunchtime on a hot day. The Germans mix their gutedel with fizzy mineral water (about half and half) so that they are still perhaps capable of spotting the difference between a crimson clover and a calendula cover crop come suppertime.

Marie-Thérèze Chappaz (www.chappaz.ch) makes several different chasselas wines in the Swiss Valais (Demeter certified). She labels them using the Swiss-French word 'fendant'. Marie-Thérèze is famed for sweet white wines made from other grape varieties, which she allows to become shrivelled (*flétri*) while still on the vine.

CHENIN BLANC

Chenin blanc grapes, which originate in the Loire region of France, make very different white wines to sauvignon blanc grapes. Sauvignon blanc's lean, green-tasting, dry white wines have strong, easy to spot flavours. Chenin blanc is fuller-bodied; its almost tannic flavours of beeswax and honeycomb are harder to pin down, and can take much longer to emerge than sauvignon blanc's. Sweetness levels vary from raspingly dry to immensely sweet (depending on the year and on how and where the wine is being made), and chenin blanc wines can be still, slightly or fully sparkling (see p. 255 for a sparkling example). Yet chenin is one of the world's classic grapes, and wine aficionados love it precisely because there is a degree of difficulty to drinking it.

Domaine des Roches Neuves, Saumur Blanc L'Insolite (Loire Valley, France)

56 Boulevard St-Vincent, F-49400 Varrains (Maine et Loire), France
T:+33 (0)2.41.52.94.02 www.rochesneuves.com

In 1990, Thierry Germain left his native Bordeaux to make wine like a Burgundian but in the Loire. If that sounds confusing it shouldn't be. 'Bordeaux was too regimented,' says Thierry 'and I thought of the Loire as being like Burgundy: a complicated jigsaw puzzle of small parcels of vines, whose incredible potential was waiting to be unlocked.' Thierry has around 22 hectares (55 acres) of biodynamic vines (Biodyvin certified) with cabernet franc for Saumur champigny reds ('Marginale', 'Terres Chaudes') and chenin blanc for a Saumur blanc called 'Insolite'. Some of the vines were planted in the 1930s. Thierry says,

> I pick the chenin blanc grapes when their fruit flavours are ripe but fresh. I don't want to pick chenin blanc too ripe or raisined. I find the biodynamic 501 spray (horn silica) a useful tool in the Loire, where bright sunny weather with plenty of clouds is the norm. In spring, the 501 helps vines to ripen their shoots while keeping the sap moving inside. Then the grapes are primed to produce ripe-but-not-overripe fruit flavours from late summer onwards until harvest.

'Insolite' has a feisty liquorice freshness in its youth, but if left in bottle for up to a decade develops a concentrated, old-vine, honeyed richness.

Domaine Huet, Vouvray Le Clos du Bourg Demi-Sec (Loire Valley, France)

11–13 rue de la Croix Buisée, F-37210 Vouvray (Indre et Loire), France
T:+33 (0)2.47.52.78.87   www.huet-echansonne.com

Like many great winemakers, Noël Pinguet was not trained in wine. The son of Vouvray's butcher, Noël married the daughter of the owner of Domaine Huet, one of the Loire's top estates for 100 per cent chenin blanc white wines (still and sparkling). Huet's still Vouvrays range from bone dry to unctuously sweet. Pinguet says,

> I trained as a mathematician, and so have a healthy scepticism for things – like biodynamics – which are not always obviously empirical. But our own tests in 1988 quickly showed biodynamics made our vines and grapes more balanced and our soils richer in worms. We have more varied wild grasses now – around thirty species – plus wild geraniums and wild tulips. These used to be a common sight in Vouvray, but disappeared with conventional farming practices.

Domaine Huet has three distinct Vouvray vineyards: a total of 35 hectares (85 acres) (Demeter biodynamic). Le Mont vineyard's stony sand turns out honeyed, obviously seductive Vouvray; Le Haut Lieu's dark clay produces rather more austere, mineral whites; and the Clos du Bourg's fine clay over soft sandy limestone grows wines with a firmer, more structured feel, wines built for the long haul. Most collectors think the sweetest wines made here (the late-picked moelleux) are the pinacle of Vouvray. They are dense, long-lived and irresistibly complex. But the tauter demi-sec wines are much more representative of what Vouvray in general and Huet in particular are all about. In a Clos du Bourg, demi-sec sweetness and acidity struggle with each other for dominance, and, with age (5–20 years or more), achieve savouriness and balance. The wine is ready once a truffle aroma appears. Demi-sec is the most food-

friendly style of Vouvray, suited to pork, fish and poultry, and even veal, plus soft cheese through to strong, hard goat's cheese.

> *Demi-sec* means half-dry or half-sweet.

François Chidaine, Montlouis Les Choisilles (Loire Valley, France)

La Cave Insolite, 30 quai Albert Baillet, F-37270 Montlouis-sur-Loire (Indre et Loire), France
T:+33 (0)2.47.45.19.14   www.cave-insolite-chidaine.com

Montlouis and Vouvray are rival wine regions lying on opposite sides of the river Loire. Both produce chenin blanc white wines, which can be still or fizzy and made in all degrees of sweetness from bone dry to incredibly sweet. François Chidaine has 30 hectares (75 acres) of biodynamic vines (Biodyvin certified), and is unusual for owning vines in both Montlouis, which is the site of his family's vines, and Vouvray, where he started acquiring vines in the late 1990s. The difference between the two is that Vouvray is more famous, its harder-textured soils making longer-lived, more structured wines than those from the softer-soiled Montlouis. What I like about the wines François makes, whether Vouvray or Montlouis, is they are more about texture than structure. Although white, the chenin blanc grape, upon which both Vouvray and Montlouis rely, can be a bit like a red wine grape, potentially producing gum-drying wines you almost have to chisel out of your glass rather than sip demurringly. In Vouvray, François makes wines like 'Les Argiles' (from clay soils) and the sweeter 'Le Bouchet' (from limier soils), which roll pleasurably off your tongue because the wine's crisp Granny Smith appley core is soft ripe rather than astringent green. In Montlouis, François makes wines with liquorice, fresh green fig and quince flavours like (in order of sweetness) 'Clos du Breuil', 'Clos Habert', 'Les Bournais', 'Les Tuffeaux' and 'Les Lys'. A good all-rounder wine for someone unfamiliar with Loire chenin blanc in general and Montlouis' version of it in particular is 'Les Choisilles', which François makes from vines planted between 1950 and 1980 on all three of his main soil types: clay for body, limestone for texture and flint for those subtle fruit flavours.

La Ferme de la Sansonnière, La Lune Vin de France Blanc (Loire Valley, France)
F-49380 Thouarce (Maine et Loire), France
T:+33 (0)2.41.54.08.08

In 1989, Mark Angeli and his wife Christine left their native Provence, where Mark worked as a stonemason, for the Loire Valley. After an 18-month search they found a dilapidated vineyard, which they gradually transformed into a thriving biodynamic farm (Demeter certified). There are 8 hectares (20 acres) of vines and 4 hectares (10 acres) of other produce, including apple trees, beehives, chickens, sunflowers, wheat, spelt and hay. The latter is to feed a small herd of cattle – which provides meat and milk as well as manure for biodynamic compost – and a horse, which ploughs the vineyards. 'The horse came about because the tractor I was using broke down,' says Mark 'and we did not have enough money to repair it. We took the horse partly because it fitted with our self-sufficient philosophy and partly because it was more cost effective.' The same thought process explains why the Angelis' vines are not trained to horizontal wires. Mark says,

> Vines that are not wire-trained do not grow as high, which makes it easier for the sap to rise. Our grapes ripen earlier with no wires than they did with wires. I also prefer the aesthetics of having no metal in the vineyard. And I save time and money, too, because there is no need to raise and lower the supporting wires every spring and autumn. So we get riper grapes while saving money...

Mark always wanted to be a farmer, saying, 'I started growing the hay because it reminded me of the scent of the hay on my grandmother's Provence farm when I was a boy. It aroused a very deep emotion in me when I smelt for the first time the hay Christine and I were growing here.' Mark's stonemason-like work in the vineyard consisted of chipping away at a vine-only monoculture, which was in environmental and financial decline, to reveal a more textured, more self-sufficient farm thriving on its new-found biodiversity.

In the cellar, Mark is minimalist, making his wines from grape juice to which little or nothing in the way of sulphites has been added. He labels them simply as Vin de France rather than as coming from the Anjou region. They include the richly raspberry-scented, pink 'Rosé d'Un Jour' from Grolleau Gris; gentle cabernet and gamay reds that take time to open and reveal their violet and plum flavours and savoury tannins, and dry to off-dry chenin blanc whites like 'La Lune', 'Les Fouchardes', and 'Le Coteau du Houet,' plus the fully sweet 'Les Blanderies'. It's hard to pick a favourite wine, but my choice would be 'La Lune', because it was the first chenin blanc I tasted 'uncensored': a chenin blanc with no added sugar, no added sulphites, no filtration, no new oak (barrels). It was rich and tangy, its stonefruit flavours untamed. It was a wine that felt good in its skin, a sensation which I dare say the people who made it, Mark and Christine, experience every day in their life as farmers.

Domaine Philippe Delesvaux, Coteaux du Layon St-Aubin-de-Luigné, Sélection de Grains Nobles (Loire Valley, France)

Les Essards, La Haie Longue, F-49190 St-Aubin-de-Luigné (Maine et Loire), France
T:+33 (0)2.41.78.18.71

Philippe Delesvaux became a wine-grower in 1978. Some of his 11 hectares (27 acres) of Loire Valley vines (certified organic) lie so near to those of Marc Angeli (see above) that they stir or dynamise their biodynamic spray preparations together in a single receptacle before each goes off to spray his own vines. Philippe also makes his own biodynamic preparations with the local Anjou branch of the Loire Valley's biodynamic farmers' group. 'It's good to have contact with other farmers who grow fruit, vegetables or cereals: something other than wine,' says Philippe, whose wife, Catherine, is a school teacher. 'We wine people tend to live in our little wine bubble. So it is good to exchange information, farming tips and techniques and to share our successes as well as our mistakes.'

Philippe makes two fine, gently herby Anjou red wines called 'Le Roc', from cabernet franc grapes, and 'La Montée de L'Épine', from cabernet sauvignon grapes. His white wines are made from chenin blanc. The dry 'Feuille d'Or' from dark schist soil has a pulpy apple-juice feel, while 'Authentique' from old vines has a riper, sweet denseness. His three sweet Coteaux du Layon wines carry the name of the local village of St-Aubin-de-Luigné. The first shows lightly raisined fruit flavours because it is made from shrivelled (*passerilés*) grapes. The second, called 'Clos de la Guiberderie', is richer, sweeter and more marmelade-like. Half its grapes are shrivelled and half are affected with a fungus called 'noble rot'. The noble rot fungus arrives in autumn when the grapes are full of sugar, and is encouraged to grow on the grapes by morning mists from the nearby river Layon. The fungus makes the already sweet, ripe grapes even sweeter, while also giving the wine a textural richness like moist honey with flavours of dessicated fruit. Philippe's flagship sweet wine called 'Sélection de Grains Nobles' is made only from the sweetest noble-rot-affected grapes, the *'grains nobles'*. The wine ages 18 months in barrel, is fully sweet (each half bottle contains over 80 grams of sugar) and has clear, concentrated honeycomb flavours, which invigorate rather than cloy. Try with nuts or blue cheese.

The Millton Vineyard, Chenin Blanc Te Arai (Gisborne, New Zealand)

Papatu Road, Manutuke, Gisborne, New Zealand
T:+64 (0)6.862.8680 www.millton.co.nz

After his father gave him a home-winemaking kit as a teenager, James Millton would ferment blackberries in his bedroom, hiding the bubbling bottles in his cupboard so his mother wouldn't see. Ever since then, James has had two missions in life: wine and  biodynamics. With his wife, Annie, James farms nearly 30 hectares (75 acres) of biodynamic vines (Demeter certified) in Gisborne on New Zealand's north island. James says, 'The hard part about going biodynamic is finding the door to the biodynamic building and then having the courage to open it. Once inside, you wonder what took you so long.' James has almost single-handedly cajoled, politely encouraged and exasperatedly berated his winemaker colleagues to live up to New Zealand's tagline of being a 'clean, green land'. It wasn't easy at first, but now New Zealand has one of the fastest conversion rates for organic and biodynamic wine-growing worldwide, with James leading by example.

At Millton, flowering herbs are sown to encourage bees and discourage pests. Vineyards are grassed to soak up rain before it dilutes flavours in the grapes. Manure for compost piles and compost teas comes from the estate's own herd of Angus cattle. 'Their presence also brought a completely different feel to our property,' adds James. He encourages his staff to participate in study days with other farmers producing different biodynamic crops like honey, kiwi fruit, flowers, beef, lamb, grain or apples. He says,

If you want your staff to create a more polycultural, biodiverse vineyard for you, then you have to give their minds some polycultural tools to work with. They also have to

learn to think. One of my tractor drivers said he wanted to work in the winery one harvest. So I asked him to write an essay on which particular grape variety he'd like to ferment, and why. I also gave him some money, enough for a decent bottle of wine. I asked him to choose a wine which inspired him and which we could share together. I can question my staff, but they should then be free to question me: whether,

James Millton with a biodynamic preparation on his vineyard in New Zealand.

for instance, my biodynamic emphasis here is the right one, meaning a focus on getting our grapes flavour-ripe by making sure the seeds inside the berries are ripe-brown rather than unripe-green at harvesting. My method is to maximise those biodynamic sprays which, in our maritime environment, bring extra warmth: to the grape seeds with horn silica [501], or to the grapeskins via valerian tea [507].

James and Annie produce acclaimed pinot noir and syrah reds, but are especially noted for their dry chardonnay, riesling, viognier and chenin blanc white wines. Chenin blanc from Millton's Te Arai vineyard comes from vines planted in 1984 on calcium-rich, silty loam soils. The bunches are picked in several stages to make sure every grape is perfectly ripe. After pressing, their juice ferments in large oak barrels, which gives the wine a hint rather than a full blast of oak and enhances its already rich fruit texture. The dominant flavours are lime marmalade, pear, papaya and pink grapefruit, with almond and honeysuckle coming through after three or four years of bottle age. A wine with the attitude to handle a Carribean seafood curry.

OTHER BIODYNAMIC ESTATES MAKING NOTABLE CHENIN BLANC WINES

...include, in the Loire, Clos de la Coulée de Serrant (www.coulee-de-serrant.com) in Savennières (Demeter certified); Eric Nicolas of Domaine de la Bellivière (belliviere.com) for Jasnières and Coteaux du Loir (Biodyvin certified); Benoît and Elisabeth Jardin's Domaine les Maisons Rouge, also for Jasnières and Coteaux du Loir (Biodyvin certified); Vincent Girault in Touraine (see p. 125), Château de Bois-Brinçon (www.chateau-bois-brincon.com) in Anjou-Coteaux de l'Aubance (Biodyvin certified); and the following, all in Coteaux du Layon: Domaine de Juchepie (www.juchepie.com) (Biodyvin certified), Domaine Cousin-Leduc (Demeter certified), Guy Rochais of Domaine de Plaisance (www.chateaudeplaisance.com) (Demeter certified), Pierre Weyand and Josette Medeau's La Star (Demeter certified), Château de Suronde (www.suronde.fr) (Demeter certified), and Domaine Mosse (www.domaine-mosse.com) (Biodyvin certified).

Marri Wood Park (www.marriwoodpark.com.au) in Margaret River, Western Australia (Demeter certified) is another good source.

CLAIRETTE

The white clairette grape is not normally bottled on its own in Mediterranean France. This is because winemakers find its crisp-tasting flavours useful when added to flabbier-tasting white wines, to make them taste fresher than they really are. However in the sun-baked village of Bellegarde, near Nîmes on the French Mediterranean coast, one biodynamic winery makes a dry, mouth-filling, reviving white wine from clairette grapes all on their own.

Terre des Chardons, Clairette de Bellegarde (Languedoc, France)

Mas Ste Marie des Costières, F-30127 Bellegarde (Gard), France
T:+33 (0)4.66.70.02.51   www.terre-des-chardons.fr

Terre des Chardons produces a humdinger Clairette de Bellegarde from its mixed 20-hectare (50-acre) farm near southern France's bullfighting centre of Nîmes. The farm is half biodynamic vines (Demeter certified) and half organic cherries, apricots, vegetables and olives. 'Clairette is a thick-skinned grape, which thrives in the same kind of really arid areas olive trees prefer,' says owner Dominique Chardon. He makes around 2,000 bottles of Clairette de Bellegarde each year from 3 hectares (7 acres) of vines, half planted before the 1940s (no one knows exactly when) and half in 1990. The vines are worked by horses. The wine ferments in stone tanks in a winery Dominique designed from untreated timber, cork and locally quarried stone so his wines would be naturally insulated from the heat. No additives are used during winemaking. Dominique's wines need decanting first, to let them breathe. His Clairette de Bellegarde has generous malty texture, and fresh flavours of lemon rind and ripe Williams (Bartlett) pears. He also produces delicious pink and red (mainly syrah) wines labelled under the Costières de Nîmes denomination.

ANOTHER LEADING PRODUCER OF BIODYNAMIC WINE IN COSTIÈRES DE NÎMES
...is Marc Kreydenweiss (www.kreydenweiss.com) from Alsace (see p. 83), who bought Domaine des Grimaudes in the late 1990s, then converted it to biodynamics (Biodyvin certified) and makes mostly red wines.

GAILLAC

The Gaillac region lies in a rollingly rural landscape along the Tarn river in southwest France. Its fascinating and truly unique range of wines is made from mainly local grape varieties, with darkly powerful, peppery reds, and white wines that can be dry, sweet, still or sparkling. These are some of the finest food wines in France.

Causse Marines, Zacmau Blanc (Gaillac, France)

F-81140 Vieux (Tarn), France
T:+33 (0)5.63.33.98.30 www.causse-marines.com

The early 1990s was a risky time to get into wine-growing in France, and in south west France in particular. It was a time of economic recession, and a period of bad harvests affected by spring frost (1991) or torrential wine harvest rains (1992, 1993). So when winemaker Patrice Lescarret bought 8 hectares of run-down vines in Gaillac in 1993, his friends thought him a fool at best, masochist at worst. Twenty years later, Patrice and his partner, Virginie Maignien, have a vineyard twice the original size at 15 hectares (40 acres), and they are planting more vines in the nearby Aveyron. The name of their Gaillac estate, Causse Marines, refers to the limestone *causses* or terraces the vines grow on, and Marinesto, a stream running through them.

Patrice and Virginie's wines have a real vibrancy and individuality. This is partly due to the fact that all their vines are biodynamic (Demeter certified), and grown from pre-World-War-Two heirloom vine cuttings. These produce lower yields and more flavourful wines than vines propagated from more modern cuttings developed for their higher yields. It is also due to Patrice and Virginie being hands-off in the winery, letting the wines make themselves as far as possible. Dry reds like 'Peyrouzelles' from syrah, duras and braucol grapes have interesting orange-peel flavours and frank tannins. The semi-sparkling (*pétillant*) white 'Préambulles' is bottled while it is still fermenting, cloudy and raw, exiting the bottle just as cloudy, and foaming with nourishing, mealy flavours. More structured are the still, saline, mauzac-based whites, 'Les Greilles' and 'Zacmau', the latter anagrammatically named by Patrice in protest at the absurd rule whereby Gaillac wines cannot carry the name of the grape variety on the label. 'Zacmau' is made from mauzac vines planted in the 1930s. The juice is fermented slowly on its yeast deposit in used barrels, giving this a lovely texture of double cream, which thickens its taut, lemongrass fruit and accentuates its saline, tonic-water tang. Around 3,000 bottles are made each year. Another dry white, 'Dencon', made (and labelled) in a similar style from the ondenc grape, shows lovely late-autumn apple softness. The sweet white 'Grain de Folie', from late-picked, shrivelled muscadelle, loin de l'oeil, semillon and petit manseng grapes, has deliciously savoury, autumnal fruit flavours and balanced sweetness.

TWO OTHER BIODYNAMIC (DEMETER CERTIFIED) PRODUCERS IN GAILLAC
...are Domaine de Gineste (www.domainedegineste.com) and Château de Mayragues (www.chateau-de-mayragues.com).

GAVI (CORTESE)

Gavi, one of Italy's trendiest dry white wines, comes from south east Piedmont and is made with cortese, a grape unique to this area. Most gavi is drunk in the seafood restaurants along the Ligurian coast to the south – in Genoa and other nearby towns – and high prices are paid for it. Most bottles are drunk too early, within a year or two of bottling whereas the two wines cited here benefit from three or more years in bottle to express their flavours fully.

La Raia, Gavi (Piedmont, Italy)
Strada di Monterotondo 79, I-15067 Novi Ligure (AL = Alessandria), Italy
T:+39 0143.743685 www.la-raia.it

La Raia is a mixed biodynamic farm (Demeter certified) in Gavi belonging to Caterina Rossi Cairo and her winemaker husband, Tom Dean. They have 85 hectares (200 acres) of oak forest and cereal crops, 25 hectares (60 acres) of vines, and an eco-friendly, rammed-earth winery. Some delightful red wines made from the grape barbera are produced here, but Tom and Caterina's main focus is gavi. They make a modern, cool, fermented style showing the typical characters of the cortese grape: a tangy, vibrant mouthfeel and pristine flavours of green apple, yellow pear and white peach. The savoury, almond characters that gavi is famed for emerge only when the wines have four or more years of bottle age. La Raia produces 50,000 bottles of gavi and another 15,000 bottles of a gavi called 'Pisé' made from cortese vines last replanted in the 1930s.

Cascina degli Ulivi, Filagnotti, Gavi (Piedmont, Italy)
Strada della Mazzola 12, I-15067 Novi Ligure (AL = Alessandria), Italy
T:+39 0143.744598 www.cascinadegliulivi.it

Stefano Bellotti's family acquired the Cascina degli Ulivi estate in Piedmont's Tassarolo hills in the 1930s. When Stefano took over in 1977, he was only eighteen, and there was but a single hectare of vines. Now there are 16 hectares (40 acres) of biodynamic vines plus another 12 hectares of arable crops and vegetable gardens. Bellotti went organic in 1980 and biodynamic in 1985 and, although he later dropped his Demeter biodynamic certification in favour of just organic certification, he is widely regarded in Italy and abroad as one of the biodynamic wine movement's deepest thinkers and most intuitive winemakers. He says,

> *I am non-interventionist in the vineyards because the more you intervene, the more work you create for yourself. We don't trim the tops of the vines because the vines are in balance. We create this balance in the soil, partly by use of the biodynamic preparations but also by creating a living carpet there by sowing cover crops.*

Cows grazing in the beautiful environment at La Raia, Italy.
La Raia

The cover crops Bellotti sows include members of the carrot family (crucifers), to poke holes in the soil for air and water; legumes, like clovers, which fix nitrogen in the soil so vines can feed; and buckwheat, whose roots build organic matter in the soil and whose purple-pink flowers attract beneficial insects (buckwheat is not a 'real' wheat in the breadmaking sense). The cover crops also soak up the rain, meaning vines have to struggle and fight for water. This makes them leaner, like hunter-gatherers looking for a meal, rather than like lazy couch-potatoes expecting to be fed fast-food in the form of soluble fertilizers. 'Leaner vines grow less,' says Bellotti, 'producing just enough leaves to get the grapes ripe without needing to be trimmed.'

Bellotti makes glacier-crisp reds like 'Mounbè' from barbera grapes and 'Nibiò' from dolcetto grapes. He also makes a dense, dry gavi white called 'Filagnotti'. It is made from the juice of cortese grapes, which is fermented using wild yeasts and aged in acacia oak barrels. 'Filagnotti' is then left on its yeast lees, until it is bottled unsulphited, with no additives whatsoever. This is a ripe, exotic white with hazelnut nuttiness from its wild yeast fermentation and a deep, fibrous texture from lees ageing. Its green-apple freshness and intriguing, dried-apricot twist in the aftertaste are well matched to oven-baked fish dishes.

GEWÜRZTRAMINER

Gewürztraminer is a white wine speciality of Alsace in eastern France. The best examples are quite full-bodied with creamily pungent flavours of rose petal and lychee, whether the wine is bone dry, incredibly sweet or anything in between. Gewürztraminer is especially good with smoked food (like salmon), terrines, and Munster cheese.

Domaine Léon Boesch, Gewürztraminer Grand Cru Zinnkeopflé (Alsace, France)

6, rue St Blaise, F-68250 Westhalten (Haut-Rhin), France
T:+33 (0)3.89.47.01.83 domaine-boesch@wanadoo.fr

Since 1640, eleven generations of the Boesch family have farmed vineyards in the Alsace village of Westhalten. Their 13 hectares (30 acres) of biodynamic vines (Demeter certified) are mainly comprised of Alsace staples like pinot gris, riesling, pinot blanc and gewürztraminer. Manure for compost and for biodynamic sprays comes from a neighbour's dairy herd. Winemaker Mathieu Boesch sprays the vines with clay powder to prevent vine diseases. 'The clay soaks up humidity which can lead to the grapes getting rot, while also keeping the grapeskins strong, without affecting the taste of the wine,' he says.

Mathieu's family's best riesling, pinot gris and gewürztraminer vines lie on the Zinnkoepflé, a steep, south-facing hill site, and one of only 51 designated 'grand cru' sites in Alsace. This is one of Alsace's sunniest, driest sites, attracting sun-worshipping pagans in ancient times. Mathieu's gewürztraminer vines are somewhat more recent, having been planted in 1970 in three small blocks by his grandfather Léon, who gave his name to the estate. The vines lie at 350 metres (1,100 feet), on a bed of 250-million-year-old, reddish sandstone plus brighter limestone fragments made up of tiny seashells. The gewürztraminer grapes are hand picked and pressed very slowly. Mathieu says,

> Pressing slowly gives a very clear juice with none of the bitter flavours carelessly pressed gewürztraminer wines can show. Then we run the juice to large, oval-shaped wooden vats and let the wild vineyard yeasts ferment the juice into wine. It takes about a year usually.

The result is a wine that oozes passionfruit and ginger aromas with a creamy honeycomb and barleysugar softness in the mouth. 'If you grow gewürztraminer in the wrong way – meaning on lifeless, compact, hot soils – you get overripe gewürztraminer grapes that taste heavy and fat,' says Mathieu, describing one smelling of old soap and talcum powder like the inside of granny's handbag.

But with ten years of biodynamics under our belts, we can see how the Zinnkoepflé soil has become much softer, earthier and cooler. We feel this is why our gewürztraminer has gained flavour intensity and complexity while also gaining in freshness, making it a much more food-friendly wine than it was before.

OTHER ALSACE GEWÜRZTRAMINER SPECIALISTS
...include Domaine Bott-Geyl (www.bott-geyl.com) for its Sonnenglanz Grand Cru (Demeter), Domaine Albert Mann (www.albertmann.com) for its Furstentum Grand Cru (Biodyvin), Eblin-Fuchs (www.eblin-fuchs.com) for its Mandelberg Grand Cru (Demeter), and Pierre-Paul Humbrecht of Domaine Paul Humbrecht (vins-humbrecht.fr) for his Steinert Grand Cru (Demeter). Their wines range from dry or dryish to sweet, or from very sweet to incredibly sweet when labelled either Vendanges Tardives (meaning 'late picked') or Sélection de Grains Nobles, a style of nobly rotten wine (as explained on p. 55).

Tawse Winery, Quarry Road Vineyard Gewürztraminer, Vinemount Ridge (Ontario, Canada)

3955 Cherry Avenue, RR#1 Vineland, ON L0R 2C0, Canada
T:+001 905.562.9500 tawsewinery.ca

Moray and Joanne Tawse's winery, in the Niagara region of Ontario, has something of the Niagara Falls about it. Liquid arrives at the top in the form of freshly squeezed grape juice, and falls down via gravity through six levels as the juice ferments, the wine  settles, ages in barrel, gets blended and then bottled and shipped.

Expansive biodynamic wine-growing at Tawse Vineyard in Canada
Tawse Winery

A geo-thermal energy system warms and cools the winery as needed, with cooling helped by the pond outside. The pond water is actually run-off from the winery; a wetland bio-filter makes it safe for birds and frogs. Increasingly, horse-drawn trailers bring the grapes in at harvest instead of tractors, and Tawse lets his sheep nibble away at vine leaves in summer. This gives the emerging grapes more of the light and heat they need. There are 40 hectares (100 acres) of biodynamic vines (Demeter certified) on two main vineyard sites along the gently sloping Niagara escarpment. Chardonnay, riesling, and cabernet franc are among the stand-outs, but Ontario's gewürztraminer in general and Tawse's version (from its Quarry Road vineyard) should catch your eye.

Tawse's winemaker, Paul Pender, says,

> Quarry Road was acquired in 2004. It had been very conventionally farmed and its clay topsoils had become really compact. With bio methods, the soil became much softer. It's the most dramatic change we have seen since farming this way.

Underneath the clay is Niagara limestone, and you can feel the chalkiness it endows to the gewürztraminer, toning down its more exuberant Turkish-delight, rose and mango flavours into something just as joyous, but more savoury and subtle. Around 2,000 bottles are made each year.

ANOTHER GOOD SOURCE OF GEWÜRZTRAMINER FROM NORTH AMERICA
...is Rudy Marchesi's Montinore Estate (www.montinore.com) in Willamette Valley, Oregon, USA (Demeter).

GRÜNER VELTLINER

Austria's signature white wine grape, grüner veltliner, produces full-bodied white wines similar to chardonnay, but with slightly more obvious flavours. These include orange and apple blossom, acacia, almond, aniseed and hints of pepper. The best grüners are world-class food wines.

Meinklang Grüner Veltliner (Burgenland, Austria)
Hauptstrasse 86, A-7152 Pamhagen, Austria
T:+43 (0)2174.21680 www.meinklang.at

Werner Michlits' family has a mixed farm with cereal crops, fruit and vines around the marshy southern edge of Lake Neusiedlersee. The lake is located in the Pannonian grasslands of Burgenland, on Austria's eastern border with Hungary. Winters are freezing, but summers are long, intensely sunny and warm, producing wines with a noticeably rich mouthfeel. Werner's farm went organic in 1995 and fully biodynamic from 2005 (Demeter certified). Werner is very proud of his long-horned Angus cattle, seeing their composted manure as a key part in keeping his soils, and thus vines, from becoming too heat-stressed in summer.

Werner's wine range includes richly plummy reds from local grapes and lightly spicy whites from pinot gris, pinot blanc and Hungarian grapes like hárslevelü and juhfark. His grüner veltliner is my favourite though: a zesty white wine with concentrated lime, yellow grapefruit and pear-drop flavours, allied to bay-leaf savouriness in the aftertaste. Un-oaked, its natural freshness makes it a good match for freshwater fish or seafood risotto. Werner makes around 30,000–40,000 bottles of it each year.

Sepp Moser, Grüner Veltliner Von den Terrassen (Kremstal, Austria)
Untere Wiener Strasse 1, A-3495 Rohrendorf bei Krems, Austria
T:+43 (0)2732.705310 www.sepp-moser.at

Niki Moser comes from Austria's most famous winemaking family. His grandfather, Lenz Moser, helped put Austria on the modern wine map from the 1950s onwards. He showed how pruning vines in a new, taller way than was usual made them easier to mechanise, and so produced bigger yields. But by the mid 1980s, the Lenz Moser company had become too big and corporate, so Niki's father Sepp bought back his portion of the family's vines. The quietly spoken Niki succeeded his father in the early 2000s. He says,

It was clear wine was reaching a technological ceiling. Technology alone was not going to allow me to make wines of individuality. I felt we needed to get back down to earth, to reconnect with what made wine so special, and biodynamics was the obvious way of achieving that. Other Austrian winemakers, not just me, sensed this. In wine terms, Austria is tiny. The Bordeaux region is more than twice as big as we are, France nearly twenty times bigger. So the idea of thinking about our wine-growing more as artisans, rather than as big-scale manufacturers, makes sense for people who drink Austrian wines and want to feel some kind of connection to our way of farming.

Niki has 50 hectares (120 acres) of vines in two Austrian regions: in Kremstal, in Lower Austria, northwest of Vienna, where the vines experience cool mountain breezes; and in Apetlon, further south towards the Hungarian border on much sunnier lowlands. 'As these two places are so different, we blend cow, sheep or horse manure in differing amounts when making biodynamic compost for each site,' says Niki. The mineral-rich soils of Kremstal are perfect for grüner veltliner. Niki's comes from terraces ('von den Terrassen') filled with rocks once ground out by glaciers. He deliberately lets the juice ferment quite warm, at 20–22°C (68–72°F). 'If I ferment it too cool the wine will taste only of candied fruits and bubblegum, and will

have no minerality or sense of place,' he says. A warmer fermentation allows the delicate, white-pepper flavours typical of Kremstal grüner veltliner to shine, in a bone-dry, pitch-perfect white. Niki makes 25,000 bottles of his grüner veltliner each year.

OTHER TOP AUSTRIAN BIODYNAMIC GRÜNER VELTLINER PRODUCERS
...include Nikolaihof (see p. 88), Toni Söller (www.weingut-soellner.at) (Demeter certified) and Bernhard Ott (www.ott.at) (certified organic).

LOUREIRO

The loureiro grape is famous for the bone-dry, bitingly crisp, almost prickly white wines it produces in the Vinho Verde region of northwest Portugal. The wines are expressly made to be sold *verde* meaning young or 'green'.

Aphros, Branco Vinho Verde (Vinho Verde, Portugal)
Quinta Casal do Paço, Padreiro (S. Salvador), P-4970-500 Arcos de Valdevez, Portugal
T:+351 96.123.4747 Website www.aphros-wine.com

After Vasco Croft, a Lisbon-based architect, took over a *quinta* (farm) in Vinho Verde that had been in his family since 1626, he renovated the house. Then, Vasco, who had studied Rudolf Steiner's biodynamic theories in his youth, converted the amphitheatre-like vineyards to full biodynamics (with organic certification). Vasco's emphasis is on plant teas to keep the vines healthy, sheep for weed control, horses for labour and bees to help pollinate the estate's native forests, nut and fruit orchards, and vines. Vasco makes his own biodynamic preparations with help from Jaõa Castella, a consultant. Castella uses biodynamic gardening and teaching as a curative tool to help children and adults with intellectual disabilities in his work with Camphill, a charitable trust that operates in 21 countries on four continents.

Vasco has 20 hectares (49 acres) of vines in Vinho Verde. Rain-bearing westerly winds from the Atlantic make this one of the world's wetter wine regions, but luckily its crumbly, sandy, granite soils drain and warm up quickly when the sun shines, making wine-growing possible. This helps Vinho Verde's wines to display a unique combination of both ripeness and tension. Vasco's white (*branco*) Vinho Verde is a forceful, round wine made from the traditional loureiro grape. It has pithy, ripe, yellow-apple texture, pin-sharp lemony acidity, and lime and tangerine flavours. Try with avocado salad and whitebait.

Vasco also makes both still and sparkling red Vinho Verde wines that have incredibly deep purple colours because the grape he makes them with (called Vinhão) has red juice (most red-skinned grapes have clear juice).

> *SLIGHTLY LIGHTER VINHO VERDE WINES THAN THOSE MADE BY APHROS*
> ...come from Fernando Paiva's Quinta da Palmirinha, an emerging biodynamic estate (Demeter certified).

MUSCADET

The Muscadet region at the mouth of the Loire, near Nantes on France's Atlantic coast, produces plump, not overly flavoured, dry white wines from a grape called 'melon'. The wines often have a slight gassy prickle when bottled directly off the fermentation yeast (*sur lie*).

Domaines Landron, Muscadet de Sèvre et Maine sur Lie Le Fief du Breuil (Loire Valley, France)

Les Brandières, F-44690 La Haye-Fouassière (Loire Atlantique), France
T:+33 (0)2.40.54.83.27 www.domaines-landron.com

Pierre Landron began establishing this Muscadet domaine from 1945. In 1990 his son Jo took over. There are around 40 hectares (100 acres) of biodynamic vines (Biodyvin certified), all hand picked, and all given to the melon de bourgogne grape variety typical of Muscadet. Jo makes a big range of Muscadet wines from a range of different soils, but it is his 'Le Fief du Breuil' bottling which he says is most representative. This is because it comes from a mix of the three main soil types in Jo's vineyards: clay, which gives a lemon-cedar feel to the wine; quartz, which is lighter and sandier and gives an exotic, creamy, orange-peel twist; and orthogneiss, a tough volcanic rock, which gives Le Fief du Breuil its precise, fumy, flinty edge. Around 20,000 bottles are made each year. Jo says the wine gets progressively rounder and fruitier-tasting the longer it ages, up to eight years, which is quite long-haul for Muscadet, as it is usually an early-drinking white wine, quaffed with the first plate of seafood it comes across – typically the local mussels with chips (*moules frites*).

ANOTHER TOP MUSCADET PRODUCER

...is Guy Bossard of Domaine de l'Ecu (www.domaine-ecu.com), who pioneered biodynamics here (Demeter certified). Guy helped the region become more ambitious by being the first to separate his Muscadets according to the different soil types in his vineyards (granite, gneiss), showing how wrong-headed it is to stereotype Muscadet as a bit flavourless and 'tasting the same wherever it is grown'.

MUSCAT

The muscat family of grapes is a large, sometimes confusingly named one, but muscat can be generally described as being white and with strong, musky-orange aromas that stand out recognisably in blind tastings. Muscat grapes are used in a wide range of wines, including styles as varied as sparkling moscato d'asti (see p. 263) and port-style, Mediterranean 'fortified' wine, created by adding brandy to still-fermenting muscat juice giving 15.5 per cent or more alcohol and considerable sweetness. The Muscat de Rivesaltes made by Domaine Cazes (see p. 238) and the Muscat St Jean de Minervois (Demeter) from Pierre Lavaysse's Le Petit Domaine de Gimios are both made this way. In Alsace, muscat is used for still white wines.

Domaine Henri and Luc Faller, Muscat Vieilles Vignes (Alsace, France)

51 route des Vins, F-67140 Itterswiller (Bas-Rhin), France
T:+33 (0)3.88.85.51.42 vin.faller@orange.fr

Luc Faller took over his father, Henri's, 8-hectare (20-acre) Alsace vineyard in 1989. He went organic in 2000 and biodynamic in 2004 (Demeter certified). He says,

Biodynamics makes you understand the importance of the biological life in the soil: bacteria, fungi, protozoa, worms and so on. If your soil is alive then your vines will have a better chance at resisting not just the usual insect pests and diseases but extreme weather too. The soil will stay cool and won't dry and crack under the sun.

The weather in Alsace can be pretty extreme because even though this is one of the most northerly French wine regions, the climate in summer is hotter and drier than some parts of the Mediterranean. Luc must be one of the few wine-growers in Alsace with no vines classified as coming from a piece of ground deemed worthy of 'grand cru' status – meaning a recognisably top site for wine. Alsace wines labelled 'grand cru' can usually sell for an extra premium price, in the same way you'd expect to pay more for a night in a five-star hotel than in a three-star one. But plenty of three-star hotels are nicer and cheaper than their five-star alternatives.

Perhaps having, on paper at least, no five-star vineyards leads Luc to work extra hard, to go that extra mile, to be both well organised and talented. He observes both his vines – asking himself whether their posture (too erect, too flacid) is right – and his vineyard – checking weeds to see whether they indicate something is wrong with the soil (too many dandelions in spring may mean the soil is too rich in nitrogen, and then it may make sense to spread a little less of his homemade biodynamic compost). His best vineyard site, Fruehmess in Itterswiller, should be classified a grand cru by the authorities (it isn't), for it produces as finely structured a dry, everyday riesling as you are likely to find in Alsace (the vines were planted in the early 1950s). But Luc is something of a muscat specialist too. Muscat is surprisingly tricky to understand (there are several sub-varieties) and drink: its pronounced musky flavours quickly become overbearingly heavy if the grapes get stressed by excess summer heat. Luc's Muscat Vieilles Vignes ('old vines'), however, is levity in wine form. The vines were planted in the mid 1960s and produce a dryish white wine with obvious grapey, lemon-fresh smells and white-peach flavours. It is perfect as an aperitif.

PINOT BLANC

It is easy to confuse pinot blanc with chardonnay, both when tasting the wines – because they are so similar: crisp, medium-to-full-bodied, with subtle rather than overbearing grapefruit flavours – and when identifying the vines: chardonnay and pinot blanc plants look remarkably similar. On a hot day, I prefer pinot blanc's slightly crisper, less full-bodied mouthfeel to chardonnay's. The best examples usually come from Alsace on the German border in France, Germany and northern Italy.

Domaine Pierre Frick et Fils, Pinot Blanc Sans Soufre (Alsace, France)
5 rue de Baer, F-68250 Pfaffenheim (Haut-Rhin), France
T:+33 (0)3.89.49.62.99 www.pierrefrick.com

Jean-Pierre Frick took over his father's 10-hectare (25-acre) Alsace vineyard in 1968. He immediately joined France's pioneering organic farmers' group, and let weeds grow freely to preserve soil structure. In 1981, Jean-Pierre joined Demeter, France's biodynamic farmers' association, and took the advice of other farmers who suggested that lightly ploughing the weeds every so often would help release nutrients, which his soil and vines desperately needed. Grape yields rose and the critics howled at how this move would dilute flavour in the wines. Once the vines had re-found their balance, Jean-Pierre felt confident his grapes could produce drinkable bottles without any sulphur dioxide being added as a wine preservative. The critics howled again at his 'no added sulphites' range of pinot blanc, riesling, pinot gris and gewürztraminer (among others), saying the wines were inferior to his (barely) sulphited alternatives. But Jean-Pierre had no time to worry about the critics. He had a steady stream of Alsace growers asking his advice about biodynamics and winemaking. Jean-Pierre, according to his fellow winemakers, 'is not one to ever close his door on you'.

The Frick wines, mainly white with a small quantity of pinot-noir red, ferment at their own pace with natural yeast, sometimes for eighteen months. To put this in context, eighteen days is more usual in Alsace. This gives Jean-Pierre's unsulphited pinot blanc incredible longevity, not in the sense that a bottle of it will survive in your wine cellar for a century – pinot blanc, Alsace's 'workhorse white grape', typically makes crisp quaffers for summer drinking – but in the sense that, once open, the bottle will yield the story of its uniquely untampered journey from budburst to bottle with rare modesty for up to ten days.

> ## OTHER GOOD PINOT BLANC PRODUCERS
> ...include Domaine François Baur (www.vinsbaur.com) in Turckheim, Alsace (Biodyvin); Stefan Sander (www.weingut-sander.de) in Rheinhessen, Germany (Demeter); Manincor (www.manincor.com) in Italy's Südtirol-Alto Adige (Demeter); Weingut Trautwein (www.trautweingut.com) in Baden's Kaiserstuhl, Germany (Demeter), where pinot blanc is labelled as weisserburgunder; and Robert Sinskey (see p. 159) in California who loves pinot blanc so much he sticks with it, even though it costs him as much to grow as chardonnay and the wines sell at far lower prices.

PINOT GRIS

Pinot gris ('pinot grigio' in Italy) is a white wine grape with pink ('gris') berries. A speciality of Alsace in France, it makes fairly full-bodied, spicy-flavoured, but not overpoweringly aromatic, white wines. These are usually dry, but in Alsace, sweeter, late-picked styles are common. Typical flavours are creamy, yellow apple, and pears and raisins in pastry, with an agreeable bitter, mandarin twist in the

> *Gris* means 'grey' in French, but, confusingly, in relation to wine, the word is used for *pink* grapes or wines.

aftertaste (if the wine is too bitter, the vines were yielding too many grapes and the winemaker then pressed them too hard). Pinot gris grapes can get quite rich in sugar while ripening, so alcohol levels of 14 per cent are normal. Pinot gris is a great match for terrine, quiche, shellfish and stir-fry.

Domaine Eugène Meyer, Pinot Gris (Alsace, France)
21a rue de Bergholtz-Zell, F-68500 Bergholtz (Haut-Rhin), France
T:+33 (0)3.89.76.13.87 vinseugenemeyer@orange.fr

The Meyer family has been making wine in Alsace since 1620 and bought their current winery, a former abbey, just after the French Revolution. In 1969, Eugène Meyer became one of the first wine-growers in France to convert to biodynamics (Demeter certified), having suffered the paralysis of an optic nerve caused by chemical vine treatments. 'My homeopathic doctor told me about

biodynamics,' says Meyer, 'but at the time most of my neighbours took me for a fool. This changed when organics and biodynamics became fashionable in the 1990s.'

Eugène's son, François, and his wife Sylvie now run the 9-hectare (22-acre) vineyard. Spare land is grazed by a neighbour's cows, which supply manure for compost – one of the best composts I have ever seen for its forest-floor smell, moist and crumbly texture and dark-earth colour. Around one third of the vineyard has a light spreading of compost each year. The grapes are hand-picked and the white wines – mainly riesling, pinot gris and gewürztraminer – are characterised by their wonderful, mouthwatering depth. Their freshness is no accident, but a result of feeding the soil with living compost so the vines can stay cool in Alsace's very dry, often torrid climate. The Meyer family's basic pinot gris, a grape that can often produce heavy-tasting wines that coat your tongue with nothing but flavourless alcoholic whiffs, is a good example of this. It has the width pinot gris typically shows in the mouth, and rather than getting stuck on your tongue, it keeps moving across, urging you to pour another glass.

Maysara Winery, Arsheen Pinot Gris, McMinnville (Oregon, USA)
15765 Muddy Valley Road, McMinnville, OR 97128, USA
T:+001 503.843.1234 www.maysara.com

From 1998, Persian-born Moe Momtazi and and his wife Flora began transforming an abandoned wheat farm just south of their home in McMinnville in Oregon's Willamette Valley into a 93-hectare (230-acre) vineyard. Soon after planting, Moe converted to organics and then almost immediately to biodynamics (Demeter certified). He got his own herd of cows to provide manure for biodynamic compost. Moe has his own vine nursery, and gets almost everything he needs for his biodynamic compost, sprays and teas from his own land. He says,

> Some people were a bit sceptical about whether what we were doing with biodynamics would work, but what could be more natural than healing vines with biodynamic teas made from local plants or manure which, after all, is just plants that have been digested? Sometimes it takes one plant to heal another.

Moe points to the trout swimming in the reservoir he uses for irrigation as proof of how sustainable wine-growing and nature can co-exist.

> The reservoir is fed by water running over our land, through both wild habitat and vineyards. Trout are incredibly sensitive and simply cannot survive in water contaminated by vineyard sprays.

Moe makes pinot-noir red wines, and dry white wines from pinot blanc and pinot gris. Moe calls his entry-level pinot gris after the Persian princess 'Arsheen', who lived in about 500 BC and was

Springtime at Maysara Winery in Oregon, USA, when the companion planting flowers beautifully. Maysara Winery

given the role of palace winemaker due to her impeccable palate. Pinot gris absolutely thrives in this part of Oregon and Maysara's example is typical of what to expect: a dry wine with soft green melon and hazelnut flavours, and an almost spritzy twist of lime in the aftertaste. Drink the youngest vintage available.

OTHER BIODYNAMIC PINOT GRIS PRODUCERS

...include, in Alsace: Domaine Barmès-Buecher (www.barmes-buecher.com) from the Rosenberg vineyard (Biodyvin), Domaine Buecher-Fix (www.buecher-fix.fr) from the Hatschbourg grand cru (Demeter), Clément and Francine Klur (www.klur.net) from the Winenck-Schlossberg grand cru (Demeter), and Andrée and Jean-Louis Trapet of Domaine Trapet-Jung (www.domaine-trapet.fr) (see p. 153), who take their pinot gris from their Sonnenglanz grand cru (Biodyvin). In Oregon's Willamette Valley, as well as Maysara, two other vineyards produce noteable pinot gris: the Sundby family's Johan Vineyards (www.johanvineyards.com), *Cont. over* and Cooper Mountain (www.coopermountainwine.com) – Oregon's biodynamic pioneer under Dr Robert Gross – both Demeter certified. Huia in Marlborough, New Zealand, opt for a deliberately fruity style of pinot gris.

RIESLING

When asked, wine experts often say they think riesling is the finest white grape of all. This may come as a shock to chardonnay lovers, but riesling has all the things a noble vine should produce. Rieslings have fine, elegant, perfectly balanced, interesting flavours; an ability to transmit a real sense of place; and they can age and develop in the bottle. Riesling is more flexible than chardonnay, because it can produce world-class wines at all sweetness levels, although riesling is at the drier end of the spectrum that is currently in fashion. Unlike chardonnay, riesling is not so good for sparkling wines, where its floral daffodil and honeysuckle aromas tend to get in the way. Riesling is taken most seriously in its homeland, Germany, and in Alsace on the French–German border.

Weingut Peter-Jakob Kühn, Amphore Riesling Trocken (Rheingau, Germany)

Mühlstraße 70, D-65375 Oestrich, Germany
T:+49 (0)6723.2299 www.weingutpjkuehn.de

Germany's Rheingau region might well claim to have produced the world's top riesling wines for at least three centuries, but there is a counter-argument that in recent years the Rheingau has been rather living off its reputation, making classic, boring, no-risk riesling. One man prepared to push boundaries is the modest Peter-Jakob Kühn, who has 20 hectares (50 acres) of mainly riesling vines (Demeter certified) in the famous Rheingau town of Oestrich. Peter-Jakob is a non-interventionist winemaker, allowing his deliciously richly textured riesling wines to find their own balance of dryness, sweetness, crispness and mouthfeel when fermenting.

However, for his very left-field Amphore Riesling, Peter-Jakob uses clay amphora rather than wooden or steel vats. This copies a technique first used in the Republic of Georgia, the so-called birthplace of wine, thousands of years ago, when wine was made in amphora with no additives. By soaking the riesling juice on the skins, as if he were making a red wine, Peter-Jakob allows the wine to pick up antioxidants (which are found in grapeskins). Antioxidants are thought to be good for human health, but they also help what would otherwise be a fragile wine to age well in bottle without the addition of any sulphur-dioxide preservative (sulphites).

The Kühns only make a few thousand bottles of their unsulphited Amphore Riesling each year. The wine has an amber-orange colour, and its intensely refreshing flavours of yeasty bruised apples and pears are more like beer, cider and perry (pear cider) than wine. This is a good wine to drink with oily fish and white meat, such as turkey. A bottle can be left open for days without spoiling (the only reason to leave the cork in the top of a half-drunk bottle would be to keep the flies out, unless it is in the refrigerator).

Amphora wines are an acquired taste, but they are becoming something of a niche among self-styled 'natural' wine producers. For another producer using amphora, see Foradori (p. 186).

Weingut Dr Bürklin-Wolf, Wachenheimer Riesling Trocken (Pfalz, Germany)
Weinstrasse Süd 65, D-67157 Wachenheim, Germany
T:+49 06322.95330 www.buerklin-wolf.de

In the mid 1990s, while odd-job winemaking and wine writing in Germany's Pfalz, I visited Weingut Dr Bürklin-Wolf. When I mentioned biodynamics to the estate's owners, the Bürklin family, they told me they wanted to be biody-namic one day. At the time, biodynamics was seen as weirdly subversive, and with 80 hectares (200 acres) of vines, including Germany's most valuable riesling vines in their Kirchen-stück plot, I thought it unlikely Bürklin-Wolf was going to indulge in something so esoteric. Yet within a few years, they were making biodynamic compost from their own horse and cow manure while burying hundreds of cow horns for biodynamic horn spray preparations.

Bürklin-Wolf's owners then asked me to work as a consultant to them, because they liked the way I saw biodynamics as a sustainable tool for growing higher quality grapes, rather than as a cult or religion. I accepted. Our first task was to make sure that, with vines spread across six villages, the daily wine-growing work was well organised enough for biodynamics to be the cherry on the cake, not the cake itself. Biodynamics alone won't make you a good wine. Red wine vineyards that distracted from the winery's main focus on riesling were sold. The money raised was used to improve the making and spreading of biodynamic compost, to buy gentler ploughs for the soil, and to make the vineyards more biodiverse by, for example, developing habitat breaks, insect hotels and bee-friendly cover crops. Sometimes less is more.

The aim with biodynamics here (the estate has Biodyvin biodynamic certification) is to help each vine produce wines that express a sense of 'somewhereness' – to carry some flavour from the site and soil it is grown on. German wines are classed according to how much sugar the grapes have at harvest; Dr Bürklin-Wolf became the first German winery to instead class its wines on the unique, site-specific flavours those grapes contain. This follows Burgundy's practice of labelling wines as coming from grand cru (GC) sites, premier cru (PC) sites, and single village (*villages*) sites. This idea is now catching on throughout German wine.

My favourite riesling from Dr Bürklin-Wolf comes from *villages* vineyards near the winery, in the village of Wachenheim. Each time I visit, the owners leave a tasting bottle of each new vintage of the Wachenheimer Riesling in the fridge. When I taste it, I look for the hallmark of a typical Pfalz riesling: something dry, full-bodied, creamy in texture, with racy grapefruit, mirabelle, spicy-peach and honey-blossom flavours, to be drunk ideally between two and eight years of the harvest.

Weingut is German for a wine estate growing all its own grapes. Use of the term indicates that the wine was grown, made and bottled on the one premises. It is used similarly to the French words *château* and *domaine* in a vineyard's name.

OTHER BIODYNAMIC RIESLING PRODUCERS IN GERMANY
...include Fuchs Jacobus (www.weingut_fuchs_jacobus.de) in the Nahe, which is self-contained and the biggest vineyard in Germany to be located on entirely steep slopes (15 hectares); Helmut Christ (www.weingut-helmut-christ.de) and Weingut Deppisch (www.weingut-deppisch.com) in Franken; the Pfeffer-Müller family's Weingut Brüder Dr Becker (www.brueder-dr-becker.de) in Rheinhessen; Rainer Haas of Weingut Jacob Christ and the Schipf family of Weingut Donnermühle (www.donnermuehle.de), both in the Rheingau; Weingut Janson-Bernhard (www.janson-bernhard.de), Weingut Pflüger (www.pflueger-wein.de), Dominik Bender (www.bender-eschbach.de) and the under-rated Rudolf Eymann (www.weingutéymann.de), all in the Pfalz; and Marküs Bürgin's Hofgut Sonnenschein (www.hofgut-sonnenschein.de) in Baden. (All these are Demeter certified.)

Domaine Marc Kreydenweiss, Riesling Andlau (Alsace, France)

12 rue Deharbe, F-67140 Andlau (Bas-Rhin), France
T:+33 (0)3.88.08.95.83   www.kreydenweiss.com

Marc Kreydenweiss took over a family wine estate when it was producing lots of bottles that sold well for cheap prices. But he decided to make life difficult by producing less wine of higher quality to sell for higher prices. 'I lost 80 per cent of my clients overnight,' he smiles.

> *I did it because I knew I had vines on some of Alsace's best bits of soil, just like my much more famous neighbours, but the wines we had been making just tasted really anonymous because we were telling our vines to produce lots of bottles with no flavours inside them.*

Marc adopted biodynamics in 1989, inspired by tasting a biodynamic chardonnay from Burgundy. He then founded the first ever biodynamic-wine producers' group, the SIVCBD or 'Biodyvin'.

Marc's signature grape variety is riesling. He says, 'I want my riesling to be dry, straight, long and slightly saline.' This probably makes the wine sound like a breadstick pretzel, but Marc is talking about riesling that really tastes of the soil, in his case blue-grey schist, a soil giving wines a wonderfully swirly internal texture. His three schist rieslings all come from his home village of Andlau: the Kastelberg, a top grand-cru site for electrifyingly dense riesling (5,000 bottles); Clos Rebberg, a brutally steep slope overlooking Andlau, where you can break your leg grape picking, but which gives wines that taste of riesling juice squeezed from a clenched-but-not-angry fist (4,000 bottles); and the village or Andlau bottling, which has the gleaming austerity riesling freaks love. Try with tuna.

Domaine Valentin Zusslin, Riesling Clos Liebenberg (Alsace, France)

57 Grand'Rue, F-68500 Orschwihr (Haut-Rhin), France
T:+33 (0)3.89.76.82.84   www.zusslin.com

The youthful brother-and-sister team of Marie and Jean-Paul Zusslin have turned this 14-hectare (35-acre) Alsace estate around since taking over from their father in 1997. Their horse, Sesame, now ploughs the entire estate. Yields have been reduced, partly by leaving fewer buds at pruning, and partly by softening the soils with regular but light doses of very well-fermented biodynamic compost. Encouraged, the vines started using some of their hitherto excess energy to put down more complex root systems, 'almost as if they were giving themselves a good stretch after a period of slumber,' says winemaker Jean-Paul. 'We get smaller, riper, brighter, more luminous berries than before,' he says. The grapes crack, rather than flop, open when you pop one in your mouth. Their pips are ripe brown (a good sign) and the skins crunchy and thick. Jean-Paul says,

> Grapes with strong skins give me more options of exactly when to pick, because I have to pick only when I know the flavours are ready. When our soils were harder, the vines were stunted underground, and their roots too shallow. If it rained, the grapes would swell up overnight. You either picked them with dilute flavours or waited until they burst and got diseased.

The Clos Liebenberg is a 3-hectare walled vineyard on a calcium-rich limestone-sandstone mix. We don't know whether the sheep that return here every winter to graze find that under the biodynamic regime the vineyard grasses are richer in the calcium they need. But the Clos Liebenberg Riesling (5,500 bottles) exhibits a snap, luminosity and voluptuously creamy depth it didn't have before.

Domaine Josmeyer, Riesling Grand Cru Brand (Alsace, France)

76 rue Clémenceau, F-68920 Wintzenheim (Haut-Rhin), France
T:+33 (0)3.89.27.91.90 www.josmeyer.com

The Meyer family is now in its sixth generation of wine-growing in Alsace. When vineyard manager, winemaker and family member Christophe Ehrhart started working here in the mid 1990s, the 26-hectare (65-acre) vineyard was already essentially organic. Christophe took six years to convert it to biodynamics (Demeter certified), having been inspired partly by his own conviction that biodynamic wine tasted better and partly by having studied wine-growing with Alsace's most influential wine teacher, Jean Schaetzel (see p. 257). Christophe says,

> I'd heard biodynamics being described as some kind of single formula or simple recipe. My sense in fact was biodynamics gives you great freedom and autonomy in your farming. There is no single way to do it, so I visited or listened to various biodynamic wine-growers in Alsace and in other regions. I think the beauty of biodynamics is that it does the exact opposite of putting you in a straitjacket. It allows you to express yourself as a farmer, and allows each plot of vines to find the best way of expressing itself.

Christophe cites two Josmeyer wines as examples:
Riesling from the Hengst grand cru [in Wintzenheim] grows on cool, dense limestone. The result is a wine that has what I call horizontality, meaning a riesling that has broad, wide flavours on the palate and broad, intense aromas which swirl around under your nose but don't immediately go right up it. In contrast, our riesling in Brand [in Turckheim] grows in a sun trap and on warmer, sandier, granitic soils. This gives a wine with a more vertical expression, both in its mouthfeel and aromas.

The flavours and smells of Josmeyer's Brand Riesling are deep and profound. You feel you can dig into the wine and keep coming up with something new. It is an absolute marvel of inner vibrancy, incisiveness and staying power. Around 3,000 bottles are made each year.

Oxen pull the plough at Domaine Josmeyer in France's Alsace region.

Domaine Zind-Humbrecht, Riesling Heimbourg (Alsace, France)

4 route de Colmar, F-68230 Turckheim (Haut-Rhin), France
T:+33 (0)3.89.27.02.05 www.zind-humbrecht.com

Olivier Humbrecht's Alsace winery has been in his family since the early seventeenth century. Olivier picks up professional wine qualifications as easily as most of us pick up our groceries, being an agronomist, winemaker and the first Frenchman to pass the almost-impossible Master of Wine exam (he studied English so he could understand the questions, and wrote his answers in English). With a science background, Olivier could be forgiven for ignoring biodynamics, which can appear to be more about nebulous, spiritual concepts than hard, scientific ones. But he decided to convert all 40 hectares (100 acres) of his vines to biodynamics after he saw the improvements it brought to his compost. He says,

As a scientist, I am naturally drawn to experimentation, so when I heard about biodynamics I wanted to try it [which he did, beginning in 1997, on around six hectares]. My father never used chemical anti-rot treatments or insecticides, and we had been making our own compost here for years, using manure from local farms. When talking to biodynamic growers, they would always stress how central to biodynamics having good compost was. But I had never been satisified with our compost, because we had not been paying enough attention to the quality of the manure or of the straw. But the first year we composted using biodynamic manure and placed the six biodynamic preparations in the piles, we saw there were many more worms, the texture of the compost was less heavy, it had the right moisture balance and it smelt so much better than before. One did not need to be a compost expert to see the differences, even after just three to four months. I could clearly see the effect of the biodynamic preparations in the compost, even if I had no scientific explanation for it. I decided I just could not continue farming my vines any way other than biodynamically.

Typically for an Alsace estate, Domaine Zind-Humbrecht produces mainly white wines. All the wines ferment in old wooden casks, not to give them an oaky flavour, but because the wood has an insulating effect. This helps the yeast, because if the wines get too cold in winter the fermentation may stop and the wine will go vinegary. Such insulation is especially important for Olivier, who lets some of his wines ferment for a year or more. Even then some wines don't fully finish their fermentation, meaning they contain a bit of unfermented sugar, leading to white wines which are off-dry and exuberantly fruity, but which leave a savoury, almost saline aftertaste. You can't make wines like this unless the vines are really connecting with the soils they grow in. A great example is Olivier's Heimbourg Riesling, grown on cool limestone subsoils located on a steep hillside swept by blistering afternoon winds. This has riesling's typical taut core wrapped in lavish layers of ripe mandarin and peach fruit. Irresistible when young, Heimbourg Riesling can nevertheless age two decades or more. Try with mild blue cheese. Each year Domaine Zind-Humbrecht makes 8,000 bottles.

OTHER ALSACE RIESLING SPECIALISTS

...include Jean-Baptiste Adam (www.jb-adam.fr) for its Kaefferkopf grand cru (Demeter), Audrey and Christian Binner for their Schlossberg grand cru (organic certification), Dirler-Cadé (www.dirler-cade.com) for its Saering and Kessler grands crus (Biodyvin), Fleith-Eschard (vins.fleith.over-blog.com) for its Saering and Kessler grands crus (Demeter), Domaine Geschickt (www.geschickt.fr) for its Kaefferkopf grand cru, Kuentz-Bas (www.kuentz-bas.fr) for its Pfersigberg grand cru (Demeter), Patrick and Mireille Meyer of Domaine Julien Meyer in Nothalten for their Muenchberg grand cru (Demeter), and the Faller family of Domaine Weinbach (www.domaineweinbach.com) for their Schlossberg grand cru (Demeter).

Nikolaihof Wachau, Riesling Steiner Hund, Kremstal (Wachau, Austria)

Nikolaigasse 3, A-3512 Mautern, Austria
T:+43 (0)2732.82901   www.nikolaihof.at

The Nikolaihof winery overlooks the Danube in the Wachau region of Lower Austria (Niederösterreich). The cellar's part-Roman foundations make it the oldest winery in Austria. Owners Nikolaus and Christine Saahs are so into biodynamics they farm their 20-hectare (50-acre) vineyard biodynamically (Demeter certified) *and* only serve biodynamic food in their winery restaurant, the Weinstube Nikolaihof, one of Austria's best. As well as producing some of Austria's top grüner veltliner white wines, Nikolaihof is also a riesling specialist. Its most renowned riesling is from the Kremstal town of Stein ('stone') from a plot called 'Hund' ('dog'). Steiner Hund was named during the Thirty Years War (1618–1648) when the vineyard was worth but a 'stone dog', because its steep terraces on primary rock were so tough to work. Steiner Hund is entirely farmed by hand and Christine calls Steiner Hund Riesling the 'difficult child', as it is as unforgiving in the bottle as it is to farm, needing a decade or two to show its incredibly powerful fruit and deeply layered, almost chiselled minerality. Try a young wine with smoked salmon, a more mature one with spinach ravioli.

IN AUSTRALIA
...Herriot Wines (www.herriotwines.com.au) in Western Australia and Mitchell Wines (www.mitchellwines.com) in Clare, South Australia, are noted for their biodynamic rieslings (both Demeter certified).

ROMORANTIN

Romorantin is a rare grape used for dry white wines in a tiny sub-region of Touraine in the Loire Valley called Cour-Cheverny.

Domaine des Huards, Cour Cheverny Cuvée François Premier (Loire Valley, France)

F-41700 Cour-Cheverny (Loir et Cher), France
T:+33 (0).2.54.79.97.90 www.gendrier.com

The Gendrier family has been making wine since 1846. Raoul Gendrier was one of the few Cour-Cheverny wine-growers to stick with the romorantin grape when plantings of it almost died out in the 1950s. In 1997, Gendrier's grandson Michel and his wife Jocelyne converted the vineyards to biodynamics (with organic certification). There are only 50 hectares (125 acres) of romorantin in Cour-Cheverny, and 7 of those belong to the Gendriers. Most of their vines were planted in the 1930s and 1950s. Their top example is named after François 1st (1515–1547), a powerful but modernising French king, who apparently decreed that romorantin be planted here. Michel Gendrier says,

> We built our own special sprayer so we could spray large areas of vines without compacting the soil with the tractor. Laboratory tests show the herbal and manure teas we have been spraying since adopting biodynamics have made our [flinty clay sand over limestone] soils richer in humus and so more worm-friendly.

The Gendriers' Cour Cheverny Cuvée François Premier has a light straw colour, rapier-like green-apple and lemon-rind freshness, and bone-dry flavours of butter, walnut, beeswax and nougat. The wine can age a decade or more. Around 15,000 bottles are made each year.

SAUVIGNON BLANC

Sauvignon blanc is an increasingly popular grape. It produces pungent white wines, typically smelling of gooseberry, nettle and cat's-pee. The best examples come from the central Loire sub-regions of Pouilly-Fumé, Sancerre and Menetou-Salon, from Marlborough in New Zealand, the cooler parts of California and Südtirol (Alto Adige) in northern Italy.

Domaine Goisot, St-Bris Exogyra Virgula (Burgundy, France)
30 rue Bienvenu Martin, F-89530 Saint-Bris-le-Vineux (Yonne), France
T:+33 (0)3.86.53.35.15 www.goisot.com

Jean-Hughes Goisot's 24-hectare (60-acre) biodynamic vineyard (Demeter certified) in St-Bris is one of the chilliest parts of north Burgundy. Jean-Hughes was initially sceptical about biodynamics, but nevertheless trialled some biodynamic oak-bark, stinging-nettle, common horsetail and comfrey sprays. He found they helped make his vines more resistant to the cold and also to diseases like rot and mildew. This meant Jean-Hughes could pick his grapes later, with more ripeness and flavour. His St Bris Exogyra Virgula is an unoaked, dry white wine from sauvignon blanc. The grapes grow on soils crammed with tiny, comma-shaped, 150-million-year-old fossilised seashells called *Exogyra virgula*. Cool-climate sauvignon blanc can taste lean, green and mouth-puckering. To avoid this, Jean-Hughes picks the grapes late and ferments the juice slightly warmer than normal. The result is a gently creamy white wine with cool, mossy flavours, which can age up to seven years in bottle. Around 25,000 bottles are made each year.

Vincent Gaudry, Sancerre Blanc Le Tournebride (Loire Valley, France)

Petit Chambre, Sury en Vaux, F-18300 Sancerre (Cher), France
T:+33 (0)2.48.79.49.25   www.vincent-gaudry.com

Vincent Gaudry is one of Sancerre's rising stars. As soon as he took over his family's 9-hectare (22-acre) vineyard in 2001, he converted it to biodynamics (Demeter certified). He sprays teas made from medicinal plants like stinging nettle, willow and common horsetail to keep the vines healthy. He says,

> *I prefer freshly brewed plant teas rather than fermented liquid manures. Fresh teas smell nicer and liquid manures risk making the vines too energetic, which would then make the wines too dilute.*

Vincent's dry Sancerre white wines, all from 100 per cent hand-picked sauvignon blanc, include Pour Vous ('for you') and A Mi Chemin ('halfway there'). Both age in oak barrels but are not at all dominated by wood flavours. Only two barrels of each (600 bottles) are made each year. His Le Tournebride (30,000 bottles), which is not oak aged, comes from vines grown on all three main soil types in Sancerre: clay limestone for body, flint for aroma and chalk pebbles (*caillottes*) for elegance. Le Tournebride has warm bread aromas, and rich pear and gooseberry freshness within.

Domaine Vacheron, Sancerre Les Romains (Loire Valley, France)

Rue des Puits Poniton, F-18300 Sancerre (Cher), France
T:+33 (0)2.48.54.09.93 vacheron.sa@wanadoo.fr

The Vacheron family produces red and white Sancerre wines you could bet your house on. They have always picked their 45-hectare (111-acre) vineyard by hand (a rarity in Sancerre), meaning sub-standard grapes never get close to their winery. They have really well-sited vineyards, some plots of which are bottled separately. Their best Sancerre rouge plot, 'La Belle Dame', has flinty soil that gives the pinot noir grapes plenty of colour and rugged bite. Sauvignon blanc gives varied white wines depending on where it is grown: dark soils in Le Paradi warm quickly and face the sun, so this wine is richly ripe; Grands Champs is nervier, and from redder soils; Guigne Chèvres is a cool soil in a sunny site, making a Sancerre sauvignon as tasty but prickly as a bush of gooseberries.

Jean-Laurent Vacheron says his family converted to biodynamics (Biodyvin certified) because it would enable their old vines to live longer (see p. 205 [Cullen]), while adding a bit of extra subtlety and complexity to their wines. Jean-Laurent says,

With biodynamics you connect more closely with your vines. You think in a more focussed way. At winter pruning, for example, we coat the vines with a winter-pruning paste. This is made from cow manure, whey, sand and clay. It costs nothing really to prepare and use, but has such a good effect, keeping the vines cleaner, healthier and more vital, so they live longer.

Old vines are at a premium in Sancerre, which enjoyed a huge planting boom in the 1980s and 1990s, when demand for Sancerre dramatically increased. Some of these vineyards, although still relatively young, are starting to die early of vine cancers, which cause the woody trunks to dry up. 'This is a sign they have lost their vitality,' says Jean-Laurent.

My favourite wine from the Vacheron family is their Sancerre Blanc Les Romains. It comes from 3 hectares (7 acres) of sauvignon blanc, planted in the late 1960s on warm flint. The wine has everything you would hope to find in Sancerre: grassy, nettley scents with generous lime-and-blackcurrant flavours, lightly seasoned with flint sparks and a touch of old oak from ageing in wooden vats.

Alexandre Bain, Pouilly-Fumé (Loire Valley, France)

148 Rue des 4 Fils Doumer, Boisfleury, F-58150 Tracy sur Loire (Nièvre), France
T:+33 (0)6.77.11.13.05 alexandre.bain@orange.fr

Sauvignon blanc is an exuberant vine, making exuberant, gooseberry-and-cat's-pee-scented, dry white wines. Well, that's the standard account anyway. In contrast, Alexandre Bain's sauvignon blanc, from Pouilly-Fumé in the deep heart of the Loire Valley, is a masterclass in understatement, with wonderful bruised-apple depth and wet-stone purity. Alexandre has 8 hectares (20 acres) of biodynamic (Demeter certified) vines. He adds no fertilizer to the soil, so the vines grow slowly enough to need only light trimming, if at all. This, coupled with Alexandre's decision to prune the bunch-bearing vine shoots lower to the ground than is common here, means the grapes produce and retain a more interesting and authentic range of flavours. When his vines are extending their green shoots upwards in the warm spring-to-summer period, he sprays them with seaweed, dandelion and stinging nettle. This prevents heat stress. When his vines start ripening their grapes as cooler weather begins from late summer to autumn, he warms the atmosphere above them with biodynamic horn silica spray 501 mixed with valerian 507 extract. He ploughs only very gently and when moon phases are at their calmest, meaning at new rather than full moon. Alexandre says Phénomène, his Percheron horse, 'is good for spring ploughing but he needs to work more tidily in winter when the earth is ploughed up around the vine trunk to keep it warm.'

Alexandre picks his sauvignon blanc grapes by hand. He bottles the wines from the old barrels they age in when the moon is in its calm 'autumn' or descending phase (two weeks per month) and during periods of high atmospheric pressure, because, he says, 'The wine looks and tastes brighter like that.'

'I want drinkability and digestibility in my wine,' he says, quietly. And he gets it.

Domaine Philippe Gilbert, Menetou-Salon Blanc (Loire Valley, France)

Les Faucards, F-18510 Menetou-Salon (Cher), France
T:+33 (0)2.48.66.65.90 www.domainephilippegilbert.fr

Philippe Gilbert never thought he would run his family's Loire vineyards. He says,
My interests lay in politics and the theatre. Combining these in a play, I wrote about the massacre at Srebrenica during the Yugoslav civil war. I began part-time here in 2000, and from 2003 assumed full control from my father. The vineyards had been farmed very conventionally, but my father never stood in my way when I said I was going biodynamic.

There are 27 hectares (66 acres) in Menetou-Salon, a smaller, less famous, but often better value region compared to nearby Sancerre, and producing similar wines: fragrantly dry sauvignon blanc whites and pinot noir rosés and reds. Philippe sensed the vineyards he took over looked tired, overly compacted and lifeless, and were 'not producing wines with the kind of narrative they were capable of. I know that sounds quite literary,' he says, a bit self-consciously, 'but if you think about it, good wines have a beginning – meaning a nice scent – then a middle when you drink them, and finally an end in their aftertaste.'

Philippe was so keen to get going with biodynamics, he even bought some biodynamic compost from the Vacheron family in nearby Sancerre (see p.92), saying 'it's better to buy top-quality compost when you embark on biodynamics, than risk making poor-quality compost just to say you made something yourself.' Philippe now does make his own compost and has stopped his father's practice of picking the grapes by machine. Wine from hand-picked sauvignon blanc grapes, 'just tastes better than the machine-picked version,' he says.

The proof comes in the Domaine Philippe Gilbert Menetou-Salon Blanc. This is tank fermented and so sees no oak (unlike Philippe's barrel-fermented Renardière version). It smells of midsummer nettles, its lemon-and-lime-citrus flavours feel comfortably pithy in the mouth, and the aftertaste is mealy, lingering and soft, because the wine was aged on its spent fermentation yeast lees. Around 50,000 bottles are made each year. Try with goat's cheese and rocket salad.

Domaine Maisons Brulées, Suavignon Blanc (Loire Valley, France)

5 impasse de la Vallée du Loing, F-41110 Pouillé (Loir et Cher), France
T:+33.02.54.71.51.57

When Roger Augé died in 1979, he left some vines in Touraine in the Loire Valley and eight children. One of them, Michel, who was 24 at the time, took the vines on but sold half of them. He then survived by earning a salary running the local wine co-operative, and also fermenting his own wine there, until he could build his own winery. Michel had already started to change the way his father's vines had been farmed, first by reducing, then eliminating weedkillers, fungicides and pesticides, while gleaning tips on organics and biodynamics from local farmers and wine-growers. Having converted his now 9 hectares (20 acres) of vines to biodynamics (Demeter certified) and built his own winery, Michel set about making wines more in keeping with his biodynamic ideals, meaning wines made to last but with no additives or fancy winemaking tricks. His sauvignon blanc is the perfect example: it comes from flint and clay soils pre-disposed to give white wines with real weight and conviction. The authorities won't let Michel label his wine sauvignon, deeming it too weird to fall into that category, so Michel calls it 'Suavignon' instead.

Young sauvignon blanc should be light bright green in colour. But if you look at Michel's Suavignon, you see a rich yellow wine that appears way past its peak. Michel says,

I soak the grape juice on the grapeskins for a few days. This helps the wine age well, because grapeskins contain antioxidants. These help wines to age, and in our blood helps humans live longer too.

Michel ages the wine in old barrels to round it out, but without giving it an oaky flavour. The result is a wine that is very different to the stereotypical 'cat's-pee on a gooseberry bush'-flavoured sauvignon blanc we are so used to. Michel's Suavignon is bottled unfiltered. It looks slightly cloudy, and is richly wholesome and filled with dry flavours of country apples and homemade cider. 5,000 bottles are made each year.

Loacker Schwarhof, Sauvignon Blanc Tasnim (South Tyrol, Italy)

Domaine Loacker, Sankt Justina 3, 39100 Bolzano (BZ), Italy
T:+39 0471.365125 www.loacker.net

The Loacker family has 7 hectares (18 acres) of vineyards in their native South Tyrol (Südtirol) region in alpine northern Italy (this is also called 'Alto Adige'). Both this, and their Tuscany vineyard, Tenuta Corte Pavone in Montalcino (see p. 173), are farmed biodynamically (with organic certification). Winemaker Hayo Loacker mixes biodynamic soil sprays like horn manure 500 with homeopathic yeast and bacteria cultures.

> We incubate these for 7–10 days, stirring in food in the form of molasses and air, which allow the micro-organism population to grow. These micro-organisms are good for the soil and are also sprayed on the vines to prevent mildew and rot, and in the winery [but not in the wine] to keep it clean but alive, rather than clean and sterile. We drink these microbial liquids too, sometimes.

This may seem wacky, but the Loacker wines taste quite mainstream and are not at all 'funky'. Their sauvignon blanc called 'Tasnim' is a good example: its fresh, green fruit, mandarin and fennel flavours revolve around a softly sour core of alpine acidity.

Weingut Maria and Sepp Muster, Graf Sauvignon (South Styria, Austria)

Schlossberg 38, A-8463 Leutschach, Austria
T:+43 (0)3454.70053 www.weingutmuster.com

Sepp Muster and his wife, Maria, took over Sepp's parents' 10-hectare (25-acre) vineyard in south Styria (Südsteiermark) in 2002, and converted the vines to biodynamics (Demeter certified). Vines were first planted in this mountainous Austrian region in the eighteenth century. Sepp and Maria have maintained the traditional wine-growing system here of letting the vines grow as high as a 6-foot-tall man (1.8 metres). This protects the grapes from frosty air that runs off the

nearby mountain plateau in spring, and allows the leafy shoots to flop over the grapes below, shading them from the intensely bright summer sun. Maria says,

> We don't then need to trim the vine shoots in summer. If we trim them, they produce too many leaves, and too much shade. This leads to grapes with unripe flavours. We want the shoots and leaves to shield the grapes from the sun while allowing dappled light to fall on them. We want the grapes to see the sun so they ripen, but we don't want the sun to see the grapes because this will burn them. We want small, ripe grapes full of flavour.

Sepp and Maria's red wines from local grapes like blaufränkisch, zweigelt and blauer wildbacher exude all of their mesmerisingly deep blackcurrant and plum flavours if you give the wine a really good swirl in the glass first. Their white wines, from riesling, sauvignon blanc and chardonnay (or 'morillon', in the local Styrian dialect) are satisfyingly ripe and understated. Their Graf Sauvignon Blanc has remarkable leanness and elegance. Its prickly nettle flavours are perfectly suited to waking your stomach up as you contemplate lunch or dinner.

Ceàgo Vinegarden, Sauvignon Blanc, Clear Lake (California, USA)

Kathleen's Vineyard, 5115 East Highway 20, Nice, CA 95464, USA
T: +001 707.274.1462 www.ceago.com

Jimmy Fetzer was the first American winemaker to give biodynamics some sex appeal. In the 1980s, Jimmy was a key figure in his

family's burgeoning wine empire. This had started as a small backwoods enterprise in northern California in the 1960s. By the early 1990s, Fetzer had become one of America's biggest wine brands, competing in the supermarket wine aisles with the likes of Benziger (see p. 204), but also creating a pioneering organic brand, Bonterra. Jimmy says,

The idea for Bonterra came about in the mid 1980s, when America's anti-alcohol lobby was at its most shrill. Our family saw wine simply as food for the table, but also as part of civilised culture. Man learnt to write at the same time he starting learning how to grow both food and wine, when changing from being a hunter-gatherer to a farmer-gardener. So we started a vegetable and herb garden by our winery visitor centre to show our customers how strong we felt the link should be between food and responsible wine drinking. The garden designer was an expert in biodynamic fruit trees. He incorporated biodynamic techniques when designing the garden, like companion planting to encourage beneficial insects, sowing and planting by the moon, using biodynamic sprays and composts. The garden proved a success with the public and made us decide to convert our vines to organics and then biodynamics.

When the Fetzer family sold Fetzer Vineyards and its Bonterra brand in 1992, Jimmy bought another Mendocino County vineyard called McNab Ranch, which he re-designed as a biodynamic 'vinegarden' to demonstrate his commitment to the idea of wine and food being inseparable, culturally and gastronomically. Jimmy then sold this vineyard (to the same company that had bought both the Fetzer Vineyards and Bonterra brand) and moved further north to California's Lake County. Here, for the first time, he planted a biodynamic vinegarden from scratch, rather than having to retro-fit vineyards originally planted for non-organic and non-biodynamic farming systems.

I did an internship with Jimmy's original family vineyard in the late 1990s. This was already Demeter certified biodynamic (its grapes are now bought by Bonterra). I wasn't the only one fascinated by Jimmy's idea of making vineyards look like visually stunning gardens. With flowers, flowering shrubs, olives, fruit trees, vegetables and livestock dotted around the vineyard, your senses – sight, smell, touch, sound and taste – are reawakened. Alvaro Espinoza also came to see what Jimmy was up to and took the vinegarden approach back to his native Chile (see p. 217). Mike Benziger (see p. 204) – who, like Jimmy, ran a big wine company and then downsized – sought Jimmy's advice when converting his family vineyards to biodynamics.

Jimmy Fetzer of Ceàgo Vinegarden in California holds an oak bark biodynamic preparation.

Jimmy's Lake County vinegarden is called Ceàgo and comprises 45 hectares (115 acres) of fruit, cypress and palm trees, olive groves, walnuts, figs, lavender fields, vegetable and herb gardens, agaves and riverbank habitat, plus 20 hectares (50 acres) of wine grapes. The vines lie on the shores of Clear Lake, California's largest freshwater lake, whose cool micro-climate has a tempering effect, especially suited to sauvignon blanc. Jimmy part barrel-ferments his sauvignon blanc to accentuate the wine's mouthfeel and broaden its gooseberry and green-pear flavours, so that the wine becomes more food-friendly. Try with grilled asparagus drizzled in Ceàgo's olive oil and seasoned with sea salt. 12,000 bottles are made each year.

Quivira Vineyards, Fig Tree Vineyard Sauvignon Blanc, Dry Creek Valley (California, USA)
4900 West Dry Creek Road, Healdsburg, CA 95448, USA
T:+001 707.431.8333 www.quivirawine.com

The fame of Sonoma County's Dry Creek Valley rests on its dry sauvignon blanc white wines and its rich aquatic life. The valley provides important spawning streams for steelhead and coho salmon, but by the late 1990s it was clear the valley's vineyards were having a negative impact on riverside habitats. Removal of wild habitats along creek sides to plant vineyards had meant the water was becoming less rich in oxygen, too warm, and more prone to erosion and silting. The fish needed cool, oxygen-rich water and clean gravel beds to spawn in. The family-owned Quivira winery played a leading role in restoring wild habitats along the creek, even replacing entire vineyard blocks adjacent to the water with the taller-growing native trees and shrubs needed to provide shade and prevent silting.

Not only did this help the fish, it helped the vines too. The riverside vegetation provided a home for the beneficial ladybirds and mites that keep vineyard pests under control. The adoption of biodynamics across Quivira's 37-hectare (93-acre) vineyard was simply the next logical step (Demeter certification). Quivira produces rich red wines from Rhône and Italian grape varieties, and zinfandel, but to my mind its flagship wine is its Fig Tree Vineyard Sauvignon Blanc. Dry Creek's warm days, very cool nights and fog-filled mornings provide Quivira's sauvignon blanc with a refreshing combination of subtle grassiness over an underlying peachy richness dabbed gently by a touch of oak from part-barrel fermentation. A great match for a dish like avocado salad or leek tart.

The old fig tree at Quivira's Fig Tree Vineyard in California, USA.
Quivira Vineyards

Richmond Plains, Sauvignon Blanc (Nelson, New Zealand)

McShane Road, Richmond, Nelson, New Zealand
T:+64 (0)3.544.4230 www.organicwines.co.nz

Richmond Plains became one of New Zealand's first certified organic vineyards in the 1990s. Since then, its new owners, Lars and Sam Jensen, have converted the 5-hectare (12-acre) vineyard in Nelson on the South Island to biodynamics (Demeter certified). Lars used to export certified organic mussels from Nelson, a major international deep-sea fishing port, and unsurprisingly he says that 'liquid manures for our vineyard soils tend to be mainly fish- and seaweed-based.' Habitat breaks established to encourage biodiversity include flax, cabbage trees, cheesewoods and the kowhai, New Zealand's national flower. Its yellow blossoms attract nectar-seeking tui birds (which are about the same size as a magpie). They are very territorial and fight off other bird species that might eat wine grapes. Two cows provide manure for biodynamic compost to soften the vineyard soil, which is loose shingle on top but potentially compact clay underneath.

Nelson sauvignon blanc offers a nice alternative to the more famous and more exuberant version from the nearby Marlborough region. As Richmond Plains' version shows, this grape's cat's-pee and gooseberry flavours can be gentler and less overtly herbaceous. Richmond Plains make about 18,000 bottles of Nelson sauvignon blanc each year.

Seresin Estate, Sauvignon Blanc (Marlborough, New Zealand)

Seresin Estate, Bedford Road (off Highway 63), Marlborough, New Zealand
T:+64 3.572.9408 www.seresin.co.nz

Michael Seresin's biodynamic (Demeter certified) vineyard in Marlborough, New Zealand, has no shortage of trainee staff. Would-be vineyard managers and winemakers from Spain, Australia, Britain, Canada, the USA, Sweden and India ask to work here, wanting to find out how Seresin makes biodynamics work on a large scale and in as self-sufficient a way as possible. Seresin has 113 hectares (280 acres) of vines, plus 55 hectares of olives and habitat.

Biodynamic wine-growing happens on a grand scale in grand scenery at
Seresin Estate in New Zealand.

Seresin Estate

SAUVIGNON BLANC
MARLBOROUGH
NEW ZEALAND

Staff use bicycles to move around the property and take it in turns to milk the estate's cows or to collect their manure from the vineyards, where the cows are allowed to graze. The manure is used in biodynamic sprays or in compost. Currently, Seresin's vineyards are becoming tractor-free zones, sprayed or composted with nothing other than estate-grown manures and plants, or with locally harvested seaweed.

A typical compost spray is made by diluting and aerating biodynamic compost made from material generated entirely on the estate: grape pomace (left over from winemaking), aged willow and poplar woodchips (a rich carbon source that worms love) from dedicated woodlots on the estate, chipped vine canes, freshly cut tall grass, freshly cut woody weeds (gorse and broom) and hay. The hay is first steeped in a slurry made from the manure of the estate's own cows and horses. The steeped hay contains micro-organisms that get the compost off to a good start, allowing it first to decompose and then recompose into a dark, humus-rich, earth-like substance in the right way.

Vineyard soils are ploughed rarely, if at all. This is kinder to worms, and prevents the soil losing carbon to the air, turning to dust, and choking and warming our atmosphere. Horses and a rig that Seresin's vineyard team designed for the purpose are used when spraying the permanently grassed vineyards. Keeping tractors out of the vineyard allows the soil to breathe, to stay light and spongy enough for local grasses, flowers and clovers to re-establish. Between fifteen and twenty-five species of wild plants can be found in a single square metre of vineyards here. All these wild plants are allowed to complete their annual growth cycle, that is, they are allowed to develop leaves, shoots, flowers and seeds. Only then are they rolled, not ploughed, to provide a mulch, which keeps the vineyard cool in hot weather, and which allows nutrients to be released slowly to the soil. Estate manager, Colin Ross, says,

If a vineyard looks as flat and linear as a tennis court, its wine will taste hard and linear too. You end up divorcing

your vines from the natural environment. By letting native plants complete their cycle of life, they express themselves, and allow your vineyard to do the same – to become more intelligent, if you like. This should then be reflected in your wine, as well as in people and animals working on the estate.

Seresin produces pinot noir reds, and whites from viognier, chardonnay, pinot gris, riesling and New Zealand's signature grape, sauvignon blanc. These different varieties are grown on fifteen different vineyard blocks with different soils, exposures and crop levels, each block picked late and in two or more vineyard passes. The way the vineyard is managed means that sauvignon can be picked late, and ripe, avoiding the cat's-pee and canned-corn smells common to unripe sauvignon blanc. The wine ferments with native yeasts and has a quite unique glacial, wet, stonefruit style allied to an insistent, rather than brash, intensity rare in sauvignon blanc. Around 250,000 bottles of it are made each year, and are sold in thirty countries worldwide. 'I think this wine shows that premium biodynamic wine on a [big scale] commercial level is possible,' says Colin.

Reyneke, Sauvignon Blanc Reserve (Stellenbosch, South Africa)

Uitzicht Farm, Polkadraai Road M12, Vlottenburg, Stellenbosch, South Africa
T:+27 (0)21.881.3517 www.reynekewines.co.za

In 2004, when I first visited Johan Reyneke in South Africa's flagship Stellenbosch wine region, he had just started converting his 20-hectare (50-acre) vineyard to biodynamics (now Demeter certified). He says,

We would have done it before, but we had a loan from the bank to pay for the vineyard and the housing we were building for our workers. But the bank wouldn't lend the money until I could prove biodynamics worked. The bank worried green would mean losing our grapes and not being able to pay the loans back.

They made us trial biodynamics on one plot of vines. When it worked we got the loan.

Today, Johan's biodynamic methods are something of a model for those wanting to farm wine grapes sustainably in South Africa's very hot climate and on its notoriously dry soils. Johan, who has a Masters in Environmental Philosophy, says,

Around 90 per cent of Stellenbosch's land is vineyard, making it among the most monocultural wine regions worldwide. We have tried to make Reyneke more polycultural. We set aside spare fields for our Nguni cattle [a local breed] to give us manure for compost and compost teas. We let native grasses grow in the vines. As the grasses die off in summer they provide a natural carpet or mulch for the soil. This keeps the soil cooler and means our grapes ripen more slowly, keeping their freshness rather than becoming overripe and burnt-tasting.

Stellenbosch's vines have been ravaged by small insects called mealy bugs. They carry a virus that weakens vines, making the wines taste bitter and thin. Johan says,

Pesticides are not the answer. This is because mealy bugs live happily in the soil on the roots of native grasses. If you constantly kill these native grasses with weedkillers, the mealy bug must find a new home. The first green plant it'll see in a monocultural place like Stellenbosch is a vine. We can stop this cycle of virus infection simply by being more tolerant of weedy-looking vineyards. What would you rather have? A vineyard that looks a bit scruffy because you are providing a habitat for a known pest, to avoid using pesticides and to keep your vines virus-free? Or a clean-looking vineyard with no weeds, but which then contains vines which look awful because they have caught a virus which makes their leaves turn an unhealthy-looking red colour?

Johan Reyneke's Sauvignon Blanc Reserve is loaded with layered, flinty mineral rather than simple gooseberry flavours. It's a great example of a *terroir*-driven wine (a wine with a sense of place), in a country where few such wines exist. 4,000 bottles are made each year. (See also Reyneke's Cornerstone Red, p.206.)

*OTHER BIODYNAMIC PRODUCERS WHOSE SAUVIGNON
BLANC WINES ARE WORTH FINDING*
...include Bruno Allion's Domaine de Pontcher in Touraine in the
Loire Valley (Demeter certified); Alphonse Mellot (www.mellot.
com) in Sancerre (Biodyvin certified); Domaine Fouassier (www.
fouassier.fr) in Sancerre (Biodyvin certified); Alois Lageder's
Tenutae Lageder (www.lageder.eu) in Italy's Südtirol – Alto Adige
(Demeter certified); Huia (www.huia.net.nz) in Marlborough,
New Zealand; and Werlitsch (www.werlitsch.com) in south Styria,
Austria (Demeter certified).

UGNI BLANC

Ugni blanc produces high yields of crisp, lightly herby, usually very
early-drinking white wines with faint citrus flavours. It is grown all
over Italy, where it is called 'trebbiano', and in southwest France,
where it makes dry white wines (one of which is profiled below) and
Armagnac brandy. The Mandelaëre family's Domaine de Saoubis
(www.mandelaere.de) produces the only biodynamic Armagnac
(Demeter certified).

Château Tour Blanc, Les Milles Fleurs Blanc (Gascony, Southwest France)

Le Tour Blanc, F-40310 Parlebosq (Landes), France
T:+33 (0)5.58.44.33.56

Château Tour Blanc is located in the rural Landes region of southwest
France. The region is famed for its goose pâté and Armagnac brandy.
In recent years some Armagnac vineyards have had their ugni blanc
vines converted from brandy to table wine, in response to changes in
people's drinking habits. Château Tour Blanc produces several ugni
blanc white wines – Sables Fauves, La Grive Blanche, Papillon de
Nuit, Les Milles Fleurs – all styled for early drinking.

Owners Philip and Sandra Kelton have 32 hectares (80 acres)
of biodynamic vines (Demeter certified). 'We leave the vineyards

grassed,' says Sandra, 'because the ground-cover creates a bit of competition for the vines, making for smaller, more flavoured grapes.' And if the weeds grow too high? 'We have an eighty-strong flock of Clun Forest sheep who keep weeds down to an acceptable height,' she says.

The bulk of the vines were planted in two periods, in the early 1900s and early 1970s. Old vines, low yields and hand-picking (a rarity in the Landes) make these refreshing, easily approachable white wines.

VERDICCHIO

Verdicchio is the name of a yellowish-green grape. The wine made from it is often said to be like an Italian version of chardonnay, meaning a rich, textured white wine with easily digestible peach, pear and grapefruit flavours.

Pievalta, Verdicchio dei Castelli di Jesi Dominè (Marche, Italy)

Via Monteschiavo 18, I – 60030 Maiolati Spontini (AN = Ancona), Italy
T:+39 0731.780375 www.baronepizzini.it

Verdicchio dei Castelli di Jesi is a mouthwatering and full-bodied dry white wine from near Ancona in the Marche region on Italy's Adriatic coast. Castelli di Jesi refers to the 'castles of Jesi': a local, medieval, fortified hilltop town. Alessandro Fenino produces one of the most deeply textured verdicchios from the 27-hectare (70-acre) Pievalta estate (Demeter certified). 'It's quite easy being biodynamic here,' he says. 'The clay or tufa soils are rich in fossilised seashells so drain really well. This keeps the grapes small, concentrated and disease-free enough for us to pick them late and ripe and with lots of flavour.'

Fenino's Verdicchio 'Dominè' (80,000 bottles a year) is a blend of his two main vineyard parcels. These are called Pievalta, which is good for elegance and flavour, and San Paolo, which is lower lying and gives the wine its breadth and texture. Dominè has a lovely, bright, light-amber colour, and savoury almond and butter flavours, with a twist of green pear and ripe lemon in the aftertaste. This is a wine that has no fear of being paired with rich, creamy dishes.

VIOGNIER

Viognier is a fussy-to-grow, fascinating-to-taste, much sought-after, niche white grape. It originates in Condrieu, a small region in France's northern Rhône, and the surrounding Ardèche. Viognier's dazzling yellow grapes produce dry white wines with melting peach and apricot flavours. Hefty alcohol levels of 14.5 per cent are normal. So are high prices: viognier's fragile spring blossoms can produce tiny grape yields. Viognier wines can undergo butterfly-like transformations with time: the initial varnish flavours can turn creamy lychee, even honeyed.

Ngeringa Viognier (Mount Barker, South Australia)
119 Williams Road, Mount Barker Summit, SA 5251, Australia
T:+61 (0)8.8398.2867 www.ngeringa.com

Thirty-something Erinn and Janet Klein's Ngeringa vineyard in the sea-breezy hills above Adelaide, South Australia, is part of a mixed farm running Scottish Highland cattle and sheep, which feed on the estate's own  hay and green manure. They also grow fruit and vegetables. Erinn and Janet took the estate on from Erinn's parents, who were Steiner-Waldorf schoolteachers. They also grew medicinal biodynamic herbs here for their successful Jurlique International range of natural cosmetics. The winery was built from biodynamic straw that Erinn and Janet grew and baled on the property.

Today, Erinn makes the wines, while Janet manages the 5 hectares (12 acres) of biodynamic vineyards (certified organic). The Ngeringa viognier grapes are hand-picked but, unusually, Erinn allows their juice to soak on the grapeskins for two days. Normally when making white wine the skins are thrown away after the grapes have been squeezed and the juice collected. Erinn says, 'I leave the viognier juice in contact with the skins to give the juice just enough extra texture to cope with fermentation in barrel,' – in this case, old French barrels. These give virtually no woody taste to the wine at all, allowing Ngeringa Viognier's dense, honeysuckle fruit to shine in its mineral-driven, savoury wrap.

The viognier grows on similar soils to those found in the best vineyards of the Rhône valley: volcanic schist with sparkly bits of mica in it. Schist gives very layered viogner, geared more to slow, reflective sipping than immediate gulping. Only 1,000–1,500 bottles of Ngeringa Viognier are made each year. Ngeringa also produces stand-out chardonnay, pinot noir and syrah.

Yalumba Organic Viognier (Riverland, South Australia)
Eden Valley Road, Angaston SA 5353, Australia
T:+61 (0) 8.8561.3200 info@yalumba.com

Yalumba is one of Australia's most respected – and still family owned – wine companies. Its owners, the Hill-Smith family, have their own conventionally farmed vineyards, but also buy in grapes for wines like Yalumba Organic Viognier. This is actually made from certified biodynamic grapes (certified organic) grown by Tony and Pam Barich on their 16-hectare (40-acre) Whistling Kite vineyard along the Murray River in southeast Australia's Riverland (www.whistlingkitewines.com.au). Tony and Pam acquired the vineyard in 1977 and farmed it organically until they switched to biodynamics, the first vineyard in the Riverland to do so. The estate takes its name from the native whistling kite, which roosts in the eucalyptus red gums along the Murray. Tony says, 'We have a favourite pair called Bonnie and Clyde who soar above the vineyard and also come in to be fed.'

Yalumba Organic Viognier shows a very obviously fruity side to the viognier grape, a real peaches-and-cream wine in terms of flavour and texture. Try with mushroom risotto.

OTHER VIOGNIERS TO LOOK OUT FOR

...are made by Mas de Libian (see p. 220) and Michel Chapoutier's Granges de Mirabel (see p. 174), both in France's Ardèche region in the Rhône valley; Millton (see p. 55) and Seresin (see p. 101), both from New Zealand; Cowhorn Vineyard in Oregon (Demeter) (www.cowhornwine.com); Phillip and Mary Morwood Hart's AmByth Estate in California for viognier made with no added sulphites (Demeter) (www.ambythestate.com); and Avonmore Estate in Heathcote, Victoria, Australia, where owners Rob and Pauline Bryans have 10 hectares (25 acres) of vines and another 110 hectares (270 acres) for cows and wild habitat (Demeter) (www.avonmoreestatewine.com).

Grgich Hills chardonnay vineyard in evening sun (see p.45).
Rocco Ceselin

WHITE WINES FROM MORE THAN ONE GRAPE VARIETY (BLENDED)

Château Morlan-Tuilière, Entre Deux Mers (Bordeaux, France)

2 Place du Lavoir, F-33760 St Pierre de Bat (Gironde), France
T:+33 (0)5.57.34.52.52 www.morlan-tuiliere.com

Château Morlan-Tuilière is one of the Bordeaux region's pioneering organic vineyards. Pierre Abel Simonneau inherited the estate in the 1965 and is a professor at Bordeaux's prestigious wine university. However, unlike many of his academic colleagues, Simonneau was never convinced that the university-tested technologies like weedkillers and pesticides that became fashionable in the 1960s were the right tools for high-quality wine. Bordeaux has more than 10,000 vineyards, but Morlan-Tuilière is among a mere handful that has never been weedkilled. Pierre Abel's son, Florent, took over in 2002 and converted the 24-hectare (60-acre) vineyard to biodynamics (Demeter certified). 'Biodynamic sprays and compost were the best way of softening our quite heavy clay soils, making them easier to work,' he says.

Two-thirds of production is given to easy-to-approach Bordeaux Rouge red wines, and the rest to dry white wines bottled either as Bordeaux Blanc or Entre Deux Mers. They are made from three different grapes: semillon (60 per cent), which provides a light golden colour and herby freshess; sauvignon blanc (30 per cent), for its gooseberry fruit; and muscadelle (10 per cent) for soft mouthfeel. Around 25,000 bottles are produced each year. The wine can be labelled either as Château Morlan-Tuilière, Château Laubarit or Château Plantadey, depending on where it is sold. Drink the most recent vintage available.

> **BORDEAUX IS ALSO RENOWNED FOR SWEET WHITE WINES**
> ...from its semillon, sauvignon blanc and muscadelle grapes in the Barsac-Sauternes region. Château Climens (www.chateau-climens.fr) is the first there with biodynamic certification (Biodyvin), and is one of the most famous vineyards in this region.

Domaine Marcel Deiss, Grand Cru Le Grand Vin de l'Altenberg (de Bergheim) (Alsace, France)

15 route du Vin, 68750 Bergheim (Haut-Rhin), France
T:+33 (0)3.89.73.63.37 www.marceldeiss.fr

If you ask Jean-Michel Deiss when he went biodynamic, he won't answer by giving you the date in 1996 he first sprayed his vines with a biodynamic preparation. Biodynamics only began, he says, 'the day my vine roots reconnected with the soil.' Jean-Michel wants his top wines to taste of the place they came from, not just of their grape variety. There are over 1,000 wineries in Alsace, and he says,

Jean-Michel Deiss enjoys a glass of one of his Alsace wines.

> *If we all make riesling exhibiting nothing other than riesling's classic petrol flavour, wine drinkers get bored. Then producers start fighting each other to sell on price alone. Corners get cut to make a margin, like forcing higher yields, which give wines with weaker flavours.*

What Jean-Michel wants is rieslings grown on Alsace's different soils like white limestone, red sandstone, blue or grey schist, thick gravel or light sand to taste different from each other. Biodynamics is his chosen tool to achieve this, he tells us, because it helps vine roots to reconnect with the soil so they can transmit that unique sense of place.

Jean-Michel has even gone a step further. From his top grand cru Altenberg in Bergheim site, he used to make separate white wines from each of the three grapes he had there: riesling, pinot gris and gewürztraminer. Now he makes just one wine from all three varieties, plus a few others he has inter-planted with the existing vines, which are all picked and blended together. The aim is to make a wine that conveys flavours transmitted by and unique to the Altenberg site, rather than a wine that tastes of its constituent varieties. The result is a brilliantly powerful, multi-layered white wine with the rich, ripe exterior typical of a dry, hot, iron-rich suntrap site like Altenberg, allied to a cool core from the marly-limestone beneath.

Domaine Matassa, Côte Catalanes Blanc (Roussillon, France)

10 Rue d'Estagel, F-66600 Calce (Pyrénées-Orientales), France
T:+33 (0)4.68.64.10.13 matassa@orange.fr

Tom Lubbe is one of the friendliest winemakers you could hope to meet, but you'd best not shake hands with him if you make an unannounced visit to his garage-like cavern of a winery near Perpignan on Roussillon's Mediterranean coast. He'd most likely be up to his shoulders preparing some of the many plant teas, herb extracts and biodynamic potions he sprays by hand on his vines. He says,

> Some of these sprays do smell, and you can't make them properly unless you're prepared to get stuck in and get yourself dirty, mixing them and stirring them by hand. But I'd rather spray my vines with homemade garlic extract than any factory-made spray. Those may well destroy the little beasties nibbling my grapes by affecting their nervous system, but they may also damage my nervous system at the same time.

The main 'beasties' Tom has to deal with in Roussillon are grape worms: tiny caterpillars that puncture grapeskins causing rot and vinegary flavours. Rather than using a chemically formulated spray to kill these caterpillars, Tom does two things. One tactic is removing leaves growing directly around the grape bunches by hand in early spring. This gets more light and air on the grapes, and annoys the shade-loving grape worms. The other tactic, Tom says, is,

Crush fresh garlic cloves, then macerate them in olive oil. After a couple of days I decant the oil into a bottle of warmish rainwater. This emulsifies out the garlic, which is very strong smelling by then. Then I give it a good shake, and leave it for a couple of days and out of direct light. Then, to get it on the vines, I dilute it in either rainwater or a plant tea I have made or in one of my biodynamic sprays. The smell seems to deter the grape worms. I only need around one or two cloves of garlic per hectare of vines for it to work. And as long as I don't spray it close to harvest, my grapes never end up smelling garlicky.

Tom also sprays fennel extract and biodynamic common horsetail 508 tea on his vines to keep them disease-free, as well as the biodynamic preparations.

With his French wife, Nathalie, Tom has 13 hectares (30 acres) of vines (organic certification). Domaine Matassa's red wines from 100-year-old carignan ('Matassa Rouge') and grenache noir ('Romanissa') have an intensely ripe, tingly savouriness to them. His dry white 'Marguerite' from muscat and viognier has grapey lemon flavours. The dry white 'Matassa Blanc' bottling made from old vine grenache gris and maccabeu just smells overpoweringly of the Mediterranean basin: its air, its wild herbs, the sea itself. The flavours are so clearly defined and intense you can easily see how well Tom succeeds in keeping his grapes healthy and ripe until they are picked in autumn.

TWO OF TOM LUBBE'S NEIGHBOURS

...in the village of Calce are also biodynamic (both Biodyvin certified): Olivier Pithon (www.domaineolivierpithon.com) who makes really creamy dry whites like D18 and Laïs, and Thomas Teibert, of Domaine de l'Horizon, who goes for a firmer style.

Domaine de la Cabotte, Colline Blanc, Côtes du Rhône (Rhône valley, France)

F-84430 Mondragon (Vaucluse), France
T:+33 (0).4.90.40.60.29 www.cabotte.com

Domaine de la Cabotte comprises 30 hectares (75 acres) of biodynamic vines (Demeter certified) and 15 hectares of woodland and scrub in the southern Rhône valley. Cabotte's owner, Marie-Pierre D'Ardhuy-Plumet, makes beautifully tense red and dry white wines with the same taffeta texture found in the best Burgundy wines just to the north, where Marie-Pierre grew up. Her father went to Burgundy in 1947 to pick grapes but married the vineyard-owner's daughter, Marie-Pierre's mother.

Marie-Pierre's dry Côte du Rhône white white is named 'Colline' after the hill the vines grow on, a sunny but exposed mineral-rich plateau at 150 metres (500 feet) along the Uchaux hills. She sprays teas from all the main plants used in biodynamics to keep the vines cool and disease-free in summer (yarrow, chamomile, stinging nettle, dandelion, oak bark) and warm in winter (valerian). Around 20,000 bottles of La Colline are made each year, from roughly equal parts of manly grenache blanc and clairette, with a splash of viognier. Marie-Pierre says,

> Although we pick the three different grape varieties several days apart, we ferment their juice together in one tank, topping up with fresh juice several times. This gives a very long, slow fermentation and means the flavour of no single grape variety can dominate the blend.

'La Colline' has satisfyingly clear, ripe, white-peach and canta-loupe-melon flavours. Try with couscous and baked vegetables.

Pendits, Dialog (Tokaji, Hungary)

Pendits Kft, H-3881 Abaújszántó, Béke út 111, Hungary
T:+47 330.567 www.pendits.com

Hungary is the only country in the world to mention its most famous wine, Tokaji, in its national anthem. The Tokaji region is located in Hungary's hilly northeast and has long been famous for its white wines. After the fall of socialism in 1991, Hungarian-born Marta Wille-Baumkauff bought a once famous but now dilapidated Tokaji winery with around 10 hectares (25 acres) of vines, including the famous Pendits, a Tokaji vineyard classified as 'First Growth' in the mid-nineteenth century. Sadly, Marta's German husband died before the vineyard and winery renovations were complete but, with help from her three sons, Marta eventually got both into shape. She converted the vines to biodynamics and is the region's only biodynamic producer (Demeter certified). She says,

The biodynamic impulse came from our three sons having had a Steiner-Waldorf education in Germany. They learnt biodynamic practices because gardening is an important part of the school curriculum. Although we are quite isolated here, we could ask other biodynamic wine-growers like Werner Michlits [see p. 69], Jean-Michel Deiss [p. 113] and Christine Saahs of Nikolaihof [p. 88] (with whom my son Stefan worked) for advice. We hand-stir our biodynamic horn manure 500 and horn silica 501 sprays. We harvest stinging nettles, willow and other wild plants to make our vines more disease resistant.

Marta replanted vines on previously abandoned stone terraces, some of which date back to the eighteenth century.

We thought it made sense to use horses rather than machines to plough weeds out from under the vines. It takes more time, but the horses are very precise and do not damage the wires and posts supporting the vines' shoots and trunks. A tractor could never plough as close up to a vine as the horse, and of course it would cause much more soil compaction. We make our compost using manure from our horses, plus manure from the sheep who graze our vines. Biodynamic farmers see sheep and horses as producing quite hot, and often therefore quite dry, manure. This is because they are both flighty animals, who can jump up off the earth. Too much of this type of manure would make too dry a compost, so we

First growth in Hungary is the offical designation of a superior-quality wine-growing plot. It is similar to the designation 'grand cru' in France.

also mix in cow manure – cows being more earthy animals – and their manure is moister. We used a fair bit of compost when renovating the vineyards, but we don't need so much now, because we can see the topsoils are softer and the soil life is returning.

From her furmint grapes, Marta makes both sweet white Tokaji wines, and dry wines, like Krakó and Holdvölgy, from single vineyard sites. Marta also makes a dry white Tokaji called 'Dialog,' which is blended from furmint and muscat grapes. Fermented in tanks rather than barrels, using native (wild) yeast, Dialog has rounded, musky flavours from the muscat, lifted by the zingy and spicy lime flavours of the furmint. Marta makes around 2,500 bottles of 'Dialog' each year.

Sedlescombe, First Release (Sussex, England)

Hawkhurst Road, Cripps Corner, Robertsbridge, East Sussex TN32 5SA, England

T:+44 (0)1580.830715   www.englishorganicwine.co.uk

In 1974 Roy Cook inherited some land at Sedlescombe in leafy Sussex, southern England. He lived there in his caravan with his German wife, Irma, and grew organic vegetables for local sale. Irma and Roy had met when Roy had travelled to Germany to learn about wine. Although the vegetables were a success, Roy and Irma felt Sedlescombe's southeast-facing slopes would be ideal for wine: a good decision, because wine soon showed signs of replacing beer as Britain's drink of choice. The first vines were planted in 1979. Since then, Roy and Irma have rented other vineyards and farm a total of 10 hectares (25 acres), making this a large-to-medium-sized operation by UK standards.

Roy and Irma were late converts to biodynamics, producing the UK's first Demeter-certified biodynamic wine from the 2010 vintage. Called – appropriately enough – 'First Release', this is a zesty dry white with crunchy green-pear flavours for early drinking. It is made from three grapes well suited to the UK's cool and often humid climes: bacchus, rivaner and solaris.

For those who would like to dip their toe into the experience of being a wine-grower, Sedlescombe have a 'renatavine' club. Members enjoy 30 per cent discount off wines produced from their rented vines as well as discounts on other wines, and regular updates on how the year's grapes are progressing. If they are in the area, members can work on their particular vines including helping with the harvest. Roy Cook says it's all the fun without the risk!

Wine-growing in a green and pleasant land: Sedlescombe Vineyard in southern England.
Sedlescombe Vineyard

PINK OR ROSÉ WINES

Pink or rosé wines are becoming fashionable once again after a long period during which it was thought to be a bit embarrassing to drink them in public.

Rosé wines look as though they are made by adding a bit of red wine to a white wine to give it a pinky-red colour, but in fact far more skill is needed. The usual method is to crush red grapes and let the fresh juice soak with the colour-laden skins for a few hours, as if making a red wine. However, after the juice has picked up enough colour from the skins it is run into a tank or barrel where it ferments into wine separately from the dark skins – just as white wine does. The skins, meanwhile, are added to a red wine rather than simply being thrown away.

The most famous wine region for rosé is Provence in France, where more than one in three bottles is pink. But good rosé or 'blush' wines are made all over the world. The trick is to usually drink them young, chilled but not over-chilled, and to buy from producers who also make good white and red wines as well as rosés. This is because making good rosé requires some of the skills needed in both white and red winemaking.

Château la Canorgue, Côtes du Lubéron Rosé (Provence, France)

Route du Pont Julien, F-84480 Bonnieux (Vaucluse), France
T:+33 (0).4.90.75.81.01 chateaucanorgue.margan@wanadoo.fr

Château la Canorgue was a star performer even before it hosted Oscar-winning director Ridley Scott in 2005 for *A Good Year*, his wine movie starring Russell Crowe, Albert Finney and Marion Cotillard. Canorgue's slightly crumbling chateau in the heart of Provence's Lubéron mountains appeared spectacular on film, but owner Jean-Pierre Margan has never been one to judge by appearances. 'Results are what drive me,' he affirms. He adopted biodynamic methods in 1993 (with organic certification), but freely admits,

> *The wackier aspects of biodynamics perplex me. I have 33 hectares (80 acres) of vines, and 88 separate vineyard plots. I cannot begin to try to prune, plough and pick them all perfectly according to lunar cycles. I worry about it, but then worry I am worrying about it. I know I stir my two biodynamic horn sprays correctly. I built a special tank in which to make decoctions and infusions from stinging nettle, willow, common horsetail and other plants to help the vines. I make biodynamic compost from [extensively grazed] sheep manure and lavendar cuttings. But I am too Cartesian. I have not understood all the biodynamic theory. I identify more with the practical side and with the results biodynamics gives us. Our vines, especially our oldest ones, now have an extra vitality about them. The result of biodynamics is clear, clearer to me than some of the biodynamic philosophy anyway.*

Jean-Pierre's Côtes de Lubéron dry white wines (from clairette, marsanne, roussanne and grenache blanc), and red and dry rosé wines (from grenache noir, syrah and mourvèdre) have such blinding clarity and freshness they reinvigorate you, even when drinking them on the hottest Mediterranean afternoon. You'd never guess by looking at Jean-Pierre's pale pink rosé that a wine with such a pale colour could contain so much flavour (damson, orange pippin apple) and texture (black olive skins), but remember that here it is results rather than appearances that matter.

Domaine Les Fouques, Cuvée de L'Aubigue Rosé (Côtes de Provence, France)

Les Premiers Borrels, Route de Hyères à Pierrefeu 1405, F-83400 Hyères (Var), France

T:+33 (0).4.94.65.68.19 www.domainedesfouques.com

Domaine Les Fouques overlooks the approaches to the port of Toulon on the French Riviera. Owners Yves and Michèle Gros and their winemaker daughter Christelle have 16 hectares (40 acres) of biodynamic vineyards (Demeter certified) plus free-range, grain-fed, heritage breeds of guineaufowl, ducks, chickens and capons. The fowl are sold oven-ready while their manure is mixed with the grapeskins left over from winemaking to make biodynamic compost. The vines occupy terraced, south-facing foothills on soils of clay schist. The clay soaks up what little rain falls so the vines don't suffer drought stress, while the schist fragments force the vines to put down intricate root systems, which helps add layers of complexity to the wines.

Around 40 per cent of production is given to dry white and red wines, and the rest to dry pink wines like Cuvée de L'Aubigue. This is made from the ideal grape for Provence rosé, the delicate but firm cinsault, which gives that herby character so typical of the region. Grenache noir, syrah and cabernet sauvignon are also blended in, the latter giving the Cuvée de L'Aubique a slighly deeper colour than many Provence rosés. Around 50,000 bottles are made each year.

OTHER GOOD PROVENCE ROSÉS
...are made at Château Romanin (see p. 227), and by Joseph Sergi at his Clos St Vincent (www.clos-st-vincent.fr) in the tiny Bellet region on sun-soaked terraces overlooking Nice (Biodyvin certified).

Domaine St Apollinaire, Côtes du Rhône Rosé (Rhône Valley, France)

Puyméras, F-84110 Vaison-La-Romaine (Vaucluse), France
T:+33 (0).4.90.46.41.09 www.domaine-st-apollinaire.com

Domaine St Apollinaire in the southern Rhône has been in the Daumus family since before the French Revolution. In 1963, Frédéric Daumas inherited the 17-hectare (40-acre) vineyard from his parents. It had never been treated with modern weedkillers, pesticides or fertilizers. Daumas, then in his mid-twenties, was a keen student of the Egyptian pyramids, Aztec calendars and biodynamics. 'Although I was not sure I understood everything about biodynamics,' he says, 'I wanted to try it. It appealed to me and suited my non-scientific way of thinking.'

In 2004 Frédéric's daughter, Elodie, took over the vineyard (Demeter certified). She is as careful and non-interventionist a wine-maker as her father. Many of the vines were planted in the 1940s and 1960s, and the wines have that glycerol-rich thickness that only old vines can give. Dry white wines from mainly grenache blanc and clairette show pine and aniseed aromas coupled with jaw-droppingly juicy fruit flavours. Reds, made from syrah and grenache noir, display evocative Mediterranean herb and savoury, dark-fruit flavours that are never overbaked. The Côtes du Rhône Rosé is a cunning bone-dry blend of grenache noir for its ruddy, ripe-plum flavours, and cinsault for its elegance and drinkability. Drink it *al fresco* on a hot day with tapenade – on toast or dipped with sticks of fresh celery.

ANOTHER RHÔNE VALLEY ROSÉ
...Tavel Rosé, is produced by the Charmasson family of Balazu des Vaussières. Tavel is the Rhône Valley's most famous village for what is often a rather burly pink wine (Demeter certified).

Clos de la Briderie, Touraine-Mesland Gris (Rosé) (Loire Valley, France)

70 Rue Rol-Tanguy, F-41150 Monteaux (Loir et Cher), France
T:+33 (0)2.54.70.28.89 www.vincent-girault.com

Vincent Girault has the Loire Valley's biggest biodynamic vineyard (Demeter certified), with 85 hectares (210 acres) on two estates: his own Clos Château Gaillard and his now retired parents' Clos de la Briderie. 'I went biodynamic in 1994 and it proved a success,' says Vincent. 'As my father is quite competitive he soon went biodynamic too.'

Vincent's winemaking style aims for good-value, early-drinking wines with ripe, zingy flavours: mint and dark berries in his mainly cabernet franc and gamay reds, and nettle and gooseberry in his mainly sauvignon blanc and chardonnay whites. His pink Touraine-Mesland wines are made from gamay noir (the beaujolais grape) and are so pale in colour they are labelled as a 'gris' – literally 'grey' – wine. Vincent says,

> I soak the freshly picked grapes in their juice at quite cold temperatures. Then I run the juice off the skins for fermentation. This preserves the delicacy of this wine's peach-skin flavours but means the wine has only the lightest of grey-pink colours. The gamay vines grow in Mesland, a sandy sub-region of Touraine. As sandy soils usually give delicate wines, it makes sense for me to respect this when winemaking.

His rosé is dry, fruity and made for unashamed summer quaffing.

Domaine Les Enfants Sauvages, Bouche du Soleil Rosé, Côtes Catalanes (Roussillon, France)

4 rue de l'Eglise, F-11510 Fitou (Aude), France
T:+33 (0)4.68.45.69.75 www.les-enfants-sauvages.com

When Nikolaus and Carolin Bantlin bought their 8-hectare (20-acre) Roussillon vineyard, the vines, which lie in two blocks, were looking rather forlorn. 'The surrounding wild scrub was vibrant and layered in its colours and vegetation,' says Nikolaus, 'but when

we looked at the vines, although they had green leaves, the vineyard looked like a desert, a monoculture.' Nikolaus, who attended a Steiner school in his native Germany, sprayed the vines with biodynamic plant teas and decoctions made from stinging nettle, horsetail, chamomile and dandelion. Manure from the estate's own sheep was spread as compost. Wild grasses were allowed to re-establish in and around the vines. Nikolaus says,

> The wild grasses look nice and smell nice, and establish a natural balance for the insects. But these grasses also keep the soil cooler and moister, especially as we are only 5 kilometres (3 miles) from the Mediterranean. Keeping cooler allows our compost to work more efficiently in the soil, to let our grapes ripen more slowly, keeping all their flavours.

The Bantlins produce creamy reds from mourvèdre, carignan and grenache noir dating from the 1950s, and mouth-filling dry white wines from mainly grenache blanc planted in the 1940s. Their Bouche du Soleil Rosé ('mouthful of sun') is made from grenache noir and syrah and has reviving redcurrant and raspberry flavours. This is a pretty pink wine from some of the prettiest-looking weedy vineyards in Roussillon.

Cefalicchio, Ponte della Lama Rosato (Puglia, Italy)

Via Andrea Dorea, 11, I-70053 Canosa di Puglia (BA = Bari), Italy
T:+39 088.3617601   www.cefalicchio.it

Brothers Nicola and Fabrizio Rossi's Cefalicchio estate in Puglia in Italy's deep south produces olives for both eating and oil, plus a lovely range of wines from 25 hectares (60 acres) of biodynamic vineyards (Demeter certified). They have introduced beehives, cows, goats, chickens and walnuts, and replanted traditional oak trees. The last time oaks grew here the Romans cut them down to build warships in the nearby port of Bari.

They make creamy dry white wines like the chardonnay 'Petraia', but the main focus is on red wines from a local grape called nero di troia or 'the Trojan grape'. Its bouncy and wild, soft blackcurrant fruit is perfectly encapsulated in Nicola and Fabrizio's 'Romanico' red (12,000 bottles). But they also make around 4,000 bottles of nero di troia as a pink wine called 'Ponte della Lama'. This gives a lovely round feeling in the mouth, but leaves you refreshed. My Puglian father-in-law would drink this with *lampascioni*, small onion-like hyacinth bulbs Italians harvest wild then cook in a water and vinegar mix. They are meltingly savoury-sweet, not over-filling and are perfect with a Puglian pink.

Cape Jaffa, La Lune Rosé de Syrah, Mount Benson (Limestone Coast, South Australia)

Limestone Coast Road, Cape Jaffa, South Australia 5276, Australia
T:+61 (0)8.8768.5053   www.capejaffawines.com.au

The Hooper family's Cape Jaffa's vineyards overlook the chilly waters of the Great Southern Ocean near the fishing village of Cape Jaffa along South Australia's Limestone Coast. Sea breezes are so cool here that workers planting Cape Jaffa's first vines in the early 1990s said it was like working in Siberia. But Derek Hooper says,

The cool weather and limestone soils augur well for the vines though, because it means our wines are naturally crisp and not too heavily alcoholic. And the strong ocean winds help reduce the risk of vine fungal diseases, making this a good place to grow grapes biodynamically.

Derek says he went biodynamic (certified organic) because 'I grew my own organic vegetables for years. I couldn't bear paying supermarkets money for hydroponically grown tomatoes. Our family always had a strong organic ethos.' He

127

sources manure and straw for compost from local farmers, and makes his biodynamic sprays with a local biodynamic group comprising mainly home gardeners from the city of Adelaide.

There are 25 hectares (62 acres) of vines at Cape Jaffa producing classy dry white wines from chardonnay, sauvignon blanc and semillon, and scented reds from cabernet and shiraz. The La Lune Syrah Rosé is as pink as a baby's bum and has a creamily dry mouthfeel plus raspberry-sherbet flavours with a twist of almond. Try with the local (sustainably fished) southern rock lobster.

Cayuse Vineyards, Edith Grenache Rosé (Washington State, USA)

17 East Main St, Walla Walla, WA 99362, USA
T:+001 509.526.0686 Website www.cayusevineyards.com

Christophe Baron studied wine in France, where his family were champagne-makers. He then worked in Australia, New Zealand and Romania as a 'flying winemaker' or hired gun, making wines to incredibly precise specifications laid down by professional buyers, usually supermarket wine chiefs. If they asked for sauvignon blanc white wines that smelt of gooseberries rather than of melon, and tasted dry but were actually a little bit sweet, then this was what they must have. This experience gave Christophe a very clear idea of how the wine market works. When he started planting his own vineyards in 1997 in Washington state's Walla Walla Valley (another place he had previously worked), he knew he could make wines everyday wine drinkers would like and accept. This, despite Washington being then still something of a niche wine region compared to its bigger and more famous west-coast neighbours to the south, Oregon and California.

Christophe also became Washington state's first biodynamic wine-grower (Demeter certified). He thinks of Cayuse as a biodiverse farm rather than as a monocultural vineyard, having adorned it with chickens, pigs, sheep, cows and two draft horses who work in the vines, as well as with fruit trees and vegetables. There are 24 hectares (60 acres) of syrah, cabernet, tempranillo, mourvedre, grenache noir and viognier for juicy-fruit red and dry white wines. Christophe's cleverly constructed rosé called 'Edith' is made from grenache noir, a grape variety usually associated with strapping Rhône reds from Châteauneuf-du-Pape but whose direct, soft-fruit style is also perfect for rosé. Christophe's grenache vines are young and their exuberant yet savoury, strawberry fruit flavours shine brightly in 'Edith'. Drink well-chilled with cold cuts of meat.

TWO OTHER NORTH AMERICAN ROSÉS OF NOTE
...come from California's Santa Rita Hills where Peter and Rebecca Work of Ampelos Cellars (www.ampeloscellars.com) make a syrah rosé from biodynamic vines interplanted with their olive trees (all Demeter certified). See also p. 174 for red wines made from syrah. Wilridge Vineyard (www.wilridgewinery.com) near Seattle, Washington state, produces a sangiovese rosé. See also p. 172 for red wines made from sangiovese.

RED WINES

Red wines get their colour by letting grape juice ferment into wine while in contact with dark-coloured grapeskins. This is why red wine can only be made from red grapes and not white (green) ones. So whereas a vat of fermenting white wine need contain only juice, for red wine everything from the grape must get tipped into the tanks: the skins, the juice and by implication also the pips (or seeds). As the sugar in the grape juice is steadily being converted into alcohol (wine) by the wine yeasts, the alcohol acts like a solvent, extracting red colour from the grapeskins. These tannins give red wine its occasionally puckering and very different mouthfeel to white wines. Because of the way they are made, red wines also contain antioxidants, which are said to make red wine especially healthy for humans by helping our blood flow more easily, putting less pressure on our hearts. To extract enough colour and tannin from the grapes, red wines ferment at quite warm temperatures, usually between 26 and 32°C (79–90°F).

Red wines can, like white wines, be made from a single grape variety or by blending more than one variety together. Some grape varieties like pinot noir (from Burgundy) show best on their own, others, like syrah, can work either on their own (in the northern Rhône) or as part of a blend, and others work best as blends: the Bordeaux grapes cabernet and merlot for example.

Red wines made mainly from very tannic grapes, like cabernet sauvignon and sangiovese, or from low-yielding vines on the very best vineyard sites (pinot noir in Burgundy, for example), will age in oak barrels before they are bottled. This is partly to give them a subtle oaky flavour if the barrels have already been used, or even overtly oaky notes if the barrels are new, but mainly to allow the tannins in the wine time to soften. Because it is porous, oak allows the wine to breathe. This contact with the air makes the tannins less jagged, smoothing them so they don't pucker your tongue so much. This is why aerating red wines, by decanting them or swirling them in your glass before you drink them, helps soften them up.

RED WINES MADE FROM SINGLE GRAPE VARIETIES

AGLIANICO

The aglianico grape was first brought to Italy's deep south by the ancient Greeks. It now produces some of Italy's most deeply coloured and richly textured reds.

Cantine del Notaio, La Firma Aglianico del Vulture (Basilicata, Italy)

Via Roma 159, I-85028 Rionero in Vulture (PZ = Potenza), Italy
T:+39 0972.723689   www.cantinedelnotaio.it

Gerardo Giuratrabocchetti's aglianico vines grow on the high slopes of Mont Vulture, an extinct volcano in southern Italy's Basilicata region (the instep of the Italian boot). Theirs are some of the last grapes to be picked in Italy each year, partly because aglianico is such a late ripener anyway, and partly because nights are so cool on the old volcano it takes longer than usual for grapes to warm up in the mornings. Gerardo has 26 hectares (64 acres) of biodynamic vines (Demeter certified). Some are more than a hundred years old. He named his winery Cantine del Notaio or 'the notary's winery' because of his day job, which is being a notary or a public legal official. His legal training has given Gerardo a keen eye for detail. He says spraying biodynamic horn silica 501 has made aglianico's vine shoots firmer, more erect and more disease resistant, and means the grapes ripen more evenly.

The top aglianico here is called 'La Firma', meaning signature, something all the legal contracts that Gerardo supervises must have. This is a purple-coloured red with an orangey-crimson tinge. You think it will taste soft and juicy but in fact the wine has such firm, warm leather, black cherry and tar flavours, you'd best drink it with one of Basilicata's tomato pasta sauces spiced with local chilli peppers.

BARBERA

The red barbera grape is a speciality of Piedmont in northwest Italy. Its incredibly versatile wines have the strength and zip to make eating rich dishes less of a chore, and the lightness of texture that means they can easily be drunk on their own.

Cascina Zerbetta, Barbera del Monferrato (Piedmont, Italy)

Strada Bozzola 11, I-15044 Quargnento (AL = Alessandria), Italy
T:+39 0131.219650 cascinazerbetta@tiscali.it

Paolo Antonio Malfatti worked in Tuscan and north Italian wineries before founding his own biodynamic farm (Demeter certified) in 1998 in Piedmont's Monferrato hills. He has 7 hectares (17 acres) of land. Half is vines and the rest is given to cereals, olives, vegetables and walnuts. As Paolo Antonio has no cows of his own to provide the manure he needs for biodynamic compost, he exchanges hay and walnuts with a local farmer whose traditional Piedmontese cows are bred for beef and can give him plenty of what he requires.

Paolo Antonio makes a greengagey, dry white sauvignon blanc, a red called 'Piangalardo' from barbera, merlot and cabernet sauvignon, and the 100 per cent Barbera del Monferrato, all handpicked. His reds have very clear but nicely wild black-plum and blackberry flavours.

Nuova Cappelletta, Barbera del Monferrato (Piedmont, Italy)

Ca' Cappellatta 9, I-15049 Vignale Monferrato (AL = Alessandria), Italy
T:+39 0142.933135   www.nuovacappelletta.it

Nuova Cappelletta is a 210-hectare (520-acre) mixed farm and vineyard in Piedmont. It is one of Italy's biggest and oldest biodynamic farms (Demeter certified since 1984). Wheat is milled into flour, cattle are sold for breeding, and alfalfa is cut in summer for use as winter feed. There are 28 hectares (70 acres) of vines, mainly local grapes like cortese for whites, and grignolino and barbera for reds. As is common here, the barbera is aged in large chestnut tanks or *botti*, which are common in this part of Italy. Owner Alessandro Uslenghi says,

> *The barbera ages in botti, not to give it an oaky taste, but to make the fruit flavours a bit softer because our clay soils give red wines of real backbone.*

Nuova Cappelletta's Barbera del Monferrato's solid, almost meaty flavours suit fireside drinking, ideally with whatever you are grilling: sliced courgettes doused in olive oil, or some well-salted beef.

Weeds are allowed to grow between vine rows at Nuova Cappelletta, Italy.

BEAUJOLAIS AND BEAUJOLAIS-STYLE REDS

The wines of Beaujolais near Lyon in eastern France have been described as light purply-red, fruity on the nose, and slipping easily down the throat. Everyday Beaujolais owes its gulpable quality to the exuberance of the gamay grape it is made from, and to the way the grapes ferment as whole rather than crushed berries in tanks that initially remain sealed. Juice which becomes wine while still inside an intact berry takes on characteristic pink-bubblegum and banana flavours and can be drunk almost as soon as it has finished fermenting. The race to get freshly fermented Beaujolais Nouveau wines into British shops on the third Thursday in November, barely two months after the grapes were picked, raised money for charity and quick profits for wine producers, but became naff. The more serious producers make outstanding beaujolais using more traditional red winemaking methods, especially from the top northern Beaujolais villages ('crus') of Brouilly, Chénas, Chiroubles, Fleurie, Juliénas, Morgon, Moulin à Vent, Régnié and St Amour.

DEMETER CERTIFIED BIODYNAMIC PRODUCERS IN BEAUJOLAIS
… include Bernard Vallette of Domaine du Bois Noir, Domaine de La Fully (www.domainedelafully.fr) in Brouilly, Aurélien Grillet's Domaine du Chardon Bleu in Morgon, and Bruno Debize. Gilles Bonnefoy of Domaine de la Madone (www.vins-g-bonnefoy.com) makes brilliant gamay from vines grown on both granitic and basalt soils in the tiny Côtes de Forez between Beaujolais and the Loire (Demeter). Doug Tunnell of Brick House (see p. 164) in Oregon also makes a very fine gamay red.

Michel Guignier, Au Bon Grés, Fleurie (Beaujolais, France)
Faudon, F-69820 Vauxrenard (Rhône), France
T:+33 (0)4.74.69.91.52 www.vignebioguignier.com

Michel Guignier is a busy man. He bottles conventionally grown Beaujolais wines as a merchant under his Domaine Les Amethystes label and makes Beaujolais from 7 hectares (17 acres) of his own biodynamic (Demeter certified) vines under his own name. Michel ploughs his steepest vines by horse, not tractor, and also has 10 hectares of biodynamic pasture for his herd of Charolais (beef) cattle. 'My cows allowed me to turn my vineyard into a self-sustaining farm organism,' he says, 'because they meant I could make my own biodynamic compost and biodynamic preparations.'

Fleurie is probably the most romantically named French wine region, and this is perhaps one reason its Beaujolais is often the most expensive. Another is the lacy smoothness the best wines, like Michel's Au Bon Grés bottling, seem to pick up from the rose-petal pink granite soils. Its firm blackcurrant-leaf, peach and red-berry fruit will, when chilled, perfectly partner a warm sausage baguette sandwich.

Christian Ducroux, Régnié (Beaujolais, France)

Thulon, F-69430 Lantignié (Rhône), France
T:+33 (0)4.74.69.20.47

Christian Ducroux inherited some vines in the Beaujolais village of Régnié from his father in his twenties, and now has around 4 hectares (10 acres). Christian first read Rudolf Steiner's *Agriculture*, the 1924 lecture series that gave birth to biodynamics, in 1980. He visited a biodynamic cereal farmer 'to check how Steiner's biodynamic theory worked in practice', and became the first Beaujolais wine-grower to convert to biodynamics (Demeter certified). Ducroux says he prefers stirring biodynamic sprays by hand rather than machine because this gives the best result. His own cows provide manure for compost. 'I chose a breed of cow from Brittany where the soil is a similar kind of granite to ours in Beaujolais,' he says. Christian sprays his vines with a range of teas, including chamomile to help the vine buds in spring, dandelion to help the vine leaves in summer, stinging nettle as an all-round pick-me-up, oak bark for mildew, and valerian for spring frost.

His Régnié radiates health and has the kind of inner depth one hopes to find in all everyday Beaujolais but rarely does. It's packed with redcurrant, blackberry and raspberry fruit flavours, with sloe in the aftertaste. Perfect everyday drinking. Around 12,000 bottles are made each year.

137

Château de Lavernette, Les Clos, Beaujolais-Leynes (Beaujolais, France)

La Vernette, F-71570 Leynes (Saône et Loire), France
T:+33 (0)3.8535.63.21 www.lavernette.com

 Xavier de Boissieu started converting his family's 12 hectares (30 acres) of Beaujolais and Pouilly-Fuissé vineyards to biodynamics (Demeter certified) in 2005 after a winemaking stint in California where he also met his wife, Kerrie. Xavier and Kerrie use their own horse manure for biodynamic compost, and harvest wild plants as teas for the vines. Their wines are suitable for vegans, smartly presented and well made, even if they are not afraid to challenge orthodoxies. For example, rather than use all their gamay grapes in the traditional way for red Beaujolais, Xavier and Kerrie set some aside for a moreish, dry, white sparkling wine called 'Granit', named after the granite soils typical of the finest Beaujolais vineyards. Their flagship red beaujolais, Les Clos, comes from vines planted in the mid 1960s in the noted village of Leynes. Le Clos starts fermenting in tank, where it gets its rich fruitiness, but unusually it finishes fermentation in barrels: the oak makes the gamay grapes' fluid banana and cherry flavours deeper, more teasing and subtle.

Domaine St Nicolas, Gammes en May Rouge, Fiefs Vendéens (Loire Valley, France)

La Croix Bégaud, F-85340 L'Ile d'Olonne (Vendée), France
T:+33 (0)2.51.33.13.04 www.domainesaintnicolas.com

Thierry Michon's 35-hectare (85-acre) biodynamic vineyard (Demeter certified) borders the salt marshes around Ile d'Olonne, along the Loire Valley's Atlantic coast. Buffeting ocean winds means Thierry, a tall lanky chap, has to train his vines back-breakingly low to the ground so they don't get blown over. Thierry also planted trees around his vines to act as spray-free buffer zones, and purchased cows for his biodynamic compost, plus grazing land for them.

Thierry makes brilliantly approachable wines from the main Loire grapes, cabernet franc for red and chenin blanc for whites. He also make a Beaujolais-style red wine from the main Beaujolais grape, gamay, calling it 'Gammes en May', a seemingly frivolous play on words. But Thierry is no fool. He grows his gamay not on clay but only on soils with patches of granite, because this is the same soil all the best Beaujolais reds come from. You could easily quaff

a bottle of his Gammes en May unthinkingly while out picnicking, but although this is a picnic red *par excellence*, its finely intricate layers of fruit allow it to stand up to food you'd eat at the table, and with cutlery.

CABERNET FRANC

The cabernet franc is one of my favourite red wine grapes, but it never gets the same kind of adulation as cabernet sauvignon, its big brother. In Bordeaux, cabernet franc is used as a minor part of the blend in red wines (see p. 189–209 for examples), its leafy crispness freshening up the merlot and toning down the cabernet sauvignon. But further north in Loire sub-regions like Chinon in Touraine and Saumur, cabernet franc is happily bottled on its own. Loire cabernet franc wines are very perfumed and crisp, tasting of liquorice, violets and blue flowers, all overlaid by pleasant aromas of mown grass. They are not too tannic and so can generally be drunk quite soon after bottling. They also offer good value when compared to their Bordeaux counterparts.

Domaine Fabrice Gasnier, Les Graves Chinon Rouge (Loire Valley, France)
Chézelet, F-37500 Cravant les Coteaux (Indre et Loire), France
T:+33 02.47.93.11.60   www.vignoblegasnier.com

The Gasnier family has been making Chinon red wines for several generations. After Fabrice Gasnier took over from his father, Jacky, he converted the 27-hectare (70-acre) cabernet-franc vineyard to biodynamics (Demeter certified). Fabrice's oldest vines were planted in the 1960s and the grapes go into his wine called Chinon Rouge Vieilles Vignes ('Old Vines'). Around 30,000 bottles are made each year and the wine ages in new and older oak barrels, although you never pick up any oak flavours when drinking it. 'I want my wine to taste of the soil and the grape,' says Fabrice, 'rather than the barrels.'

Fabrice's biggest production wine is called 'Les Graves', referring to the gravelly soils his vines grow in at Chinon's two best villages, Cravant les Coteaux and Panzoult. The gravels here contain lots of sand, making them perfect for cabernet franc, a vine that thrives on warm, free-draining soils. Fabrice makes around 50,000 bottles of 'Les Graves' each year. This wine ferments and ages in cement tanks. It has warm, bracing red fruit infused with mint, and a smooth, gliding texture. This is the classic wine of the Paris bistro, a lunchtime red designed to sit well in your stomach so it never weighs you down bodily.

Domaine les Chesnaies, Danaé Chinon Rouge (Loire Valley, France)

Les Chesnaies, F-37500 Cravant les Coteaux (Indre et Loire), France
T:+33 (0)2.47.93.13.79   www.chinonlambert.com

Pascal and Béatrice Lambert are the third generation to farm this 14-hectare (35-acre) Chinon vineyard. They converted to biodynamics in 2004 (organic certification) and produce wines of incredible elegance and purity. Vineyard work is meticulous. Oats and other cereals are sown in autumn. These cleanse the soils, and are ploughed in at springtime to improve soil tilth. In winter the pruned vines are cleansed of disease organisms with an old-fashioned mix of sulphur and lime, which is popular with fruit growers. Biodynamic compost is applied to the soil. It is made from straw, green waste from a local market, cow manure and wood chips. The latter are rich in carbon – which worms love – and the kind of smaller micro-organisms that soils need if they are to stay healthy and friable in the Loire's damp climate. Teas formulated from an array of medicinal plants (chamomile, common horsetail, dandelion, fennel, lavendar, rosemary, sage, stinging nettle and valerian) are used to stimulate the vines' immune systems. The grapes are hand-picked.

Chenin blanc wines with mineral and citrus notes range from the bone-dry Anjou blanc 'La Potardière' or Chinon blanc 'Les Chesnaies' and 'La Rochette', to the fully sweet Coteaux du Layon 'Clos des Bonne Blanches'. The key Chinon red wines include 'Cuvée Marie' made from cabernet franc planted in the 1930s and 1950s. This has a thick, old-vine texture to it. 'Les Terrasses' is its simpler, young-vine counterpart, bottled with no added sulphites. 'Les Graves' comes from gravelly ground, which brings agreeable opulence to cabernet franc's sometimes lean frame. 'Perruches' is a cabernet franc red wine of absolute clarity from the sandy clay soils after which the wine is named. My pick, 'Danaé', is a cabernet franc from flinty soils. Its fruit is finely balanced between plum-stone crunchiness and ripe-plum skin, melt-in-your-mouth juiciness. Les Chesnaies is one of those rare wine estates from which you could drink a different bottle of wine every night for a week – red, white, dry or sweet, even their rosé 'Mathilde' – and be stimulated every time.

Château Tour Grise, 253 Rouge, Saumur Puy-Notre-Dame (Loire Valley, France)

1 rue des Ducs d'Aquitaine, F-49260 Le Puy-Notre-Dame (Maine et Loire), France
T:+33 (0)2.41.38.82.42   www.latourgrise.com

Philippe and Françoise Gourdon are the seventh generation of their family to make wine at this fourteenth-century chateau in Saumur. Its underground cellars stretch for several miles in Saumur's soft, sandy clay. There are 20 hectares (50 acres) of biodynamic vines (Biodyvin certified), mainly chenin blanc for white wines and cabernet franc for reds. Minimal intervention is practised in both vineyard and winery, with prevention rather than cure the aim. Excess buds are removed from the vines in spring to give each grape bunch plenty of sunlight. The vines are not trimmed because, 'trimming produces too many side shoots, causing disease and unripeness,' says Philippe. Weeds are allowed to grow between the rows because this forces the vines to put down deeper, more complex root systems. The best red wine, called '253', is made from 100 per cent cabernet franc grapes grown on warm clay and limestone soils. Hand-picked, the grapes ferment very slowly in egg-shaped vats for several weeks. The result is a brightly coloured red with ripe, revivingly frank flavours of violet and hawthorn.

OTHER BIODYNAMIC LOIRE ESTATES PRODUCING GOOD CABERNET FRANC REDS
...include Matthieu Bouchet's Domaine du Château Gaillard (see also p. 125) in Saumur (Demeter certified), Nicolas Grosbois (www.domainegrosbois.fr) in Chinon (Demeter certified), Manoir de la Tête Rouge (www.manoirdelateterouge.com) in Anjou-Saumur (Biodyvin certified), Domaine des Rouets in Chinon (Demeter certified), Clau de Nell (www.claudenell.com) in Anjou (Demeter certified), Domaine Breton (www.domainebreton.net) for Bourgueil and Chinon (Demeter certified), Louis-Jean Sylvos of Château de la Roche en Loire (chateaudelaroche.com) in Touraine Azay le Rideau (Demeter certified), and Domaine des Roches Neuves (see p. 50).

MALBEC

Malbec is a red grape that is more famous today for the reds it produces in Argentina than in its French homeland of Cahors. In the Middle Ages, Bordeaux would beef up its reds with malbec grapes grown up-river in the Cahors region of southwest France. Cahors produced red wines so deeply coloured they became known as 'black wines'. These were useful to Bordeaux merchants looking to pass off their own weedy, dilute-looking reds as having more stuffing than they really did. Malbec makes such forcefully tannic reds on the cool limestone terraces or *causses* of Cahors that today's winemakers there have had to soften them up using modern techniques, like bubbling oxygen through the wines, which makes the tannins less aggressive, as if the wine had softened in bottle for many years.

Malbec makes more obviously juicy, sexy wines quite naturally in the much warmer climes of Argentina, where malbec vines were taken in the nineteenth century by European emigrés. Malbec from Cahors and from Argentina, while very different, are two absolutely classic red wines full of energy and personality.

Cosse-Maisonneuve, Les Laquets (Cahors, Southwest France)
Matthieu Cosse, Domaine Le Sid, F-46800 Prayssac (Lot), France
T:+39 (0)5.53.66.76.42 matthieu.cosse@gmail.com

Professional winemaker Catherine Maisonneuve and former rugby player Matthieu Cosse began making wine from an old malbec vineyard in Cahors in 1999. They gradually added more vines, and adopted biodynamic practices (with organic certification) across what are now 18 hectares (45 acres) of vineyard. They produce various site-specific Cahors bottlings, including 'Le Combal' at the bottom of the quality scale, from vines on heavier soils close to the river local Lot, and 'Le Sid' at the top of the scale, from vines overlooking the river from sunnier, drier, more interesting ground. In the middle is 'Les Laquets' from vines planted in 1957, after the devastating 1956 frost, on a curly limestone tongue of land that produces a Cahors wine with a typically bluebell tinge in its cavernously deep colour and a pruney liquorice chew to its fruit. Either you drink it freshly bottled, or you wait for five, or – better – seven years for the ripe-fruit flavours to turn into a broad, savoury cedar.

Bodega Noemía di Patagonia (Río Negro Valley, Argentina)
Ruta Prov 7, Km 12, Valle Azul (Río Negro), Argentina
T:+549 298.4.530412 www.bodeganoemia.com

Hans Vinding-Diers was sent to Argentine Patagonia's Río Negro Valley to make wines for an upmarket British grocery chain store. While there, the Danish-born, Bordeaux-trained winemaker discovered some malbec vines planted in the 1930s and decided

Hans Vinding-Diers combines biodynamic techniques with expertise from wine's old and new worlds.

to make wine from them in a fruit-packing warehouse. 'It was the only place with air-conditioning to keep the wines from overheating,' he remembers. With his Italian partner, Noemi Cinzano, he built a winery, and planted new vines using cuttings from the original 1930s vines. They acquired more 1930s vines in a different, better location, and adopted biodynamic practices for the entire 13-hectare (32-acre) vineyard (Demeter certified). Hans says,

We got some cows and used their manure to make our first biodynamic horn manure 500 in 2006. We had three different kinds of horns: the correct ones from female cows, some not correct and two from a bull. After six months underground the manure in the correct horns had turned into humus, as the biodynamic literature suggests. In the others we found the manure was raw and exactly as it had been buried. It made our general manager, who was a bit sceptical about biodynamics, completely buy into the idea.

Hans used gravity rather than pumps in the fruit-packing warehouse, and does the same in the new winery he has designed to avoid pumping. The cement tanks allow the grape seeds (pips) to be drained out while wines are still fermenting. 'Seeds make the wines taste bitter,' he says. Harnesses suspended from the roof over the fermentation tanks mean the grapeskins, which are full of colour and flavour, can be safely punched down into the fermenting juice by human feet, rather than using a mechanical pump. The 100 per cent malbec 'Bodega Noemía' red is a very rich, almost over-powering wine packed with colour, tannin and dark-cherry flavours. Pour it into a wide-bottomed decanter and leave at room temperature for two days before you broach it.

BIODYNAMIC MALBEC PRODUCERS TO LOOK OUT FOR
...include, in Argentina: Fabril Alto Verde (www.fabril-altoverde.com.ar) and Alpamanta (www.alpamanta.com); and in and around Cahors: Domaine des Savarines (www.domainedessavarines.com), Mas del Périé (www.masdelperie.com), Château Vent d'Autan (www.cahorsAOC.com) and Domaine de Lafage (domainedelafage.free.fr/). (All are Demeter certified.)

MONDEUSE (SAVOY)

The mondeuse grape thrives in the Savoy's Alpine foothills, producing well-coloured juicy reds with appealing peppery overtones.

Prieuré St Christophe, Mondeuse Cuvée Tradition (Savoy, France)
F-73250 Fréterive (Savoie), France
T:+33 (0)4.79.28.62.10

Michel Grisard's family were vine and plant nurserymen in Savoy in the French Alps bordering Switzerland. In 1983 and in his mid-thirties, Michel decided to stop working with his father and two brothers to strike out on his own. The vineyards were amicably divided between them, and Grisard became, in his words, 'a good chemical wine-grower'. Then, a decade later, Michel began adopting greener methods 'for two reasons,' he says.

> *First, wine is a food to me, and I find it abnormal that we wine-growers use so many chemical products; and second, when I tasted organic and biodynamic wines I saw that the methods can produce the best quality, too. I spread tonnes of chemical fertilizers in my vines when I was younger, but chemical fertilizers had made me forget that wild plants never needed to wait for man to feed them to survive all these years.*

Grisard has 6 hectares (15 acres) of biodynamic vines (Demeter certified), and because his vines are on such unrelentingly steep slopes he uses a quad bike to spray them with biodynamic teas.

Grisard makes beautifully piercing, dry white wines laden with hazelnut flavours from roussette, a local grape also known as altesse. His red wines are considered Savoy's best examples from the local mondeuse grape. Two styles are made, the 'Prestige', which ages in oak for over twelve months and is released only in the very best years, and the cheaper 'Tradition'. Made every year, this ferments in tank then in spring is run to older barrels for a few months before bottling. It has a dark, plum colour and clear, pure, glacial flavours of cranberry, crystallised raspberry and red plum. An uplifting red, perfect for lunch.

MONTEPULCIANO D'ABRUZZO

Montepulciano d'Abruzzo is a dark, ripely chewy red from about halfway along Italy's Adriatic (eastern) coast. Much montepulciano is made by co-operatives, like Orsogna (profiled below) whereby farmers pool resources to save money.

Co-operative Olearia Vinicola Orsogna, Coste di Moro Montepulciano d'Abruzzo (Abruzzo, Italy)
Via Ortonese 29, 66036 Orsogna Chieti (CH = Chieti), Italy
T:+39 0871.86241 www.oleariavinicola.it

The Orsogna co-operative is among Abruzzo's largest, producing both olive oil and wine. The co-op's 600 members have 1,200 hectares (nearly 3,000 acres) of vines producing 20 million bottles annually. Nearly 10 per cent of the vines are Demeter certified biodynamic, from a dozen small growers with mixed, essentially self-sufficient farms. Their other produce includes olives, figs, apricots, honey bees, table grapes, cereals, hay and forage for livestock, pigs, poultry, goats, cows and ewes for yoghurt and ricotta and pecorino cheeses. 75 per cent of the rest is certified organic.

The co-op makes two wines from Demeter-certified biodynamic grapes. The dry white wine called 'Civitas' is a well-made, satisfying quaffer that can handle even hefty local dishes like minestrone soup or the local fish broth. Civitas is made from a grape called pecorino (not to be confused with the ewe's milk cheese also called pecorino). The co-op's montepulciano d'Abruzzo red 'Coste di Moro' is one you can really get your teeth into, with ripe blackcurrant and strawberry fruit flavours becoming gamey as the wine is swirled in your glass. It is made mainly from the montepulciano grape (which is not to be confused with a red wine called Vino Nobile from a Tuscan town called Montepulciano). Try with local dishes based on goat, lamb and roast pork, or risottos based on sweeter-tasting fare like pumpkin, for a wine less than four years old, or artichoke, for a wine with more maturity.

OTHER SOURCES OF MONTEPULCIANO D'ABRUZZO
...are Nicola and Paola Matteucci (www. vinimatteucci.com) and Antonio Battista's Aquaviva estate (Tel +39 085.880786) (both Demeter certified).

Care of the vines and grape picking is done by hand at Fattoria Caiarossa, Italy.
Fabio Muzzi

147

PINOT NOIR

Pinot noir, the great red wine grape of Burgundy, is a heartbreaker for both wine-growers and wine drinkers. As a grape, pinot noir is notoriously tricky to grow, and you can easily lose your shirt paying over the odds for its often over-hyped, under-flavoured wines. In hot climates pinot noir makes jammy-tasting red wines with no centre: so-called 'doughnut wines'. In humid climates pinot noir grapes easily rot, producing thin, dusty reds. But the best pinot noir red wines are so other-worldly and have such sensuous, hedonistic, velvety red-fruit flavours they can stimulate tears of joy among pinot-philes. Burgundy in France produces the world's best (and most expensive) pinot noir reds, but is being challenged by Oregon and California in the USA, Australia, New Zealand and even parts of Germany.

Domaine de la Romanée-Conti, Romanée-Conti Grand Cru Monopole (Burgundy, France)

F-21700 Vosne-Romanée (Côte d'Or), France
T:+33 (0)3.80.61.04.57   www.romanee-conti.fr

Domaine de la Romanée-Conti in Burgundy produces the world's most sought-after pinot noir red wines. Many wine lovers even consider 'the Domaine', as it is known, the world's most prestigious winery. The Domaine's 32 hectares (75 acres) of vines certainly includes the most prized collection of pinot noir vineyards in the world. All carry Burgundy's top grand cru classification, as does the Domaine's sole white wine vineyard, Le Montrachet. The Domaine's main pinot noir vineyards around the village of Vosne-Romanée include Richebourg, Romanée-St-Vivant, Échézeaux and Grands Échézeaux (other wineries also own vines in these plots) plus La Tâche and Romanée-Conti, the single vineyard after which the Domaine is named. Both the Romanée-Conti and La Tâche vineyard sites are wholly owned by the Domaine, and as monopolies can be described as *monopoles* in French.

The Domaine is co-owned by two families called de Villaine and Leroy. Both also have their own Burgundy vineyards, separate from those of the Domaine. All of these other vineyards are now certified either organic or biodynamic (for other wines from the Leroy family, see p. 152). The Domaine first moved towards organic methods in the late 1980s, making compost by mixing its pruned vine canes and the grape residues left over from winemaking with cow and horse manure. By the late 1990s, a biodynamic programme was in place. Aubert de Villaine co-runs the Domaine and converted his own vineyard, which produces excellent dry Aligoté white wines in Bouzeron (see also p. 148), to certified organic methods in 1986. Regarding the adoption of biodynamics at the Domaine, Aubert says,

It seemed to give the vines a boost. This was especially noticeable in virused vines, whose self-defence mechanisim seems to be stimulated by biodynamics. Perhaps this is because the vine develops a thicker, stronger root system.

Vines carrying a virus can, like humans, still function, but can also show signs of weakness, in the vine's case producing grapes that perhaps lack a bit of ripeness, colour or flavour.

The Domaine makes teas and decoctions from common horsetail 508, stinging nettle, chamomile, yarrow and dandelion and dilutes them with rainwater. They plough 6 hectares by horse, and the other 26 are worked by light-weight tractors. They follow lunar rhythms whenever new vines are planted, whenever vines are sprayed with biodynamic treatments and, for certain plots only, at pruning. Sensibly, weather conditions alone guide their decisions regarding working the soil and spraying against disease.

Picking a single pinot noir from the Domaine's stellar line-up is no easy task, but of the two wholly owned (*monopole*) vineyards, La Romanée-Conti itself would be most people's desert island choice. The wine's colour is never particularly deep, but its floral smell, mouth-expanding flavours and lace-like texture are incredibly, uniquely sensual.

Grand cru is an official French term for vineyards producing potentially the highest quality grapes in terms of their ripeness, complexity and flavour. Only 32 vineyard plots in Burgundy are designated as grand cru, or 'great growth'. *Premier cru* or *1er cru* ('first growth') is the second-highest classification level in Burgundy.

*Burn Cottage Vineyard in South Africa allows other plants
and shrubs to thrive alongside the vines.*
Burn Cottage Vineyard

Domaine Leroy, Romanée St Vivant Grand Cru (Burgundy, France)

15 rue de la Fontaine, F-21700 Vosne-Romanée (Côte d'Or), France
T:+33 (0)3.80.21.21.10 domaine.leroy@wanadoo.fr

Domaine Leroy is another of Burgundy's most fabled sources of pinot noir red wines (see also Domaine de la Romanée-Conti, see p.148; and Domaine d'Auvenay, p. 39). Owner Lalou Bize-Leroy says her minimalist approach – ultra-low yields, least possible ploughing and biodynamic practices (Demeter certified) – coupled with some top vineyard sites (22 hectares – 55 acres – in total) means her vines can almost self-regulate. The only time they are trimmed is in winter, at pruning. Lalou has all but abandoned trimming vine shoots in summer because the vines are in balance. She says,

> *The more you trim the tops of the vines, the bushier and leafier they become below. The grape bunches then become too shaded from the sun and, lacking light and air, the risk of disease and uneven ripeness increases.*

Lalou's stellar line-up of pinot noir reds includes the premiers crus Brûlées and Beaumonts in Vosne-Romanée and grands crus Chambertin, Clos de la Roche, Richebourg and Romanée St Vivant in this and other neighbouring villages. The Romanée St Vivant comes from 1 hectare (2.5 acres) of pinot noir in Vosne-Romanée, which were last fully replanted in 1924. Their tiny berries, combined with clay-rich topsoils, give a notably deep-coloured red for pinot noir. The flavours are multi-faceted, combining black and red fruits, leather, musk and earth with a texture that showcases intriguing robustness with an elegant fragility. People can, and do, spend hours analysing these wines, partly because they cost so much money to buy, even if you can find a bottle (no more than 6,000 are made each year), but mainly because the wines are so interesting and comforting both to study and enjoy – like running your fingers over cloth with the finest of weaves.

Lalou Bize-Leroy is also a co-owner of Domaine de la Romanée-Conti (see p. 148).

Domaine Trapet Père et Fils, Gevrey-Chambertin 1er Cru Clos Prieur (Burgundy, France)

51 route de Beaune, F-21220 Gevrey Chambertin (Côte d'Or), France
T:+33 (0)3.80.34.30.40 www.domaine-trapet.com

Jean-Louis Trapet is a Burgundy wine-grower who is constantly looking to evolve. He joined the family domaine in 1987 and in the early 1990s put its 11 hectares (25 acres) of vines – mainly pinot noir in Gevrey-Chambertin – on an organic path. In 1992 he stopped using weedkillers because of environmental concerns. But he faced a conundrum when dealing with mildew and other fungal diseases, which ruin the grapes. Jean-Louis says he could have used a small amount of fungicide, which penetrates the sap of the plant and protects it from within. These so-called systemic sprays are not allowed in organics or biodynamics. But the alternative was to rely more on copper-based sprays like Bordeaux mixture (copper sulphate mixed with lime). These are allowed in organics and biodynamics, even though copper residues dripping onto the soil can be toxic to soil microbes. So Jean-Louis discussed the issue with other wine-grower friends including Jean-Claude Rateau, and with a cousin growing biodynamic cereals, then converted to biodynamics because he felt it to be the best tool to reduce and even potentially eliminate altogether the need for any such copper-based sprays (Demeter certified). Jean-Louis says,

> Biodynamics taught me to understand that it was better to prevent diseases arriving on my vines, than to try to cure vines of disease by spraying them after the disease had arrived. By then it is too late. We time spraying [horn silica] 501 in spring very precisely. We spray it once or twice, between the moment the vine shoots have produced their first leaves but just before what will become the grape bunches have started appearing on the shoots. The idea is the [horn silica] 501 mobilises the sugars in the vine's green parts by connecting the vine with the sun's heat and light. The sun is rising higher in the sky each day and the vine shoots are growing higher each day. This stretches the vine by making it tighter and

more disease resistant, as if the vine is so swollen with sugars that she is bulging her muscles so much the disease organisms can't get in.

The red wines Jean-Louis makes – the top ones being grands crus Chambertin, Chapelle-Chambertin and Latrichières-Chambertin, and Gevrey-Chambertin premiers crus Clos Prieur and Petite Chapelle – show singularly ripe, concentrated, clear, fruit flavours, all with a dashingly vibrant mouthfeel. Jean-Louis makes the wine using minimal sulphur dioxide preservative ('sulphites'), giving his pinot noir an extra level of purity and leaving its wondrous detail exposed. Splashing these wines into a wide-brimmed decanter to give them some air first really helps loosen them up. Jean-Louis Trapet and his wife, Andrée, who is from Alsace, also own Domaine Trapet-Jung (see p. 79).

Domaine Jean-Claude Rateau, Beaune Rouge 1er Cru, Aux Coucherias (Burgundy, France)

Chemin des Mariages, F-21200 Beaune (Côte d'Or), France
T:+33 (0)3.80.22.98.91 www.jc-rateau.com

Jean-Claude Rateau discovered biodynamics as a teenager while studying at the wine school in Beaune. He met a very elderly man who, after the end of the Second World War, was one of the first in France to practise non-interventionist winemaking and wine-growing on his vines in Beaujolais. Inspired, Jean-Claude converted his vegetable garden to biodynamics in 1974. 'It was easy, the plot was small but the result was extraordinary on the vegetables.' As soon as Rateau rented his first vines in 1979 these went biodynamic too.

Jean-Claude Rateau nurtures the soil of his vineyard on the French Côte d'Or.

I like biodynamics because it sees nature as something complex and intelligent, and as comprising lots of different relationships between living things.

Jean-Claude is not someone who preaches what he practices, at least not openly. But he has always given free advice to wine-growers curious to follow his biodynamic lead, including to all of Burgundy's aristocrats – those with vines in much better (mainly grands crus) sites than his.

Jean-Claude's 8 hectares (12 acres) of vines are mainly in lowlier sites classified as *villages*, but he does have some premier cru sites. Aux Coucherias on the edge of the town of Beaune is among his best. 'Coucherias is a very dry site, sheltered from the rain and on very deep, free-draining limestone fragments left over from quarrying,' says Jean-Claude. It produces as wholesome an everyday pinot noir as you will find, with a tidy mix of earth and quiet rather than shouty, wild, red-fruit flavours.

Domaine Chandon de Briailles, Savigny-lès-Beaune 1er Cru Rouge Les Lavières (Burgundy, France)

Rue Soeur Goby, F-21420 Savigny-lès-Beaune (Côte d'Or), France
T:+33 (0)3.80.21.52.31   www.chandondebriailles.com

Domaine Chandon de Briailles in the sleepy Burgundy village of Savigny-lès-Beaune has belonged to the de Nicolay family since 1834. The current winemaker, Claude de Nicolay, trained in her native Burgundy but then went to work in New Zealand and Oregon in wineries specialising in pinot noir, Burgundy's signature red grape. She says,

> The aim was not to come back to Burgundy and then try to copy what everyone thinks a stereotypical New World pinot noir red will be like: very ripe, very soft and rather jammy tasting. The aim was more to see how our competitors were making their pinot noirs, and also to see if we in Burgundy could learn something from their approach. Just because we have been making pinot noir in Burgundy since the Middle Ages and the time of the Cistercian monks does not mean we cannot keep learning.

When Claude returned to Burgundy and, in 1988, began making the family wines, the 14-hectare (35-acre) vineyards were in a state of neglect, having been leased out to other growers. By the early 1990s she had adopted organic methods, and by the mid 2000s had gone biodynamic (Demeter certified). 'The 2008 vintage was tough,' says Claude, referring to the high disease pressure that year. 'One local sceptic asked us what we were going to do for 2009, and I said, "Last year we had one foot in biodynamics, and now we have both there. We're not giving up."' Claude's desire to learn rather than believing she knows it all saw her ask for advice from Frédéric Lafarge (see below) down the road in Volnay. She followed his advice and changed the pruning of vineyards that had been cultivated for high yields while leased out. The new regime allowed more sunlight and airflow around the bunches, reducing the risk of disease. Then she started sowing grasses to soak up rainwater, ensuring the grapes would have thicker, more disease-resistant skins and more concentrated flavours.

But this is not a domaine looking to produce concentrated, thunderous pinot noir reds, as Claude says herself, although it could do, especially from its top grand cru holdings in Corton, for example (fine chardonnay whites from Pernand-Vergelesses and Corton are also made here). Instead, the Chandon de Briailles reds are pretty pinot noir wines with an easy-to-appreciate smoothness and levity, the Savigny-lès-Beaune Premier Cru Les Lavières being the perfect example.

Domaine Lafarge, Volnay (Burgundy, France)

Rue de la Combe, F-21190 Volnay (Côte d'Or), France
T:+33 (0)3.80.21.61.61 www.domainelafarge.com

Burgundy's Lafarge family bought their first Volnay vineyards during the French Revolution, handing them from father to son ever since. Frédéric Lafarge took over here in 1978 and converted to biodynamics from 1997 (certified organic). As, historically, the mayor of Volnay was often a member of the Lafarge family, appearances are critical. Hence some Volnay villagers were initially rather distressed to see Lafarge's vine plots take on a scruffier look under the biodynamic regime, because Frédéric happily let weeds grow to improve soil structure. Now Frédéric's advice is often sought by neighbouring wine-growers keen to improve their vineyards. He says,

Biodynamics is one aspect of improving wine quality, but you also need to get the basics right, like pruning the vines so the bunches are evenly spaced. This gives them more air and sunlight, keeping them healthier and making life much easier in the vineyard and winery.

Lafarge makes a number of consistently outstanding Volnays from premier cru vineyards like Clos des Chênes, Caillerets and Clos du Château des Duc, but his basic Volnay red is as good an introduction to pinot noir in general and Burgundy in particular as you are likely to find. It is a deep, multi-textured red that has savoury layers of hedge fruit and red earth flavours, which unfold brilliantly over four to twelve years.

Château de Monthélie, Monthélie Rouge 1er Cru Sur la Velle (Burgundy, France)

Rue du Pied de la Vallée, F-21190 Monthélie (Côte d'Or), France
T:+33 (0)3.80.21.23.32

Although Eric de Sûremain's family owns a huge château in Monthélie and is related by birth to some of Burgundy's most famous families (notably to Anne-Claude Leflaive; see p. 39), Eric is a very down-to-earth farmer. When Eric took over here in 1978, he carried on using the organic practices he learnt from his father. But Eric wanted to go further, and in 1990 he helped found a group of Burgundy growers keen to exchange ideas about how better to protect and improve their vineyards. Soon Eric was spraying biodynamic horn manure 500 on his soils. He says,

I could see the soil structure change, becoming softer to walk on. So it made sense for me to get three people to spray horn

manure by hand using back sprayers rather than to do it using a single heavy tractor.

Eric has 11 hectares (28 acres) of pinot noir and chardonnay grapevines in the south central Burgundy villages of Rully (mainly white wine) and Monthélie (mainly red). Eric's oldest pinot noir vines were planted in 1959 high above the town of Monthélie in Sur la Velle, a premier cru site. This is fragrant yet firm pinot noir, with wild redcurrant fruit and a moreish dark-plum twist in the aftertaste. Drink within four to eight years of the vintage. Around 8–12,000 bottles are made annually.

Les Champs de l'Abbaye, Côte Chalonnaise Rouge Clos des Roches (Burgundy, France)

9 rue des Roches Pendantes, F-71510 Aluze (Saône et Loire) , France
T:+33 (0)3.8545.59.32 alainhasard@wanadoo.fr

Alain and Isabelle Hasard met while studying at Montpellier University, a world leader for teaching the art and science of vineyard management. But Alain and Isabelle were studying in the university's medical faculty, and only got into wine when Alain started working in wine shops. They started renting, then buying, vineyards in southern Burgundy's sleepy Côte Chalonnaise region. Meticulous work in their chardonnay and pinot noir vineyards produced low yields of high quality grapes giving wines that soon had the critics purring. Alain uses a back sprayer for his biodynamic vineyard sprays, deciding by eye whether a vine plot needs the earthy impulse given by a soil spray like horn manure 500, or the extra light and heat forces the horn silica 501 atmosphere spray encourages.

The flagship vineyard here is the walled Clos des Roches, which Alain and Isabelle rent. Its pinot noir vines were planted in 1959. They produce a scrumptious red with a tingly vibrancy that reaches every part of your mouth. The red-fruit flavours are tongue-coatingly ripe, reflecting the fact the vines face due sunny south; but texturally the wine has incisor-like bite because the limestone soils beneath are rich in ruddy clay. The Clos des Roches produces just 1,500 bottles each year from its 0.7 hectares (1.7 acres).

OTHER PINOT NOIR PRODUCERS OF INTEREST IN BURGUNDY

...are Gilles and Fabienne Ballorin for Morey St Denis and Marsannay (Demeter certified), Domaine Arlaud (www.domainearlaud.com) in Gevrey-Chambertin (Biodyvin certified), Domaine (Nicolas and David) Rossignol-Trapet (www.Rossignol-Trapet.com) in Gevrey-Chambertin (Demeter certified), Comte (Louis-Michel) Liger-Belair (www.liger-belair.fr) for grands crus in Vosne-Romanée, Domaine Marquis d'Angerville (www.domainedangerville.fr) for Volnay and Pommard (Demeter certified), Christine and Didier Montchovet (www.montchovet.fr) for Beaune Rouge and Pommard, Thiébault Huber (www.huber-verdereau.com) for Volnay and Pommard (Demeter certified), and Fréderic Rossignol in Pommard (Demeter certified).

Robert Sinskey, Three Amigos Pinot Noir, Los Carneros (California, USA)

6320 Silverado Trail, Napa, CA 94558, USA
T:+1 707.944.9090 www.robertsinskey.com

Robert Sinskey and his wife Maria committed to converting their California vineyards to organics because they were worried about the declining health of both their soils and their vines. Converting was no easy task logistically,  because their Napa Valley vineyards are located in both the Stag's Leap district (where the winery is) and much further south towards San Francisco in the cooler, more ocean-influenced Los Carneros region. Los Carneros is where the Sinskeys' Three Amigos ('Three Friends') pinot noir comes from, so named because it comes from three vineyards called Amigo 1, 2 and 3. First planted in 1982, the

Three Amigos contain some of the oldest pinot noir vineyards in this part of California, including 'heirloom' cuttings which first arrived in California in the early twentieth century. They produce low yields of classically flavoured – some would say old-fashioned – pinot noir reds filled with gentle redcurrant, *sous-bois* and mushroom flavours.

When Robert began sowing his vineyards with clovers, medics and fescues to stop his soils from drying hard under the summer sun, grazing sheep in them over winter, and feeding them (vines, not sheep!) with his homemade compost, he was seen as being misguided at best, stupid at worst. This was in the mid 1990s, when Napa Valley's wine industry was booming and organics was seen as desirable only if you wanted uneconomically low yields of unhealthy grapes for wines no one would ever drink. Times and attitudes changed, and when Robert adopted biodynamics in the early 2000s (Demeter certified) he did it step by step, buying material for key biodynamic sprays like horn manure 500 and horn silica 501 from those with more experience than he, before learning how to make his own.

What I like about Robert's approach is that he proves you get more by doing less: he has kept his unfashionable heirloom pinot noir vines and refused to drown his wines with an excess of new oak (he also makes fine chardonnay and pinot blanc whites as well as sumptuous cabernet reds. Most of all, Robert has shown that the more you leave the soil alone, by leaving it untidily weedy-looking rather than ploughing it clean, the happier the vines seem to be. Pinot noir shows its class in Carneros because this region has a similar kind of 'cool climate' to the grape's Burgundy homeland. The refreshing nature of Robert Sinskey's Three Amigos Pinot Noir demonstrates there is no point choosing a cool climate for your vines if your topsoil gets furnace hot in summer, as it will if weeded and ploughed. Cooler soils allow pinot noir grapes to ripen more slowly and retain more of their delicate flavours. With grass protecting the soil it stays cooler on top and moister underground, which encourages the worms who, thanks to all that homemade compost, started recolonising and cleansing the Sinskey vineyards from the mid 1990s.

Littorai, The Haven Pinot Noir, Sonoma Coast (California, USA)

Littorai Wines, 788 Gold Ridge Road, Sebastopol, CA 95472, USA
T:+1 707.823.9586 www.littorai.com

If I had a dollar for every non-Burgundian winemaker I'd met telling me he was looking for the perfect spot to plant the perfect pinot noir vineyard and hence make the perfect pinot noir red wine, I could have given up wine writing years ago. I first met Ted Lemon, Littorai's founding owner, in 1993 when he had just returned to the US from France. While away he'd succeeded in turning a really good Burgundy estate (Guy Roulot's in Meursault) into an even better one (Ted was the first American to run a Burgundy domaine, having come to France initially to study medieval French rather than wine). Back in California, Ted was making cerebral Burgundy-style wines in the Napa Valley for a well-respected French family. However, at that time America didn't seem to want effete, tight, mineral-rich French-style chardonnays and pinots, it wanted big, muscly, fast-food wines that shouted oak, high alcohol and gobs of fruit. When I told Ted I thought his chardonnay was the best I had tasted from California, he told me he was starting his own winery (Littorai) making pinot noir and chardonnay grown only in the coolest reaches of California's otherwise balmy Sonoma Coast – cool vineyard sites in a warm climate being the holy grail for chardo- and pinot-philes.

I didn't hear much of Ted for nearly another two decades, until I tried a New Zealand pinot noir from Burn Cottage (see p. 168), a vineyard Ted had helped meticulously plan to run as biodynamic from the start. They'd hired Ted because they liked what he was doing at Littorai, where he is producing pinot noir and chardonnay wines (no certification) that engage all of your senses while also really getting into your mind. Ted's 'The Haven' pinot noir (from 1.6 hectares or 4 acres) is pale red to look at, almost like a deep rosé rather than a proper red, but the intensity and brightness in the colour is the really significant clue to what you'll find when you

161

smell the wine and then drink it. It expresses what in biodynamic-speak one might describe as a tension between fire and water. It has strong inner vibrancy, which shows the vines are really connected to their surroundings: soils made by firey volcanoes in a landscape dampened by Pacific coastal winds and fogs, and lit by a dynamic interplay of light and shade that is constantly being reconstructed, because the prevailing winds and air temperatures change so quickly where the vast Pacific ocean meets the big American landmass.

'Biodynamics is really a way of getting both your vines and you as a farmer to engage all of your senses,' says Ted, whose three children attend a local Steiner-Waldorf school, a type of 'biodynamic education' that encourages children to engage and express their senses of touch, sight, smell, sound and taste, rather than stuffing them too early with purely academic knowledge. I like Ted's pinot noirs (he also makes chardonnay) because they tell me something I didn't know about pinot noir in general and about Californian pinot noir in particular. They taste clear and clean and ripe and balanced and all those tick-box things wine writers love spotting as they taste, but most of all perhaps I like Ted's wines because they engage my spirit as well as my bodily senses.

CALIFORNIAN BIODYNAMIC PINOT NOIR ...is also made by Benziger (see p. 204) in Sonoma County, and by Porter Bass (www.porterbass.com), de Loach (deloachvineyards.com) and Porter Creek (www.portercreekvineyards.com), all in Russian River (all Demeter certified).

Bergström Wines, Bergström Vineyard Pinot Noir, Willamette Valley (Oregon, USA)

18405 NE Calkins Lane, Newberg, OR 97132
T:+1 503.554.0468 Website www.bergstromwines.com

Josh Bergström's parents, John and Karen, swapped city life in downtown Portland, Oregon, for the state's Willamette Valley wine country in 1997. While they were leasing vines and planting their own in the Dundee Hills, Josh finished his winemaking studies in

California before heading to Burgundy for more study plus some hands-on experience. His aim was to find out just how those darned Burgundians make such incredible pinot noir reds and chardonnay whites. The late 1990s was an exciting time to be in Burgundy as far as biodynamics was concerned. Established wine-growers were starting to accept, and students were even being taught, that a diet of weedkillers and fertilizers was tiring Burgundy's soils and weakening the vines. Life needed to be encouraged back into the soils, the biodynamic options for this being either manure-based compost or manure-based soil sprays . When Josh returned to Oregon he brought back with him some biodynamic ideas for the vines, and a determination to make wines that tasted as if they had made themselves, with minimal interference from him as winemaker.

Josh has 9 hectares (23 acres) of estate-grown biodynamic pinot noir and chardonnay to work with (Demeter certified). Pinot noir in the flagship Bergström Vineyard was planted from 1999, a former nut orchard with soils containing basalt. This is a dark, hard, heat-retaining rock, of volcanic origin. Although the basalt in the soil is no longer hot like molten lava, in biodynamic terms it still brings a 'hot' influence to the vineyard. If pinot noir feels too hot it will ripen too quickly, making a wine smelling of caramel, fudge or toffee (molten sugar). To negate this potentially hot basalt influence, Josh boosted the cool, dark earthiness of the vineyard soils by sowing cereals and clovers as cover crops or 'green manures'. They help build soil structure, and make the earth more 'earthy'. This provides the vines with a cooler, earthier place to stand in, and helps them ripen their grapes more slowly. That coolness is expressed in the Bergström Vineyard pinot noir through its minty, mentholated, red-fruit flavours, which have the lushness that makes pinot noir so obviously irresistible to drink, and also through its mouthfeel, which has the firmness of texture that makes those flavours satisfying and interesting too.

Brick House Vineyards, Evelyn's Pinot Noir, Willamette Valley (Oregon, USA)

18200 Lewis Rogers Lane, Newberg OR 97132, USA
T:+1 503.538.5136 www.brickhousewines.com

In early 1990, Doug Tunnell swapped a career as a high-profile TV news reporter for wine-growing. 'Wine ran in the family,' he says. 'My surname derives from French Hugenot [Protestant] ancestors who fled [Catholic] France in the late seventeenth century and were barrel-makers or *tonneliers*.' Doug and his partner, Melissa Mills, have 12 hectares (30 acres) of mainly pinot noir, chardonnay and gamay vines in Oregon's Willamette Valley (Demeter certified). He says,

> *Organics came about because of my love of freshwater line fishing. The idea of chemical run-off from vineyards going into local rivers bothered me. We planted the vines on what was a really heavily sprayed filbert [hazelnut] orchard, sowing rye grass around the baby vines as a way of stopping what was left of the topsoil sliding away in the spring rains. The vineyards are now biodynamic, and we see biodynamic compost as key in keeping our soils vital and healthy. We use cow manure from a local organic dairy and seed the piles with the biodynamic compost preparations. We stir our biodynamic spray preparations in an old barrel.*

I find Doug's wines really satisfying to drink. His dry white chardonnay wines are rich and always focussed, his red gamay noir (from the Beaujolais grape) is vibrant but far from the one-dimensional Beaujolais stereotype, and his pinot noir reds consistently deliver rich textures and flavours with a fine balance between sweet-tasting ripe red fruit and savoury tannins. I would love to send Doug back to his ancestral French homeland because I am sure he'd thrive in Burgundy, winning the respect of his peers there as he has done in Oregon. His signature pinot noir, 'Evelyn's', is named after his mother. Barrel matured, it has deep, ripe-cherry and chewy-blackberry flavours that steadily evolve after the wine is poured. A wine to take your time over.

Hochkirch, Steinbruch Pinot Noir, Henty (Victoria, Australia)

Hamilton Highway, Tarrington, Victoria 3301, Australia
T:+61 (0)3.5573.5200

John Nagorcka's 8-hectare (20-acre) Hochkirch vineyard is tucked along the foot of the Grampian mountains in southwestern Victoria's Henty sub-region. The vineyard forms part of a mixed biodynamic farm producing wool, grain, lamb, beef and pork (Demeter certified). John planted his first vines in 1990. Unirrigated and deliberately spaced close together to compete with each other for food and water, they produce low yields of incredibly concentrated grapes. With such good raw material, John's winemaking style can be as hands-off as his grape growing, leading to wines with a very natural feel.

Dry whites are produced from semillon and chardonnay, with reds from syrah (shiraz) and pinot noir. The unfiltered Steinbruch Pinot Noir is especially expressive of Hochkirch's fine-grained, reddish soils. The grapes are hand-picked, then go into open-topped fermenting vats with a good proportion of whole as opposed to crushed berries. This prolongs the fermenation because the fermentation yeast can't convert all the sugar in the grapes until all the berries have become crushed by John slowly hand-plunging them over a period of days. A long, steady fermentation produces a wine that needs to be left a while after pouring for its ripe fruit flavours and barrel-aged, savoury oak tannins to meld together. Once the wine has settled in your glass, a very pure, ethereal pinot noir appears, which you'll find it hard to tear yourself away from.

Lark Hill, Pinot Noir (Canberra District, Australia)

521 Bungendore Road, Bungendore, New South Wales 2621, Australia
T:+61(0)2.6238.1393 www.larkhillwine.com.au

Dr Dave and Sue Carpenter's Lark Hill vineyard was the first to be planted in Australia's unusually high, windy and semi-arid Canberra district in 1978. Their 5-hectare (12-acre) biodynamic vineyard lies in an environmental protection zone and is home to many species of birds and wildlife (certified organic). At 860 metres (2,860 feet), the vines endure high swings between hot day- and very cool night-time temperatures. Vines struggle to grow on the poor soils, and grape yields are tiny. Of the grapes planted, chardonnay, riesling and especially pinot noir thrive. The Carpenters use whey and canola oil to protect the vines from fungal diseases. They fertilise with fish and seaweed extracts, and control weeds by deep mulching, which also protects the soil from erosion and keeps it cool during the heat of the day.

Dave, Sue and their winemaker son, Chris, all have science and winemaking backgrounds. In their in-house lab, they conducted analyses over several years, which showed that grape juice from their biodynamic vines contained higher levels of the nutrients that yeast needs to ferment wine, than juice from the non-biodynamic grapes they were purchasing. Dave says,

Being biodynamic has certainly not caused us to abandon science. We had been alerted to problems in fermentations caused by low nutrient levels when fermenting grapes we purchased from conventional growers in the Canberra District. Such juices needed a great deal of [added] yeast nutrient prior and during fermentation to avoid off aromas [eggy, cheesy smells] and stuck ferments.

'Stuck ferments' occur because the yeast lacks the food it needs to complete its job of turning grape-juice sugar into wine. Dave's conclusion, based on his own data and industry data taken over several years across the district was that the conventional farming use of soluble or 'chemical' fertilizers might temporarily fix a lack of nitrogen for vines, but it then leads to a lack of the right nutrients for fermentation in grapes. He says, 'Heavy application of inorganic fertilizers to address nitrogen deficiency simply exacerbated the imbalance in grape juices and wines.' In other words the more artificial nitrogen you feed the vines as soluble fertilizers, the more artificial nitrogen (in the form of yeast nutrients) you will then need to give to the wine to get it to ferment properly.

Dave and Sue no longer buy any grapes, and get rave reviews for their biodynamic wines. Their pinot noir has

intensely clear, ethereal, cherry fruit flavours and a satin-like texture. The fruit takes on classic meaty and gamey notes as the tannins soften with age. Around 4,500 bottles are made each year.

Felton Road, Pinot Noir, Bannockburn (Central Otago, New Zealand)

Bannockburn, RD2 Cromwell, Central Otago, New Zealand
T:+64 (0)3.445.0885 www.feltonroad.com

It is easy to see why Felton Road's owner, Englishman Nigel Greening, is so bullish about biodynamics. Greening has 32 hectares (79 acres) of biodynamic vines in New Zealand's Central Otago region (Demeter certified). He says,

> People were a bit sceptical about biodynamics when we started converting in around 2002. But then we even had a famous vine expert, who is one of the world's most dedicated opponents of organics and biodynamics, saying how well balanced our vines were. The only block of ours he seemed less enthusiastic about turned out to have been irrigated with water contaminated by a neighbour who'd been using weedkillers on his spare land to keep the scrub and brushwood down and prevent a fire hazard.

Now scrub around the Felton Road vineyards is not weedkilled but is instead devoured by a small but energetic herd of goats. The goats are not trusted to perform weed control under the vines. 'They'd eat the irrigation lines, the grapes, everything they could find,' says Nigel, so he uses under-vine mulching instead. For the mulch, he lays straw to block the light weeds need to grow.

> Laying our biodynamic compost under the straw keeps the soil cool and allows the compost to feed the soil with nutrients slowly, so that the vines can access what they need when they need it, without the risk of pushing them to grow too fast. It also means we need to irrigate less, so our pinot noir grapes are becoming smaller and thicker-skinned, and the wines are then more robust and savoury.

Around 30 per cent of the grapes in Felton Road's pinot noirs go into the fermenting vats uncrushed. The grapes gradually split and release their juice as the fermentation unfolds. 'This gives a slow build-up to fermentation and produces red wines with softer tannins, with the intricacy we want our schist-based soils to give to our wines,' says Nigel.

Central Otago pinot noirs are characterised by dark cherry rather than raspberry or strawberry flavours. Felton Road's signature Bannockburn pinot noir is very floral, ripe without being overripe, with delicate spice flavours and quintessential pinot noir character. The wine is at its best between seven and ten years of the vintage shown on the label. Felton Road also makes two noticeably diverse single vineyard wines called 'Block Three' and 'Block Five'.

Burn Cottage Vineyard, Pinot Noir (Central Otago, New Zealand)

PO Box 183, Cromwell, Central Otago, New Zealand
T:+64 (0)27.2403352 www.burncottage.com

Marquis Sauvage got into wine while studying business at graduate school in Denver. 'Although I was a good student I didn't really fancy the world of corporate affairs. In fact, I preferred wine, so I opened a wine bar in Denver instead. This then grew into a wine import business to keep the bar stocked.' His love of pinot noir eventually saw Marquis buy some bare land just south of the 45th parallel on New Zealand's south island, in Otago, an emerging mecca for pinot noir. From 2003 he planted 11 hectares (25 acres) of mainly pinot noir grapes, with advice from Peter Proctor (see p. 237) and Ted Lemon (see p. 161). 'I feel that New Zealand pinot noir gets as close structurally to Burgundian pinot noir as is possible outside Burgundy itself,' he says.

Marquis grew up on his parents' 25,000-head cattle farm in Kansas, and the first thing he did after acquiring his vineyard-to-be was buy eight Highland heifer milk cows.

We used their manure to compost all the waste vegetation we cleared off the land in order to plant the vineyards. We made dozens and dozens of small biodynamic compost piles over a period of two years. When we planted the pinot noir vines we filled each hole with one kilo of biodynamic compost. We planted 55,000 vines. We also planted shrubs and trees for shade, as habitat breaks to attract beneficial insects, or as wind breaks. Each tree got five kilos of biodynamic compost in its hole.

What was a rabbit-infested wasteland has been transformed into a vine oasis, with regular applications of biodynamic and seaweed sprays on both the vines and the soil. As well as cows, Burn Cottage has chickens and sheep. Estate manager Jared Connolly says,

The thinking behind this is for pasture health. From a parasite point of view each animal will graze at a different level, with the cows mowing the grass low but the sheep mowing it lower still. So the sheep eat those parasites the cows won't have reached. Then the chickens come in and eat any parasites left either right low down in the grass, which neither the sheep nor the cows could reach, and also the chickens pick parasites out of the the animals' dung while also spreading the dung around via their scratching. It's a healthy system from a self-sufficiency point of view.

Burn Cottage's pinot noir is scented, alluring, velvety and wholesome, with a flamboyant and quite remarkable inner brightness to it, especially seeing as the vines are still so young. Less than 7,000 bottles are made each year.

MORE GOOD SOURCES OF BIODYNAMIC PINOT NOIR
...include Vynfields (www.vynfields.com) in Martinborough, New Zealand. Also, Dutchman Jacob Duijn (www.duijn.de) makes one of Germany's most concentrated pinot noirs from low yield vines in the warm, southerly Baden Ortenau region. In Argentina, Bodega Chacra (www.bodegachacra.com) has pinot noir vines dating back to the 1930s. (All Demeter certified.)

Burn Cottage Vineyard in New Zealand plants wind breaks of shrubs and trees, which also foster biodiversity.
Burn Cottage Vineyard

SANGIOVESE ('BRUNELLO')

As we will see in the section on blended red wines, sangiovese is combined with other Italian and French grapes to make chianti. But a little further south, sangiovese is made into 100 per cent varietal red wines around the Tuscan hilltop town of Montalcino. Here the sangiovese is called 'brunello', hence Brunello di Montalcino.

SANGIOVESE OUTSIDE ITALY
...Ridgely Evers and Colleen McGlynn's DaVero estate (www.davero.com) in California's Dry Creek Valley is a sangiovese – and olive oil – specialist (Demeter certified).

San Giuseppe, Brunello di Montalcino (Tuscany, Italy)

53020 Castelnuovo dell'Abate (SI = Siena), Italy
T:+39 0577.835754 www.sT: ladicampalto.com

This isolated Montalcino estate was first planted with olives in the 1920s but had been largely abandoned until Stella di Campalto, whose mother was from nearby Florence, took over in the mid 1990s. From 1999–2002 Stella planted a 6-hectare (15-acre) sangiovese (or 'brunello') vineyard to make Rosso and Brunello di Montalcino. She says

I never used antibiotics either for myself or my two children. I wanted my trees and vines to be as strong and as disease resistant as possible. Having read about biodynamics I thought it seemed the best way of achieving this.

Stella uses a back sprayer when applying biodynamic preparations to her vines, and also sprays garlic infusions to discourage pests like grape berry moths. Her grapes are hand-picked and sorted in the field to eliminate anything substandard.

The rocky, stiflingly warm soils here look like they'd produce impenetrably brutish brunello red wines, laden with colour and tannin. In fact, San Giuseppe's brunello is a pale but bright peony red with powerful, rich, and warmly compelling *sous-bois* flavours, which become elegantly gamey with age. The wines need five to eight years in bottle to show their best. Decant and serve with wild boar stew.

Pian dell'Orino, Rosso di Montalcino (Tuscany, Italy)

Loc. Pian dell'Orino 189, 53024 Montalcino (SI = Siena), Italy

T:+39 0577.849301   www.piandellorino.it

Caroline Pobitzer's family are wine merchants from Südtirol (Alto Adige) in northern Italy. In 1997 they bought a ruined house in Tuscany's Montalcino region to use as a holiday home called Pian dell'Orino. Caroline's German partner, Jan Erbach, began renovating Pian dell'Orino's small, abandoned brunello (sangiovese) vineyard while renting three other local vineyards. The couple have 6 hectares (15 acres) in total, all of which Jan converted to biodynamics (organic certification). Jan's previous job had been planting a biodynamic vineyard for the Loacker family (see p. 96). They had hired Jan knowing he had written his winemaking thesis on controlling insect pests using non-chemical methods. He says,

> *Biodynamics encourages you to get closer to natural rhythms. One year you might have a problem with wasps, but the following year you might not see a single wasp in your vineyard. Understanding that this chronobiology exists in nature is so important. Rudolf Steiner [the creator of biodynamics] was the first writer I'd read who'd understood. The teas I make from local plants [fennel, yellow fleabane] really help stimulate the vine's self-defence mechanism against pests and diseases.*

When making his brunello, Jan can blend sangiovese grapes grown on four very different soil types. This builds complexity into the wine and is one reason Pian dell'Orino's red wines, the early drinking Rosso di Montalcino and the more age-able Brunello di Montalcino, have such interesting textures. The other reason is Jan has a very light touch in the winery, allowing the inherently bright fruit flavours in his sangiovese grapes to almost radiate in pure, refreshing, bright-crimson-coloured red wines with smooth, luminous textures.

SYRAH (SHIRAZ)

When bottled on its own in the great wines of the northern Rhône (Côte Rotie, Hermitage, Cornas), syrah produces big, sometimes brutish but often long-lived reds, whose violet, cherry preserve, liquorice and cassis flavours are infused with appealing notes of roasted meat and black pepper. In the southern Rhône, Mediterranean France, California, Italy and Australia (where it is often referred to as shiraz) syrah is regularly used with other red grapes as part of a blend.

M. Chapoutier, Les Varonniers Rouge, Crozes-Hermitage (Rhône, France)

18 avenue du Docteur Paul Durand, F-26600 Tain L'Hermitage (Drôme), France
T:+33 (0)4.75.08.28.65   www.chapoutier.com

Michel Chapoutier took over his family's ailing Rhône wine-growing and wine-merchant business in 1991, buying their shares with a bank loan. The seventh generation of the Chapoutier family to run the firm, and preternaturally hyperactive, Michel launched a successful, one-man sales campaign, making some marketing gaffes but also learning from them. He burnt the old wooden fermentation vats, which had vinegary staves that were tainting the wines. He restructured vineyards in prized Rhône appellations, replacing missing or lifeless vines with better cuttings. These vineyards, and new ones he bought in the Ardèche, Roussillon and Provence were gradually converted to biodynamics (Demeter certified). For eastern France, Michel strategically sited his composting area to make it easier to source the raw materials (organic cow and sheep manure, lavender stems) and to transport the finished biodynamic compost to whichever vineyard needed it most. In the meantime, he continued the family merchant business, buying in grapes and wines from contracted growers, while developing joint ventures in other parts of France, in Australia (Beechworth)

and in Portugal's Douro (Port region). Invariably he chose sub-regions or individual vine plots on his favourite granitic soils while trying (not always successfully) to convince his partners to follow his biodynamic lead (Cape Jaffa's Hooper family proved an exception; see p. 127).

Michel says he loves granite because the wines leave an almost indelible imprint on your tastebuds. He even labels his St Joseph syrah red and its deliciously dense, old viney, dry white Marsanne counterpart as 'Les Granits'. They form part of his Sélections Parcellaires (single vine plot) series. He also makes Crozes-Hermitage red and white from granite soils labelled Les Varonniers, after the name of the plot they are grown on. The red version of Les Varonniers, from 100 per cent syrah, is my favourite value red wine in Michel's huge range. This is a serious red, full of ripe tannins and bricky red fruit, making it easier to drink, digest and therefore enjoy than Michel's denser and vastly more expensive Sélections Parcellaires syrah from iconic regions like Côte Rotie and Ermitage (as he calls Hermitage).

The wine trade hasn't always taken kindly to noisy, excitable, relentlessly self-promoting tall poppies like Michel Chapoutier. But he attracts talented people (vineyard managers, winemakers) to work for or with him, he has a great eye for vineyards, and his so-called gimmickery – like becoming the first winemaker to label his wines in braille (in 1996) – can be visionary (no pun intended). But most of all his wines, whether from granite, schist, clay or limestone, northern hemisphere or southern, red or white, have invariably given me real pleasure to drink.

ANOTHER BIODYNAMIC CROZES-HERMITAGE PRODUCER TO NOTE ...is David Renaud of Domaine les Bruyères (www.domainelesbruyeres.fr), who stopped sending his grapes to the local co-op in 2002 to start making his own wine instead.

Château Maris, La Touge, Minervois La Livinière (Languedoc, France)

Chemin de Parignoles, F-34210 La Livinière (Hérault), France
T:+33 (0)4.68.91.42.63 www.mariswine.com

Bertie Eden of Château Maris

Bertie Eden is an Englishman with a keen sense of history. In part this is because one of his uncles was Anthony Eden, British prime minister in the 1950s and also a key founding figure in the world's first organic farming organisation, the UK's Soil Assocation. But Bertie's sense of history goes back even further: he says that when he roams his Minervois vineyards in France's Languedoc, 'The excitement is knowing I am walking across tracks and fields created and farmed by the Romans, land with over 2,000 years of history producing top-quality wine.' Bertie's mission is to use biodynamics (Demeter certified) to ensure his 40 hectares (98 acres) of Minervois survive another 2,000 years. He says,

> *We prefer our Percheron horse to tractors, and spray plant teas from local wild herbs for pests and diseases. We plough and prune to lunar cycles and make around 500 tonnes of cow-manure-based biodynamic compost a year. The real stuff at a real size! We sow winter barley, beans, peas and radishes between the vine rows as food for the vines, the soil and its worms, and to prevent erosion. Soil erosion is absolutely the biggest threat to the Languedoc. The further you take your vineyard away from monoculture [ie. just growing vines] to something more biodiverse the better.*

Bertie installed rainwater showers and dry loos for staff and collects rainwater for all his biodynamic teas and sprays. He also built a winery made of hemp-lime bricks and wood. It was built by hand, without machines or cement. 'Our hemp bricks actually absorb carbon dioxide from the atmosphere,' he says, 'but they are also great at keeping the wines cool, so there is no need for refrigerated chilling.' Bertie even grew his own hemp for the bricks in nearby fields. 'A winery made of wood, lime, and earth can breathe, and if one day I decide to knock my winery down, it can be safely thrown back to nature.'

Bertie makes a big range of generously proportioned red wines from southern French staples like grenache and carignan, but it is his 'La Touge' syrah red that has an extra degree of class. La Touge comes from an area of Minervois called La Livinière on clay-limestone terraces with a unique layer of schist on top. The soil drains quickly but gives the vine roots the kind of cool foundation they need in the hot Mediterranean climate if the grapes are to ripen without becoming jammy. 80,000 bottles of 'La Touge' are made each year.

(For another Minervois red, see p. 229.)

Amerighi Stefano, Syrah (Tuscany, Italy)

Via Molino Nuovo 1, I-52045 Foiano della Chiana (AR = Arezzo), Italy
T:+39 0575.648340 amerighi@inwind.it

Stefano Amerighi grew up on his parents' farm near Cortona in southeast Tuscany. Cortona's continental climate and soft, free-draining hill slopes are seen as producing Tuscany's definitive syrah. Stefano planted an 8-hectare (20-acre) syrah vineyard, which was biodynamic from the time of planting (Demeter certified). He makes compost and his biodynamic preparations in the surrounding woodland. He sprays stinging-nettle tea to stop the vines from heat stressing, but Stefano says he likes to 'cool the soil down with compost, compost teas and tall-growing cereals like wheat and oats sown as cover crops. Cutting these forms a mulch, which protects the soil from the sun, keeping it cooler for the vine roots.' Stefano's flagship syrah red has caressingly soft, ripe raspberry flavours styled for drinking within three to six years of the vintage shown on the label. Around 10,000 bottles are made each year.

177

Kalleske, Eduard Syrah (Barossa Valley, South Australia)

PO Box 650, Greenock, South Australia 5360
T:+61 (0)8.8563.4000   www.kalleske.com

John Kalleske is the fifth generation of his family to farm in South Australia's parched Barossa Valley, which is famed for its shiraz (syrah) red wines. He has 50 hectares (120 acres) of vines, plus 160 hectares (400 acres) of land for arable crops and livestock. John used to sell his grapes, becoming the first Australian whose shiraz was chosen for the country's iconic Rhône-style red wine three years running. The company who made it then got taken over by a beer conglomerate. He explains,

> *They started sending technicians here in white overalls holding computer print-outs. They said I'd get higher yields by changing how I pruned. But I've never irrigated my vines and knew that there's a skill in making sure vines can produce the right quantity of healthy grapes, which don't raisin through lack of water. Going for the higher yields on the computer print-out would have produced small, raisined grapes, which are uneconomic for me and useless to the winery buying the grapes. They downgraded me, meaning I'd be paid less per kilo of grapes. So I renovated one of our barns, bought some fermenting tanks and started making my own wine.*

Critical acclaim followed, especially for the Kalleske syrah 'Eduard' whose vines, planted between 1905 and 1960, had produced the grapes John sold into Australia's top red. He says,

> *I always thought these were our worst vines. When I took over from my father [who farmed conventionally] I sensed our farm was becoming weaker. I went to an organic seminar and then trialled organic and biodynamic methods by feeding those vines with compost. Although the vines started looking different I thought the composting had been a waste. But tests subsequently showed how these soils were our only ones with textbook balance on the estate. So there was a logic to why these grapes, of all the grapes we grew, were so highly valued by prized buyers looking for grapes to end up in Australia's top red.*

John then converted the whole farm to biodynamics (organic certification), with a particular emphasis on compost and soil sprays like horn manure 500. 'These keep our soils cooler, making them able to retain more rainwater, which is what unirrigated vines need in a hot, dry climate like ours,' he says. The Kalleske Eduard Syrah has opulent menthol, thick tar and juicy blackberry flavours overlain by glossy oak. Decant and drink with rabbit stew.

Paxton Vineyards, Quandong Farm Shiraz (McLaren Vale, South Australia)

PO Box 18, McLaren Vale, SA 5171, Australia
T:+61 (0)8.8323.8645 www.paxtonvineyards.com

David Paxton forged a career planting and then managing vineyards for some of Australia's biggest wine names during the country's 1990s wine boom. 'Managing the vineyards also meant finding clients to buy and ferment the grapes,' says David, now in his early seventies.

Biodynamics started when my vineyard manager, Toby Bekkers, told me he'd consistently found sugar levels seemed to rise noticeably in the grapes around full moon. This gave us an advantage because we couldn't sell grapes if the sugars were too low. So we bought a biodynamic moon calendar and started pre-booking [fermenting] tank space for grapes in client wineries. Even if our competitors' grapes started becoming richer in sugar at the same time as ours, we knew ours were first in the queue at the wineries. The worst thing that can happen at harvest is having grapes that are ripe enough to sell and buyers who want them but who have run out of space in the winery.

But when he started converting his 71-hectare (175-acre) vineyard in McLaren Vale (see also p. 181) to biodynamics (NASAA certified), David met some hostility.

It was as if I had brought some kind of ritualistic voodoo religion to McLaren Vale. But we found biodynamics to be a cheaper way of farming. The soils are richer, the vines are better balanced and the grapes are higher quality. Switching from soluble liquid fertilizers to solid compost and sprays made from the manure of our own cows has made weeds easier to manage. And we don't have to trim the vines so often. We get less disease and grapes with more flavour and less sugar, meaning tastier wines with less alcohol. And we have fewer problems in the winery when fermenting the wines too.

The first vines David converted to biodynamics were shiraz in Quandong Farm. Its sandy loam over limestone soils produce a deeply coloured shiraz with rich flavours of dark chocolate and black cherry overlaid with vanilla from oak-barrel ageing. Bottled unfiltered.

OTHER BIODYNAMIC SYRAH PRODUCERS WORTH NOTING
...include Ferraton (www.ferraton.fr) for Côte Rotie and Hermitage (Ferraton is now owned by Michel Chapoutier, profiled on p.174), and Mathieu Barret of Domaine du Coulet in Cornas (Biodyvin certified), – both in the northern Rhône; from California, Araujo (see p. 203), and the Ciolino family's Montemaggiore (www.montemaggiore.com) in Dry Creek Valley; Botobolar (www.botobolar.com) in Mudgee, NSW, Australia (organic certification) and Jason and Rebecca O'Dea's Pig in the House (www.piginthehouse.com.au) in Cowra, NSW, Australia (ACO biodynamic certified); and Millton in New Zealand (see p. 55).

TEMPRANILLO

Tempranillo is the main grape of Rioja, Spain's most famous red wine. It produces warm, quite deeply coloured reds with inviting flavours of liquidised cherries and blackberry fool. As well as the three producers profiled here, good examples come from Verdad (www.verdadwines.com) in California and Joseba Escalera in Navarra, Spain (both Demeter certified).

Dominio de Punctum, Tempranillo Lobetia Tinto, Tierra de Castilla (Castilla-La Mancha, Spain)

Ctra. N-301 km 162 (Madrid-Alicante), 16660 Las Pedroñeras (Cuenca), Spain
T:+34 912.959998 www.dominiodepunctum.com

Dominio de Punctum in central Spain only produced its first wines in 1999. Under Jesus Fernández and his winemaker sister, Ruth, the estate recently converted to biodynamics (Demeter certified). There are 110 hectares (270 acres) in the Castilla-La Mancha region. The vines lie on an arid plateau at 800 metres (2,600 feet). Jesus says,

> *In such dry conditions we risk losing our soil to erosion, either by the wind or the sun. To prevent this from happening, we spray biodynamic horn manure 500 at least three times a year. We fill around 200 horns with cow manure each year, using manure from a dairy farmer whose herd lies in a less arid region 125 miles [200 km] away. We pay him in wine.*

Jesus adds, 'In spring, though, it can be very cold here, so we spray valerian tea to keep the vines warm if frost threatens.' Dominio de Punctum's 'Lobetia' red is a tempranillo with approachable flavours of red plum, garnished with a sprig of mint. This is a wine for simple everyday drinking, not for keeping. Around 200,000 bottles are made each year.

Gemtree Vineyards, Luna Roja Tempranillo (McLaren Vale, South Australia)

184 Main Road, McLaren Vale, South Australia 5171
T:+61 (0)8.8323.8199 www.gemtreevineyards.com.au

At 130 hectares (321 acres), the Buttery family's Gemtree Vineyard is one of the largest in South Australia's exciting McLaren Vale region (see also Paxton, p. 179). Four generations of the Buttery family have grown grapes here, but Melissa Buttery says becoming greener required planning. 'I needed to make it work financially, especially as we have a pretty big vineyard.' Melissa encouraged the local University of Adelaide to test how vines reacted differently to conventional,

Gemtree
VINEYARDS

Luna Roja
Tempranillo

McLAREN VALE
2011

750mL   WINE OF AUSTRALIA   75cL

organic and biodynamic methods. She says, *The university data will help all of us in McLaren Vale be clearer about how different ways of growing grapes work. But our own observations so far are that organics and biodynamics give us healthier, richer, more friable soils containing more worms and other microbes, that our vines are becoming less bushy and more disease resistant. You just have to change your mindset to think that not every single weed you see needs to be chemically destroyed. Just because weedkillers have always been used does not mean they are automatically the best way to deal with weeds. Then you can start realising how weeds can even be beneficial, soaking up rain around harvest and stopping soils becoming airless and too compact.*

Melissa convinced her father to abandon weedkillers on a small plot of vines as a trial, before converting Gemtree's entire vineyard to biodynamics (Ausqual certification) and establishing a wetland habitat. One of the first plots to be converted was tempranillo for a wine called 'Luna Roja'. Its lush, mouth-awakening blueberry and bitter cherry flavours are given a light dusting of vanilla from barrel ageing.

Sunny skies above Gemtree Vineyards in South Australia
Gemtree Vineyards

AmByth Estate, Tempranillo, Paso Robles (California, USA)

510 Sequoia Lane, Templeton, CA 93465
T:+1 805.305.9497 www.ambythestate.com

Don't bother asking Phillip and Mary Hart the size of AmByth, their California estate. 'Um, it's difficult to be absolutely definite regarding size,' says Phillip. 'An accurate guess would be 17 acres [7 hectares] of vines and 2 acres [less than 1 hectare] of olive trees.' Phillip and Mary began planting their vines, olives, apple and nut orchards from 2001, soon after acquiring hilly land in Paso Robles, on California's baking-hot central coast, between San Francisco and Los Angeles. They named it 'am byth', which means 'forever' in Welsh. Phillip was a chef with a passion for wine, and both he and Mary found they usually preferred wines that came from environmentally friendly dry-farmed vines than from vines grown with the help of irrigation. They felt it made sense to inter-plant the vines at AmByth with olive trees. The presence of the trees means calculating the exact size of the vineyard is tricky, but the olives do provide more shade. This keeps Mary and Phillip's beehives cool, and makes life easier for their chickens, sheep, horned cows and peacocks. They roam the vineyard and olive grove providing weed control. The cow manure is collected and used for biodynamic compost, AmByth having been planted as biodynamic (Demeter certified).

The main reason for the olive trees was to keep the vineyard cooler, allowing the grapes to produce wines containing ripe but not excessively alcoholic flavours. The olives include varietals like lechen de sevilla, picual, arbequina and manzanilla, all of which are Spanish. Phillip and Mary have also chosen grape varieties that thrive in Spain's hot climate, like mourvèdre (mataro in Sanish), grenache (garnacha), carignan (carineña), and of course tempranillo. Because there is no irrigation, all the vines can be grown low, as individual bushes, with much more airflow around them and less risk of disease than with irrigated vines grown in cramped, hedge-like rows. The grapes are so healthy and balanced, AmByth can bottle its wines with little or no winemaking interventions. Around half AmByth's wines are made with no added sulphites. Their tempranillo is endowed with rich, dark-cherry and chocolate flavours. It's a big wine for a long *al fresco* lunch that won't knock you out on a hot day.

Avondale Wines, South Africa

TEROLDEGO

The teroldego grape was facing near-extinction from its Alpine base in Trentino, northern Italy, until a remarkable local wine-grower called Elisabetta Foradori championed it. It is known for deeply coloured red wines potentially jam-packed with lively menthol and raspberry flavours.

Foradori, Granato Vigneti delle Dolomiti (Trentino, Italy)
Via Damiano Chiesa 1, 38017 Mezzolombardo (TN = Trento), Italy
T:+39 0461.601046 Website www.elisabettaforadori.com

Elisabetta Foradori is often described as a revolutionary but in her quietly spoken way she says she prefers to be known simply as someone who favours the natural evolution of things. Elisabetta wanted to prove to her neighbours that teroldego, a local grape, was being undervalued. In the 1970s local growers started pushing teroldego's yields too high. The results were all-but-flavourless, cheap, simple picnic reds. Elisabetta felt that teroldego should be made into age-able wines of distinction. She replanted her vineyards with teroldego cuttings producing low yields of highly flavoured grapes, and fed her soils biodynamic composts rather than yield-friendly fertilizers.

Elisabetta ferments her teroldego grapes for her 'Sgarzon' and 'Morei' labels in clay amphora. Their low height makes it easier for her to punch the grapes down into the fermenting juice by hand, and their curved shape means the wine ferments more steadily than in vertically walled tanks. If this all sounds too retro, Elisabetta also uses traditional vats made of chestnut and oak barrels in which to ferment and age the teroldego grapes for 'Granato', a red with feisty dark-cherry flavours. Although most of Elisabetta's 23 hectares (57 acres) of biodynamic vines (Demeter certified) are teroldego she also has a small amount of nosiola, a rare white grape producing nettle-fresh dry and mouthwateringly sweet wines.

ZINFANDEL

Zinfandel is a red grape, which arrived in California from Croatia during the mid-nineteenth-century gold rush. It is a versatile grape producing pink (blush) wines with lipstick-like sweetness; jammy-tasting red wines for quaffing ('jug wines'); as well as more serious 'zins' with rich, raisiny fruit flavours, gum-friendly rather than drying tannins, and alcohol levels so generous you'll want to share a bottle with a big meal and probably at least two friends.

Frey Vineyards, Biodynamic Zinfandel, Redwood Valley (California, USA)

14000 Tomki Road, Redwood Valley, CA 95470, USA
T:+001 707.485.5177 Website www.freywine.com

Frey Vineyards in northern California's Redwood Valley is an iconic name in organic and biodynamic wine-growing. Paul and Marguerite Frey planted vines in the 1960s on their newly acquired property, purely to help pay the property taxes. When the winemakers who bought their grapes started winning gold medals, the Freys realised perhaps they should build their own winery. They did it using lumber discarded during the construction of California's north–south Highway 101. Frey now has around 100 hectares (250 acres) of biodynamic vineyards (Demeter certified) and buys grapes from around another 200 hectares of certified organic and biodynamic vineyards.

Even their rivals admit the Freys have been 'years ahead' in terms of how they nurture their vineyard soils, with herbs, melons, tomatoes, squash and garlic growing in between the rows. Recently winter wheat, barley, oats and rye have also been grown in the vine rows and are harvested using a mini-combine. The grain is turned into bread, while the vines benefit because cereal crops are very good at making soils more worm-friendly and water retentive. 'This is all part of maintaining our biodynamic vineyard as a self-sustaining living organism,' says Katrina Frey, who met her husband Jonathon Frey (the eldest of Paul and Marguerite's twelve children) in the mid 1970s while studying biodynamic gardening.

Frey produced the world's first ever wine for which both the grapes and the winemaking were Demeter certified: a 1996 vintage made from zinfandel grapes with no added sulphites. All Frey wines, whether from their own biodynamic grapes or purchased organic ones, are made with no added sulphites and ferment naturally with wild yeasts. Their biodynamic zinfandel shows the chewy, juicy, warm raspberry and dried cherry fruit typical of this variety, with none of the raisin-like flavours that mar some California zins. Frey make round 13,000 bottles of zin each year. Drink from three to five years of the harvest year on the bottle.

OTHER BIODYNAMIC ZINFANDEL PRODUCERS
...include Quivira Vineyards (www.quivirawine.com) in Dry Creek Valley, California, USA (see p. 99), and also Mattern (www.matternvineyards.com) in Mendocino County, California, USA, which has vines dating from the 1930s (Demeter certified). In Western Australia, Jamie McCall's Burnside (www.burnsideorganicfarm.com.au) in Margaret River produces zinfandel and offers holiday accommodation in rammed-earth flats (ACO certified).

Frey Vineyards in California grows wheat between the vine rows.
It improves the soil and is harvested for bread.
Frey Vineyards

RED WINES MADE FROM MORE THAN ONE GRAPE VARIETY

BORDEAUX AND BORDEAUX-STYLE BLENDED RED WINES

Bordeaux in southwest France is the biggest and probably most famous fine wine region in the world. With 120,000 hectares (300,000 acres) it has more vineyards than South Africa or Germany or Chile, and more than New Zealand and Canada combined. Although Bordeaux makes dry white wines and late-picked sweet ones, its signature is its red wine or 'claret'. Around 80 per cent of Bordeaux wine is red. The two main grapes used are cabernet sauvignon for its firm blackcurrant flavours and merlot for smoother, plummier ones. Supporting roles are given to other grapes like cabernet franc, which is also grown in the Loire (see p. 139–142 for some examples), and malbec, which is also grown slightly further south in Cahors and in Argentina (see p.142–145).

The term *claret* is a particularly British one for red Bordeaux wine. It is not used in France, and in the US it is a rarely used word for Bordeaux-style wine. It derives from the name of a French wine, 'clairet', that was common in England when Aquitaine (which then included the Bordeaux region) was ruled by the English throne from the twelfth to the fifteenth century.

Bordeaux is famous for blends because Bordeaux red grape varieties taste best in combinations rather than as 100 per cent cabernet sauvignon or 100 per cent merlot. Cabernet sauvignon tastes lean on its own, but with a dollop of merlot it becomes richer and more satisfying. On its own, merlot tastes plump but a bit simple, yet with a little cabernet added the

189

merlot gains more line and length in the mouth. The exact per
centages in blends of each grape vary from year to year, depending on
the weather. Bordeaux's bright but wet Atlantic-influenced climate
and free-draining soils produce ripe, elegant wines, which are firm
rather than overtly fruity, but which, if given time in bottle to soften,
are very easy to digest.

As an iconic red wine, Bordeaux is much imitated by winemakers
outside France, often most successfully in Australia and California,
as some of the examples of Bordeaux-style wine below demonstrate.

Château Pontet-Canet, Pauillac (Bordeaux, France)

F-33250 Pauillac (Gironde), France
T:+33 (0)5.56.59.04.04 www.pontet-canet.com

Pontet-Canet was the first really high-profile
Bordeaux château to go biodynamic (Biodyvin
certified), from 2005. Château owner Alfred
Tesseron took the biodynamic plunge having
seen biodynamics in action at Château Champ
des Treilles (see p. 198), a vineyard owned by
Pontet-Canet's vineyard manager Jean-Michel
Comme. Pruning was reorganised at Pontet-
Canet so each individual vine (700,000 in total) could be painted
with a protective biodynamic pruning wash made from cow manure,
clay and whey within 24 hours of being pruned. Tractors were
re-fitted for spraying seaweed powders on the vines in spring as a
pick-me-up. Horses started to replace tractors for ploughing under
the vines in autumn and spring. Chariots were designed so the men
driving the horses could stay seated and see when the animals were
getting too close to the vines.

Sceptics say that vineyards like Pontet-Canet, which make super-
high-priced wines, can easily afford to pamper their vines, but Alfred
Tesseron, who had one or two early setbacks with biodynamics in the
tough 2007 vintage, argues that what they are doing should be rightly
understood neither as easy, nor as expensive pampering:

If it was that easy why isn't everyone doing it? With
biodynamics we save money because the horses compact the
soil much less than the tractors, and they are far less likely

to kill vines by knocking them over. Replacing vines that get knocked over is very complicated and time-consuming, and also expensive in terms of bottles lost. Vineyard plots which before biodynamics produced wine good enough only for our second label [Les Hauts de Pontet] now provide us with grapes good enough for the top label.

Pontet-Canet has 80 hectares (200 acres) planted with the classic Pauillac red wine mix of around two-thirds cabernet sauvignon, one third merlot and small per centages of cabernet franc and malbec. Pontet-Canet's wines were once written off as among Pauillac's biggest underperformers: weedy, light, vegetal. Now the wine shows all the attributes of classic Pauillac: intense flavours of cedar, cigar box, blackcurrant, even mint, with richly textured tannins that take around a decade to soften into drinkability.

Château Peybonhomme les Tours, Premières Côtes de Blaye Rouge (Bordeaux, France)

F-33390 Cars (Gironde), France www.vignobles-hubert.com

Château Peybonhomme les Tours is another large vineyard, even by Bordeaux standards, at 64 hectares (158 acres). Jean-Luc and Catherine Hubert bought Peybonhomme, and Château La Grolet (28 hectares) in nearby Bourg, in 1997. They converted both to biodynamics (Biodyvin and Demeter certified). The early ripening merlot grape dominates (around 70–75 per cent) because it is so well suited to both the terrain of fairly gentle clay slopes and to the local climate. This climate could be described as bright, breezy and Atlantic-influenced, because the Gironde estuary, which the vines overlook, soon flows into the Atlantic to the northeast.

Jean-Luc says,

It takes around three days to spray each vineyard with biodynamic preparations like horn manure 500 and horn silica 501, but we can save time when applying our favourite plant teas by combining these with normal vineyard sprays. We find fresh stinging nettle and common horsetail 508 teas work best in keeping the vines healthy in our Atlantic climate.

191

The grapes for Château Peybonhomme les Tours are de-stemmed (to avoid stalky flavours), fermented in cement vats and then, after nine months or so, wines in the different tanks are blended together ready for bottling before grapes from the new harvest arrive. The result is red Bordeaux wines with appealing plum flavours and firm but not aggressive tannins styled for everyday, medium-term drinking. Wines from the best plots are aged in oak barrels and bottled under the 'Quintessence' label, and have a recognisable vanilla sheen.

Château Falfas, Côtes de Bourg Rouge (Bordeaux, France)
F-33710 Bayon (Gironde), France
T:+33 (0)5.57.64.80.41   www.chateaufalfas.fr

Falfas became Bordeaux's pioneering biodynamic vineyard (Biodyvin certified) after it was purchased by Véronique Cochran in 1989 with her husband John. Véronique grew up on a small Loire vineyard called Domaine du Château Gaillard, which was converted to biodynamics in 1962 by her father François Bouchet – the first such conversion in France. Bouchet had become France's leading biodynamic wine consultant by the late 1980s when his daughter arrived at Falfas.

Vines have been grown at Château Falfas since 1612, when the château was built to survey boat traffic on the Gironde, the estuary connecting the port of Bordeaux with the Atlantic Ocean. Vines, like those at Falfas, which directly overlook the Gironde are said to make the best red wines from this part of Bordeaux, the hills or *côtes* of Bourg. Falfas produces absolutely classic red Bordeaux (claret) from its 22 hectares (55 acres) of merlot, cabernet franc, malbec and cabernet sauvignon vines. The rich clay topsoils here give Château Falfas its profound scarlet colour, while hard limestone subsoils help generate mouthwatering flavours of menthol, juniper and blackberry. It usually pays to drink bottles from a good year between five to ten years of the harvest. I find decanting Falfas a day, or even two, before I intend to drink it really helps loosen the wine up, making it even more expressive. Falfas ages wine from its oldest vines in its newest oak barrels, bottling it under the Le Chevalier label.

Château La Fleur Cailleau, Canon-Fronsac (Bordeaux, France)

Vignobles Paul Barre, F-33126 Fronsac (Gironde), France
T:+33 (0)5.57.51.31.11 www.vignoblespaulbarre.com

Paul Barre has two biodynamic vineyards along the Dordogne river in Bordeaux's hilly, secluded Fronsac sub-region: La Grave in Fronsac itself and La Fleur-Cailleau in the finer Fronsac sub-region of Canon-Fronsac. Together that is 7 hectares (16 acres) of vines (Demeter certified).

Paul's was the first biodynamic wine I tasted. It tasted different. I asked him why. He wouldn't tell me. I marched him into his vineyard. He asked what I thought of his vines. I said his vines looked much stronger and more erect than those of his neighbours. I got down on my knees and dug my hands into his soils, which smelt really healthy too – the healthiest I had ever smelt in Bordeaux. I suggested this was why his wine tasted different. He agreed it probably was. Then he told me he was 'biodynamic'. He had no time to explain what this meant, but gave the names of a couple of other biodynamic Bordeaux estates (one of which was Château Falfas). Since that day, which was two decades ago in 1993, I have been following biodynamic wines.

What I like about Paul's red wines (both La Grave and La Fleur-Cailleau) is they tell you more about the soil they were grown in than any book can, because they break the rules and the assumptions made by previous generations. This is partly because of Paul's wine-growing choices, planting vines from a genetically diverse range of cuttings rather than from genetically standardised clones, for example. But it is mainly due to Paul's biodynamic choices. He sees biodynamics as being able to balance Bordeaux's Atlantic (wet, cloudy, earthy) climate because it provides you with a tool like horn silica 501, which brightens the soil, the vines, their grapes and the wines they give us. Paul's wines are not blockbusters – far from it. But they have an inner brightness and distinctly layered quality that Fronsac wines are supposed not to have, but should do.

Seresin Home vineyard, New Zealand
Seresin Estate

Château Canon St Michel, Canon-Fronsac (Bordeaux, France)

Lamarche, F-33126 Fronsac (Gironde), France
T:+33 (0)5.57.24.94.99 www.vins-millaire.fr

I helped make wine in the Canon-Fronsac region as a teenager. As well as discovering biodynamics there (as I describe in the Preface and in the entry for Château La Fleur Cailleau on p.193), I discovered how Canon-Fronsac's sandy limestone or *molasse* soil gives its mainly merlot (flesh) and cabernet franc (bones) red wines real bite and freshness, qualities sometimes lacking in the far pricier wines of neighbouring Pomerol and St-Émilion. This is perhaps why owners of weaker Pomerol and St-Émilion vineyards would buy Fronsac reds as 'medicine' to beef up their own wines after their vineyards – which are generally lower lying than Canon-Fronsac's – were badly frosted in the mid 1950s.

The 1950s was also when the grandfather of the current owner of Canon St Michel, Jean-Yves Millaire, began buying vines here. After Jean-Yves took over in 1998, he converted first to organics and then biodynamics (Biodyvin certified). Jean-Yves says,

Fronsac is no place to be only half-hearted if you want to make good wine. You really have to work at your wine-growing, pruning wisely in winter to prevent the vines over-cropping then giving you big yields of rustic-tasting red wines, and having the courage to wait for all the grapes to ripen fully.

Jean-Yves produces around 15,000 bottles each year of his Canon-Fronsac red from 6 hectares (15 acres) of merlot (70 per cent), cabernet sauvignon (15 per cent), malbec and cabernet franc (15 per cent combined). Aged in a mix of new and older barrels, this wine demolishes the argument that Canon-Fronsac's reds lack elegance and refinement. The fruit flavours are clear, direct and deep, and the tannins broad, smooth and savoury.

Château Moulin du Cadet, St-Émilion Grand Cru Classé (Bordeaux, France)

F-33330 St-Émilion (Gironde), France
T:+33 (0)5.57.55.00.50 moulinducadet@wanadoo.fr

Château Moulin du Cadet lies just north of the ancient hilltop town of St-Émilion, a UNESCO world heritage site and source of world-famous red wines. Alain Moueix converted its 5 hectares (11 acres) of merlot to biodynamics (Biodyvin certified) in 2002 after he took over for his father and sister. He says,

The vines lie on limestone, a type of soil that can block iron from reaching vine roots. Like humans, vines turn anaemic if they lack iron. They get yellow leaves and produce an unripe wine. We found spraying the vines with iron-rich stinging-nettle tea and spraying the soil with horn manure 500 loosened everything up: the vines, the soil, the wine.

The grapes are hand-picked and ferment in small cement vats.

Alain comes from one of Bordeaux's most famous winemaking families and says since going biodynamic the grapes ripen slightly earlier and the wines are easier to ferment, meaning their texture is softer, not so mouth-puckering. Alain also says with biodynamics he can ferment the grapes more slowly than he used to, getting wines with rich colours and flavours, with no alcoholic burn in the after-taste. Before Alain arrived, the wines here really were anaemic and washed out. Now they have bite and attitude, clarity and body, and lots of savoury layers. This is the kind of bottle I open, then drink one glass from each evening with my dinner from Monday to Friday (five generous glasses). Each night the wine gives me a different chapter from the same narrative. About 25,000 bottles are produced each year. Alain Moueix also runs another brilliant biodynamic St-Émilion estate, Château Fonroque (www.chateaufonroque.com) (Biodyvin certified).

Château Champ des Treilles, Ste Foy Rouge (Bordeaux, France)

F-33250 Margueron (Gironde), France
T:+33 (0)5.56.59.15.88 www.champdestreilles.com

After Jean-Michel Comme took over the vineyard first planted by his immigrant Italian grandparents in the 1920s, he went to see Véronique Cochran's biodynamic Château Falfas (see p. 192). 'It was important for me to meet someone like Véronique, who worked with biodynamics in a really practical rather than an overly philosophical way,' says Jean-Michel. He converted Champ des Treilles' 10 hectares (25 acres) of vines to biodynamics (Biodyvin certified). The vines, which produce both dry white and red wines, are located in Ste Foy, one of Bordeaux's most easterly sub-regions. Ste Foy's especially dry and sunny climate proved ideal for biodynamics (Ste Foy has always had a strong core of organic estates). The Champ des Treilles vines lie on loamy soil, which is rich in flint and easy to work. The vines are planted deliberately close together and are left grassed. This is so each vine produces only small volumes of richly flavoured grapes. Only the soil under the vines is ploughed, by horse, not tractor. The wines are hand-picked, with around 30 per cent given to grassily uplifting dry white wines (from semillon and sauvignon blanc) and the rest to red wines.

The Château Champ des Treilles Bordeaux Ste Foy Rouge bottling (sometimes called 'Le Petit Champ') is one of those perfectly weighted red wines that make drinking wine so pleasurable. It's ripe but not jammy, mineral but not earthy, and savoury both to smell and taste. Serve slightly cooler than room temperature. An oak-aged and more merlot-dominated version of this red wine is labelled 'Grand Vin'.

Château Haut Garrigue, La Source Rouge (Bergerac, Southwest France)

F-24240 Saussignac (Dordogne), France
T:+33 (0)5.53.22.72.71 www.hautgarrigue.com

Seán and Caroline Feely's 10-hectare (25-acre) biodynamic vineyard in Bergerac – which neighbours Bordeaux to the east – is a hit with wine-loving Anglophones (Demeter certified). Visitors can rent vines under the Feelys' 'Vine Share' scheme, but it's doubtful they'll ever know those vines as well as Seán, who does all the vineyard and winery work himself (there are no employees). He says,

> *I'd like to work the soil with animals, horse ploughing like my grandfather did, but the reality is that with 10 hectares and as a one-man workforce I don't have the time. I follow the lunar calendar very closely in timing soil cultivation, as I believe this, along with the biodynamic compost, biodynamic preparations and teas, have had a tangible impact on our soil life – more earthworms, better humus formation, no erosion and great earthy odours from the soil. In winter I prune mostly to the descending moon, when the vine's nutrients are concentrated underground in the roots, rather than in the canes I am pruning off. I don't want to think that every time I cut a cane off I am taking the vine's energy reserves. In spring, I tie the pruned vine canes to the supporting wires under an ascending moon, when the sap is in the upper part*

*of the vines so the canes are more pliable. I break almost no
canes like this.*

Seán makes his own teas from stinging nettle, willow and the
biodynamic common horsetail 508 to help keep mildew and odium
under control, and combines them with copper-based sprays like
Bordeaux Mixture.

*Like all wine-growers I see eliminating copper sprays
completely as the holy grail. But I only use half the amount
allowed under the organic and biodynamic rules. I am
hoping to reduce copper use even more using sage infusions
and wild fennel tea, which have worked really well in our
vegetable garden. I do all my spraying at dawn, before the
sun is too high, so that sprays don't burn the foliage.*

The Feelys' dry Bergerac white wines, made from sauvignon
blanc or semillon or both, show lovely greengage and green-melon
flavours. Reds based on merlot and cabernet sauvignon include 'La
Source', whose juicy liquorice and fresh purple fruit flavours are
streamlined tidily by ageing in oak barrels.

Château Jonc Blanc, Les Sens du Fruit Rouge (Bergerac, Southwest France)

F-24230 Vélines (Dordogne), France
T:+33 (0)5.53.74.18.97 jonc.blanc@free.fr

Franck and Isabelle Pascal left
Paris in 1999 for Bergerac in the
Dordogne in southwest France. Here
they became, in their own words,
paysans-vignerons, meaning 'peasant
wine-growers'. They now have 16
hectares (40 acres) of biodynamic
vineyards (Demeter certified). Franck lives up to his peasant billing
by using a vast array of plant teas, extracts and tinctures to keep his
vines healthy. The biodynamic common horsetail 508 preparation is
sprayed on the soil to keep fungus disease organisms in their rightful
earthy environment, preventing them from jumping up onto the
vines. Franck makes infusions by macerating dried plants in alcohol

and distilled water. He uses absinthe to inhibit insects, and willow, oak bark and alder buckthorn (*Rhamnus frangula*) to counteract mildew. To control pesky insects he sprays a liquid extract made from ivy (*Hedera helix*), and also clay powders. Franck says,

> *The ivy treatment sticks to the insects' wings, while the bentonite powder inhibits their ability to breathe. It also helps dry any humidity on the vines, which in turn reduces the risk of fungus disease.*

Stinging nettle, dandelion, thyme, rosemary and savoury are also sprayed to help stimulate the vines. 'Humans use these medicinal plants to stimulate and maintain better digestion,' says Franck, adding with impeccable logic, 'If your digestion or your breathing or your blood become blocked you are going to get quite ill, quite soon.'

Franck's wine-growing approach creates grapes, and wines, of really incredible lift and purity. No additives are used (or needed) during winemaking. One quarter of production is given to highly individual white wines made from sauvignon blanc and semillon, which have subtle and crystalline flavours of mirabelle plums, ginger barley and mint. Around 35,000 bottles of red wine are made, with the top Bergerac rouge labelled 'Les Sens du Fruit'. This is a play on words when pronounced in French, meaning their wines are the essence of fruit itself. Here the dominant fruit flavours are crunchy blackcurrant and soft, dark plum, as one would expect from a red dominated by cabernet sauvignon and merlot grapes. I think you can taste in these wines a sense that every single grape that went into them thoroughly enjoyed its time growing in Isabelle and Franck's vineyards.

Domaine du Pech, La Badinerie du Pech Rouge (Buzet, Southwest France)

F-47310 Ste Colombe en Bruilhois (Lot et Garonne), France
T:+33 (0)5.53.67.84.20 www.domainedupech.com

Magali Tissot (a cousin of the Jura's Stéphane Tissot, see p. 43) and her partner Ludovic Bonnelle took over her late father's 17-hectare (42-acre) vineyard in Buzet, southwest France, in 1997. They became less interventionist in both vineyard and winery with each passing year, converting the vineyards first to organics, then biodynamics (Demeter certified). Ludovic says the vines get both Atlantic (cool, wet) and Mediterranean (drier, hotter) weather, 'so we are flexible in how we farm the vines.' But some practices are always followed.

For example, Ludovic says prunings are not burnt.

They are left to decompose over winter between the vine rows. This is what happens in the forest – the environment where vines thrive in the wild – and maintains that forest-floor likeness in terms of how the soil feels and smells, due to the beneficial bacteria the decomposing prunings attract. And by recycling the vine's wood, no nutrients are lost to the vineyard.

The vineyard soils are aerated using a special plough that lifts but does not turn the soil. Ludovic says,

By not putting the topsoil in the subsoil or the subsoil in the topsoil we maintain a carpet of native grasses and flowers in the vines. We make vine teas from these plants. These teas are a cornerstone for vine health. And the way these wild plants grow in the vineyard are like a book, which allows us to read the health of the soil in our vines.

The vines grow on a hill, or *pech* in local dialect, around the winery, hence the name. The red wines are made from foot-trodden merlot, cabernet franc and cabernet sauvignon grapes. They are bottled with minimal or no sulphur-dioxide preservative, either as Buzet, the name of the local region, or simply as Vin de France (table wine). 'Pech Abusé' has brick leather flavours, 'Jarnicoton' has softer, more obvious fruit, while the 'La Badinerie du Pech' bottling combines merlot's red-plum denseness with cabernet franc's more lithe blueberry freshness. Decant at least a day in advance.

OTHER PRODUCERS OF BIODYNAMIC BORDEAUX-STYLE REDS IN SOUTHWEST FRANCE

...are Henri-Paul Guillot at Château du Grand-Roc (Demeter certified) and the Faurichon de la Bardonnie family at Château Laroque (Demeter certified), which are both in Bergerac. In nearby Duras, Alain Lescaut's Domaine du Petit Malromé (www.petitmalrose.com) is also biodynamic (Biodyvin certified).

Araujo Estate, Eisele Vineyard, Napa Valley (California, USA)

2155 Pickett Road, Calistoga, CA 94515, USA

T:+001 707.942.6061   www.araujoestatewines.com

The Eisele vineyard in northeastern Napa Valley was first planted in the 1880s and produces one of California's iconic cabernet sauvignons. However, by the late 1980s, Eisele, which now has vines replanted in the 1950s, was starting to struggle. New owners, Bart and Daphne Araujo, began replanting the 16-hectare (41-acre) vineyard, and adopting biodynamic methods (Demeter certified). Jeff Dawson, who had also advised the late Apple Inc. supremo Steve Jobs on biodynamic landscaping projects, created habitat breaks or 'insectories' at Eisele. These encouraged beneficial insects, which predate hot weather vine pests like mites and leafhoppers. The insectories were planted with aromatic herbs (fever few, sage, fennel), flowering shrubs like butterfly bush (*Buddleia*) and the medicinal plants used in the biodynamic preparations.

When discussing the aims of his biodynamic compost and soil spray programme, Jeff says,

> *It helps cool Eisele's soil and make it more earthy, Eisele lying in a hot pocket of Napa Valley. Compost additions and soil sprays were timed to the full moon cycle, a time of fertility and growth, maximising their effectiveness. If the earth is more alive your vines are less likely to suffer heat stress. The grapes ripen without shrivelling, giving clearer rather than baked-fruit flavours.*

Eisele's Bordeaux-style red is made from mainly cabernet sauvignon, with smaller portions of merlot, petit verdot and cabernet franc blended in. Its classy, initially rather impenetrable, inner core of cool blackcurrant fruit needs eight to twelve years in bottle for its deftness, brightness and elegance to become clear.

Benziger, Tribute, Sonoma Mountain (California, USA)

1883 London Ranch Rd, Glen Ellen, CA 95442, USA

T:+1 888.490.2739 (within USA) www.benziger.com

Mike Benziger's family ran a wine import business in his native New York. The first job Mike got after he graduated in 1973 was in a California wine store. Two decades later, Mike was heading up Benziger of Glen Ellen, one of America's most successful wine brands, based on irresistibly soft chardonnays. 'We were a big company,' says Mike, 'and we had the choice of up-scaling to become absolutely huge, or down-sizing and getting back to our roots. We chose the latter.'

A big part of Mike's quest to get back to his roots involved biodynamics. He says,

I've always been into quantum mechanics and the idea that everything in our universe is connected at a sub-atomic level. And biodynamics makes you understand that plants are intimately connected to forces both here on the earth and to the universe around and beyond it. But biodynamics is a team sport. It is not going to work if it is just the owner who is fanatical about it. So we invested time in getting everyone, from the vineyard and winery crews to the marketing people, involved. We took our vineyard crews [of mainly Latino origin] to other biodynamic vineyards so they could see biodynamics in action and ask how biodynamics worked, whether it worked and how it would affect their daily working life without us employers being around. They soon realised a lot of it was what they already knew: turning waste streams like organic matter from the winery into fertility streams by recycling it as compost. You have to get total buy-in, from the people pruning the vines to the team selling the wine, for biodynamics to work.

Mike's four biodynamic Sonoma vineyards total 40 hectares (97 acres) (Demeter certified). His top estate-bottled wine, Tribute, is a luxuriant, Bordeaux-style red, barrel aged for 24 months, and made mainly from cabernet sauvignon, with merlot, cabernet franc and petit verdot blended in. You can drink it young, but its deep, dark-fruit flavours become more diverse, interesting and mellow after at least five years of bottle age.

Cullen Wines, Diana Madeline Cabernet-Merlot (Margaret River, Western Australia)

Caves Road, Cowaramup, Western Australia 6284, Australia

T:+61 (0)8.9755.5277 www.cullenwines.com.au

In the mid 1960s Dr Kevin Cullen and his wife Diana Madeline pioneered the planting of vines in Western Australia's Margaret River region, 180 miles (300 km) south of Perth. The red Bordeaux grape varieties, especially cabernet sauvignon and merlot, loved Margaret River's loamy soils and temperate, Indian Ocean-influenced climate, and soon Margaret River was considered one of the best regions outside Bordeaux for Bordeaux-style red wines.

Conviviality at Cullen Wines in Western Australia.
Cullen Wines

Cullen, of course, is one of its iconic producers. Kevin and Diana's daughter, Vanya, took over from her late parents in 1989, and converted first to organics, then to biodynamics (certified organic). 'My parents were environmental pioneers,' she says, 'successfully battling against bauxite mining in the 1960s on the Western Australian coast.' Cullen became Australia's first carbon-neutral winery and vineyard in 2006.

Diana Madeline, Cullen's flagship Bordeaux-style wine, is made mainly from vines Diana and Kevin planted in 1971 in Margaret River's central Wilyabrup sub-region. Vanya says,

We have so many old vines our family agreed biodynamics was the best way to keep those old vines going while also enhancing their individuality.

Diana Madeline is typically made from two-thirds cabernet sauvignon and one third merlot, cabernet franc, malbec and petit verdot. The wine's densely ripe redcurrant fruit flavours soften in oak barrels for fifteen months before bottling. After eight to fifteen years in bottle, classic savoury, cedary flavours start to emerge. Around 30,000 bottles are made each year.

Reyneke, Cornerstone Red (Stellenbosch, South Africa)

Uitzicht Farm, Vlottenburg 7604, South Africa
T:+27 (0)21.8813517 www.reynekewines.co.za

South Africa's modern wine industry is helping to right some of the historic wrongs of the apartheid era. A number of 'empowerment' projects have been created to give workers from historically disadvantaged ethnic communities more autonomy. Under apartheid such workers might have been paid in wine or brandy. The result was chronic alcoholism, with workers effectively shackled to jobs in wine. The empowerment project that Reyneke Wines launched in 1998 is, in my view, the most meaningful in the Cape. While other empowerment projects ran the risk of being managed from the top down, with whites deciding what blacks needed, the four (black) families who worked at Reyneke had complete autonomy.

They wanted to live in their own homes away from the Reyneke estate. For the first time they could enjoy a separation between their work and family lives. Johan Reyneke diverted money from his farming and wine activities into buying land, then building homes via a trust, which gave the families ownership of their homes. Johan took the loan out himself initially and then waited three years for the banks to come on board. The banks were unconvinced Johan's biodynamic wine-growing philosophy could be profitable. Nevertheless, Reyneke's working families now have three-bedroomed homes in the local town. After paying off the bonds Johan had underwritten for the houses, money was diverted towards bursaries for educational study. Johan says,

Johan Reyneke's vineyard makes Cornerstone red wine as part of an empowerment project for the estate's workers.

> *Our cellar master, George, is illiterate having left school aged ten to work in vineyards to supplement his parents' income. His wife Linda left school aged fourteen, but did learn to read and write. Both asked to work here, Linda doing housework. George and Linda's daughter Lizanne was able to start school aged five, when the money from the Cornerstone wine range began coming in. Lizanne is now aged nineteen, in tertiary education and heading for a career in the hospitality industry. Throwing money at people like George, Linda and Lizanne is not sustainable socially. However, giving people like them a stake in society, a home that is both a place to live and capital, is the basis upon which economic upliftment can be built. Allowing kids to get an education instead of being exploited as manual labourers is a truly sustainable way of getting our country and its people back on their feet.*

Johan makes the Cornerstone red from mainly cabernet sauvignon and merlot grapes, plus a little syrah. Ageing the wine in barrel gives structure to its deeply vibrant, juicy plum flavours. The grapes are purchased (Johan has no cabernet or merlot vines) from certified organic vineyards. 'However,' Johan says, 'biodynamics teaches you that for real sustainability everything is connected, and if you respect the environment you have more chance of respecting not only yourself, but your fellow man. That's really where Cornerstone springs from.'

Southbrook Vineyards, Whimsy! Winemakers' Red, Niagara on the Lake (Ontario, Canada)

581 Niagara Stone Road, RR4, Niagara-on-the-Lake, Ontario L0S 1J0, Canada
T:+1 905.641.2548 www.southbrook.com

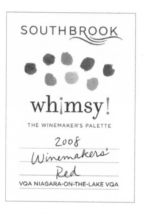

Bill and Marilyn Redelmeier built their first Ontario winery in century-old barns on Bill's family's cattle farm. The couple now have a new winery surrounded by their biodynamic vineyards (Demeter certified) in a warmer and more wine-friendly spot in Ontario, not far from the Niagara Falls. There are 25 hectares (60 acres) of vines with another 30 hectares (75 acres) of neighbouring pasture for biodiversity and to provide space for animals, especially sheep (good grazers of weeds), horses (potentially to replace vineyard tractors) and cows (for manure for compost). Bill says,

> So far we've not used a great deal of solid compost, since our vineyard was planted in a field that had been fallow for many years. We just try to stimulate the soil life that is already there with biodynamic compost sprays. We also rely on willow, horsetail and stinging nettle to use as teas on the vines for disease prevention. Some of the tea plants we wild harvest from our own land. We've been focusing on cover crops like grasses, fescues and clovers to keep the soil airy, well fed and well drained. As well as sowing seeds we find there are also many native plants that grow of their own accord, providing flowers for insects and seeds for birds. We've seen our beneficial insect and bird population increase dramatically in the last few years. The Niagara region, much of which is part of the world biosphere, has rich biodiversity, so if a farm provides the conditions for life, it comes of its own accord.

Niagara's clay soils and its dry summer climate produce small-berried grapes rich in colour and flavour. You can see this in Southbrook's Bordeaux-style Winemakers' Red, a bumptiously crimson-coloured, plum-textured cabernet sauvignon, merlot and cabernet franc blend laden with a well-judged mix of blackcurrant and strawberry fruit and vanilla oak (from barrel ageing).

CHIANTI-STYLE REDS

Chianti is the classic red wine of Tuscany, a fresh, tangy wine traditionally drunk young in the bars of Siena and Florence. The best modern chianti is also made as a more serious, age-able red for wine lovers, a wine with biting red-plum flavours that take on softer balsamic notes as the wine gets older. Chianti and Chianti-style reds are made mainly from the sangiovese grape blended with a seasoning of other local grapes or French ones like cabernet sauvignon and merlot (for 100 per cent sangiovese reds, see p. 172-73).

Fattoria La Vialla, Casa Conforto Chianti Superiore (Tuscany, Italy)

Via di Meliciano 26, 52029 Castiglion Fibocchi (AR = Arezzo), Italy
T:+39 0575.430020 www.lavialla.it

Visiting Fattoria La Vialla in central Tuscany is like taking a step back in time. The owners, the Lo Franco family, have managed to pre-serve their 1,350-hectare (3,335-acre) estate as a biodiverse, mixed farm rather than doing what so many other Tuscan estates of this size did from the 1960s onwards, which was to concentrate on a single crop, like, say, wine or olives, as was believed to be more cost effec-tive. La Vialla has 190 hectares of biodynamic vineyards for its mainly Chianti red wines (Demeter certified).

Fattoria La Vialla in Tuscany, Italy, is an unusually diverse farm and vineyard.
Fattoria La Vialla

It also has 14,000 olive trees for oil (produced in La Vialla's own mill), 1,250 sheep for meat and for milk for pecorino cheese, plus 800 chickens for meat and eggs. There are also over 200 hectares of arable land for cereal crops, providing wheat for bread, pasta and biscuits; plus pastures, bee hives and fruit trees for preserves, sauces, jams and honey. The remaining 700-odd hectares is woodland (oak, chestnut and pine), which provides firewood and wooden stakes for the farm and vineyard.

What the Lo Franco family have found is that having such a diverse range of crops is qualitatively better and gives their products an edge in the market. To make enough biodynamic horn manure 500 for all its crops, La Vialla buries a staggering 600 manure-filled cow horns every autumn. Green waste from all the different crops gets recycled into well-maintained piles of biodynamic compost, which then gets spread wherever it is needed. You don't have to be a soil microbiologist to see the difference in colour and texture between La Vialla's dark, smooth, crumbly-looking soils and those of La Vialla's conventional neighbours, which are bleached and full of large, hard clods of earth that look more like rocks. I don't think you can make good wine in general or good Chianti in particular from cement-like soils. La Vialla's Chianti Superiore 'Casa Conforto' is made mainly from sangiovese. It's a pretty, country lunchtime wine with supple red-plum and cherry flavours that leave a refreshing aftertaste. Try with Tuscan sausages accompanied by white (cannellini) beans in tomato sauce.

Tenuta di Valgiano, Colline Lucchesi Rosso (Tuscany, Italy)
Via di Valgiano 7, I-55010 Lucca (LU = Lucca), Italy
T:+39 0583.402271 www.valgiano.it

Tenuta di Valgiano has 16 hectares (40 acres) of biodynamic vines (Demeter certified) plus 10 hectares (25 acres) of olives for oil in the Colline Lucchesi, the hills around the city of Lucca in northwest Tuscany. Owner, Laura di Collobiano, says,
> Our vines are on the lower slopes of the Appenines [Italy's mountainous spine] and we are not far from the Mediterranean. So we get Mediterranean heat allied to

mountain freshness and humidity: a combination which can cause our soils to become very dry and compact in summer but also rather sticky under winter rain.

In 1999 Saverio Petrilli began managing Valgiano's vines and they adopted biodynamics. 'We can see the positive effect [horn manure] 500 has had on our soils, making them easier for the vines to find the food and air they need for deeper rooting,' he says. 'But we have also worked very hard at understanding the types of plants we should sow between the vine rows as cover crops.' These include grasses and cereals to build organic matter, clovers to add nitrogen – which both soil microbes and vines need as food – to the soil, and deeper-rooting plants like winter radishes. 'These help maintain the looser, richer, healthier soil-structure the [horn manure] 500 is trying to create,' says Saverio.

Valgiano produces one of my favourite dry white Tuscan wines, 'Giallo dei Muri'. This is made mainly from vermentino (for body), plus trebbiano (for freshness) and malvasia (for texture). However reds from a mix of sangiovese, merlot and syrah are Valgiano's main focus, with two oaked wines called 'Palistori' and the single vineyard 'Scasso dei Cesari' being the flagships. Valgiano's entry-level Colline Lucchesi Rosso is more approachable but still needs decanting for its grainy tannins and menthol fruit to express their inner charm and warmth.

Fattoria Caiarossa, Toscana Rosso (Tuscany, Italy)

Loc. Serra all'Olio 59, I-56046 Riparbella (PI = Pisa), Italy
T:+39 0586.699016 www.caiarossa.com

Fattoria Caiarossa lies on the Tuscan Mediterranean coast, just south of the famous city of Pisa. So far so very Italian, until you realise Caiarossa's owner is a Dutchman called Eric Albada Jelgersma, who also owns two famous Bordeaux châteaux, Giscours and du Tertre in Margaux. Also, the bulk of Caiarossa's eleven different grape varieties (both red and white wines are made here) are more usually associated with Bordeaux, Burgundy, the Rhône

and Provence rather than Italy. The biodynamic approach here (Demeter certified) is also more French than Italian in terms of which biodynamic sprays, composts and teas are used, and when. For example, Maria Thun's barrel compost (see p. 28), rarely used by Italian biodynamic wine-growers but very popular with their French counterparts, is sprayed on Caiarossa's soil in autumn. This cow-manure-based spray makes sure leaves falling off the vines can decompose quickly into the soil and in a healthy way. If they don't decompose properly this makes it easier for disease organisms (like mildew or rot) on the leaves to survive until the following spring, when they can jump up onto the vines, causing problems.

There are a lot of falling leaves to decompose in Caiarossa's 16-hectare (40-acre) vineyard. This is because its vines were planted twice as close together than would be common in a Mediterranean vineyard on either the French or Italian side of the border. The aim of this is to ask each vine to produce fewer grapes but of higher quality. Caiarossa's claret-coloured winery is dug into a hillside to make use of gravity during winemaking, to reduce the need to pump the wines.

Caiarossa's flagship red wine (not to be confused with its junior partner called Pergolaia) is a clever blend of Bordeaux grapes like merlot, cabernet sauvignon, cabernet franc and petit verdot, plus Tuscany's sangiovese (the main Chianti grape), and a light seasoning of syrah and mourvèdre from Rhône-Provence. Although it ages in small French oak barrels rather than the much larger oak vats more typical of Tuscany, the wine is not weighed down by soupy, oaky flavours. Instead, the fruit flavours of red cherry and strawberry are bright and zippy, and the wine has a satisfyingly velvety mouthfeel with a savoury aftertaste typical of Tuscan red wines. Overall this is a classy Tuscan red with a perfectly judged French influence.

MORE TUSCAN BIODYNAMIC PRODUCERS MAKING SANGIOVESE-BASED RED WINES
...include the Giglioli and Rinaldi families at Casale (www.casalebio.com), Dante Lomazzi at La Colombaia (www.colombaia.it), Enrico Bramilla of Poggio Tre Lune (www.poggiotrelune.com), and Irmgard Schick, all in Chianti. Near Tenuta di Valgiano (profiled

on p. 212) in the Colline Lucchesi are Gabriele da Prato's Podere Còncori (www.podereconcori.com) and Giovanna Tronci's La Fabbrica di San Martino (www.fabbricadisanmartino.it). Along the Tuscan coast, biodynamic producers include Emilio Falcione's La Busattina (www.labusattina.blogspot.com) in Sovana, Elena Celli Duemani (www.duemani.eu) in Riparbella, Daniele Mazzanti's La Cerreta (www.cerreta.it) and Dominique Mosca's La Maliosa (www.fattorialamaliosa.it). (All these vineyards are Demeter certified.)

Fattoria Caiarossa's distinctive red winery works by gravity so the wines can be moved as naturally as possible.
Fabio Muzzi

CHILEAN BLENDED RED WINES

Chile is often described as a 'paradise' for wine-growing. Irrigation is plentiful from Andean snowmelt and Chile's soils and climate are perfect for organics and biodynamics. There are few pests. One main one, a hot-weather mite, dehydrates vines. However, the mite is a problem only on vines that get covered in dust (which mites like) from careless tractor driving, or that have been sprayed with anti-mite pesticides. These kill both the mites and their natural insect predators. Worries about the effect these pesticides were having, not just on mite predators and the eco-system but also on people working in the vines, reached a peak in the late 1990s. This was when two Chilean vineyards, Antiyal and Viñedos Emiliana, went biodynamic. Their success inspired other Chilean estates to do likewise, such as the Chilean-owned Seña (www.sena.cl), the French-owned Casa Lapostolle (www.casalapostolle.com) and the American-owned Aguatierra (www.aguatierra.cl).

Viñedos Emiliana, Coyam (Colchagua Valley, Chile)
WTC Building, Avenida Nueva Tajamar 481 Of. 905, South Tower, Las Condes, Santiago, Chile
T:+56 2.353 9130 www.emiliana.cl

Emiliana is the world's biggest biodynamic vineyard, with 583 hectares (1,440 acres) certified by Demeter and another 340 hectares (840 acres) certified organic. Emiliana's Chilean owners, the Guilisasti family, converted their first vineyard, Los Robles ('The Oaks') in the Mediterranean-like Colchagua Valley, to biodynamics from 1999.

At the time Los Robles was producing anonymous, watery wines. A combination of improved nuts-and-bolts wine-growing – involving less and better-targetted irrigation – and full-on biodynamics – such as more biodiversity and livestock, increased self-sufficiency, and compost and plant teas for the vines –

meant Los Robles started producing red wines to rival Chile's best. The debut 2001 vintage of its top red 'Coyam' was voted Chile's best wine at the inaugural Chilean Wine Awards, judged blind by an international panel. Coyam is an oak-aged, southern-France-meets-Bordeaux-style blend of nearly 60 per cent merlot, carmenère, cabernet and petit verdot (Bordeaux grapes), plus 40 per cent syrah (a Rhône grape) and mourvèdre (a Provence grape). Coyam's success saw Emiliana convert all its vineyards located across all of Chile's main wine sub-regions to organics or biodynamics. These vineyards produce less expensive, more everyday wines (red and white) than Coyam.

Emiliana's biodynamic muse, Alvaro Espinoza of Antiyal (see immediately below), says,

> Emiliana didn't go biodynamic to be the world's biggest biodynamic vineyard, but because Chile is an easy place to farm in a greener way, biodynamics keeps producing better quality grapes than before, our staff prefer farming this way and sales suggest people who drink our wine prefer the end result too.

Antiyal, Maipo Valley (Maipo Valley, Chile)

Camino Padre Hurtado 68, Alto Jahuel, Buín, Chile

www.antiyal.com

Alvaro Espinoza came from a traditional Chilean wine family but his own career has been less conventional. Alvaro's father taught winemaking at Chile's top university but sent his son to study in Bordeaux, telling him not to return to Chile just to make carbon copies of Bordeaux's famed  red wines. Alvaro developed a passion for Bordeaux-Mediterranean red wine blends combining Bordeaux's lean elegance with the more mouth-filling wildness of the Rhône and Provence.

Alvaro also developed a passion for biodynamics when working in California at Bonterra (see p. 241) in 1998. He returned to Chile and planted a tiny (a quarter of a hectare – half an acre) biodynamic

Alvaro and Marina Espinoza created Chile's first 'garage' wine.

cabernet sauvignon vineyard in his back garden in a residential area in the Maipo Valley near Chile's capital, Santiago (Demeter certified). These cabernet grapes, plus syrah and carmenère from Alvaro's mother's 2-hectare (5-acre) vineyard, were fermented in Alvaro and his wife, Marina's, garage. This was Chile's first so-called 'garage' wine. Alvaro and Marina called it 'Antiyal' or 'son of the sun' in the indigenous Mapuche language. Antiyal's untamed blackberry, leather and baked-earth flavours wowed the critics. Its tiny scale challenged Chile's preoccupation with churning out container-loads of fresh, fruity, inoffensive wines. Alvaro says,

Ordinary consumers quite rightly love these simple, fruity wines. Not every wine can come from a tiny vineyard like Antiyal. But neither should every wine come from huge vineyards farmed anonymously by numbers. Antiyal shows how the more self-sufficient, biodynamic approach can work, like working with animals such as alpacas. They provide manure for compost and eat weeds. The nutrients these weeds contain are then recycled back into the vineyard giving the grapes a stronger sense of place than when fertilizers are used. Adding the biodynamic preparations to your compost means your vines can connect to the natural rythms of the earth below and the moon and stars above. Of course this sounds too esoteric for most people. So the best way of showing that biodynamics works is by making wines people enjoy drinking.

Alvaro's subsequent work consulting to Emiliana (see p.216) is his attempt to show how the small-scale biodynamic approach of Antiyal can work even for much larger vineyards.

RHÔNE AND MEDITERRANEAN-STYLE BLENDED REDS

In the northern Rhône the syrah grape tends to be used on its own. However in the southern half of the Rhône Valley, Provence, Corsica and the rest of the Mediterranean regions Languedoc and Roussillon – called 'the Midi' for short, because the midday sun is so hot overhead – red wines are made from a large range of grape varieties blended together. This makes for more balanced wines. As well as syrah these grapes include grenache noir, mourvèdre, carignan, cinsault and several others.

The wines will of course vary in smell, taste and mouthfeel depending on where they were grown, which grapes they were blended from and in what proportions. Syrah has firm red fruit, grenache's black fruit is softer, juicier and more open-knit, while mourvèdre can be a bit of a clenched fist, when young anyway. But generally these red wines are warm fruited, and rich in tannin and alcohol. In my view they generally work best with food, benefit from being served cool but not chilled, or at least not too warm anyway (around 12°C – 54°F – will do), and they really improve with decanting, or lots of swirling anyway, so the tannins loosen up and any eggy, just-bottled smells disappear, allowing the rich fruit flavours to come to the fore.

Mediterranean France has the perfect climate for organics and biodynamics. There has been an explosion of interest in this way of farming in the last decade, often led by people from outside the region looking for a change of scene or lifestyle and a second career as green-fingered wine-growers. These new wine-growers frequently acquire small plots of well-sited old vines, which were being sold by old timers. Grapes from these old vines had in most cases been sold to local co-operatives, many of which are in severe financial difficulty, leading to the retirement of the former plot owners.

Château de Bastet, Cuvée Spéciale Rouge (Côtes du Rhône, France)

Route d'Ales, F-30200 Sabran (Gard), France
T:+33 (0)4.66.39.97.07

In the mid-nineteenth century, Château de Bastet did have some vines but was more geared to silkworm farming for the cloth manufacturers of nearby Lyon. The current owners, the Aubert family, arrived here in 1934. Jean-Charles Aubert extended the vineyard to 65 hectares (160 acres), then converted it to biodynamics in the 1990s (Demeter certified). He says,

> I did this after having arranged to visit a biodynamic vineyard whose wine I had tried and liked. [The vineyard belonged to Michel Chapoutier, see p. 174]. This made me curious. After the visit it was obvious to me that biodynamics was the system to have if you wanted high-quality grapes.

Jean-Charles' daughter Julie now runs Château de Bastet, where vines are contained by natural buffer zones and water for vineyard sprays is taken from the estate's own natural springs. They make a very drinkable range of dry white and red Côtes du Rhône wines. The 'Cuvée Spéciale' red is half grenache noir and half syrah. A versatile wine for enjoying rather than waxing lyrical about, it is loaded with soft, punchy, wild-cherry fruit. You can drink it slightly chilled on a hot day, or slightly warm on a really cold one.

Mas de Libian, Bout d'Zán Rouge (Côtes du Rhône, France)

F-07700 St Marcel d'Ardèche (Ardèche), France
T:+33 (0)4.75.04.66.22 www.masdelibian.com

The Thibon family live in a hunting lodge dating from 1670 with an incredible view overlooking the southern Rhône and Provence mountain ranges of the Dentelles de Montmirail, Mont Ventoux, and the Alpilles (see p. 227). In the mid 1990s, Hélène Thibon convinced her parents – who never used pesticides here – and two sisters to start making and bottling their own Côtes du

Rhône wines rather than sending their grapes to a local co-operative. After this they took the next step and converted the farm's fruit trees, cereals and 25 hectares (60 acres) of vineyards to biodynamics (Demeter certified). Mas de Libian's oldest vines are part-ploughed by a horse called Nestor. The arid, stony-clay soils allied to often cool, buffeting mountain winds mean the vines produce loose bunches of small, concentrated, perfumed berries.

The Bout d'Zán ('stick of liquorice') red from 80 per cent grenache noir and 20 per cent syrah is part-aged in large, old chestnut casks before bottling (into 50,000 bottles each year). The wine has a forthright mountain crispness, the black plum and cherry fruit taste as though they are cut into thick chunks rather than thinly sliced. A lunchtime picnic wine you wish you'd saved more of for dinner.

Domaine Chaume-Arnaud, Côtes du Rhône-Villages Vinsobres (Côtes du Rhône, France)

Les Paluds, F-26110 Vinsobres (Drôme), France
T:+33 (0)4.75.27.66.85 chaume-arnaud@wanadoo.fr

Valérie Arnauds's parents' southern Rhône Valley estate produced melons, herbs and vegetables, which were sold to wholesalers, and also wine grapes, which disappeared into anonymous blends in the local wine co-operative. In 1987 Valérie, who had just qualified as a winemaker, borrowed a wine press and some small fermenting tanks and made her first wine from 5 hectares (11 acres) of her parents' Côtes du Rhône vines. In 1989, and with her husband, Philippe Chaume, whose day job was selling and maintaining winemaking equipment (presses, tanks, filters, bottling lines), Valérie took over the whole of the family estate. This now comprises 35 hectares (86 acres) of the Côtes du Rhône. Philippe and Valérie's wines were already some of the most highly rated in the southern Rhône by the time they adopted biodynamic methods (Demeter certified) in the early 2000s. So why change an already winning formula? Valérie says,

> We knew we had good vineyard sites: both the vines I
> inherited from my parents, plus those we purchased in 1994

[on the plateau in the village of Vinsobres]. But we also knew from tasting biodynamic wines made by friends in the Rhône [like François Vallot of Domaine du Coriançon (see immediately below)] and other French regions that biodynamics could help our vines express their terroir [or sense of place] even more intensely.

A good example is their Côtes du Rhône red made from 60 per cent grenache noir, 15 per cent each syrah and mourvèdre, and 5 per cent each carignan and cinsault. The wine can be labelled Vinsobres, after the village in which the grapes grow. Rhône reds can often be richly flattering and gluggable, but they can also leave you feeling drowsy after just one glass. The Chaume-Arnaud Vinsobres, however, has a really uplifting crunchiness, which shows, I think, how well the vine roots are connecting with the soft limestone subsoils that this village is famous for. The fruit flavours are clear and defined, and the tannins have a liquorice-like chewiness that is enticing and reviving. Around 60,000 bottles are made each year.

Domaine du Coriançon, Côtes du Rhône-Villages Vinsobres (Côtes du Rhône, France)

Quartier Hauterives, F-26110 Vinsobres (Drôme), France
T:+33 (0)4.75.26.03.24   www.domainevallot.com

François Vallot was in his early twenties in 1976 when he took over his family's Côtes du Rhône vineyard upon the death of his father. François was the fourth generation of his family to be a wine-grower, and he happily ran the vineyard for nearly thirty years for his three brothers and two sisters. However, in 2003 he decided to go it alone. He took his share of the vines, which was 30 hectares (74 acres), and within the year had converted to biodynamics (Demeter certified). François has two wooden dynamiser machines in which to stir his biodynamic vineyard spray preparations like horn manure 500 and horn silica 501. He says,

Each stirrer holds 250 litres (66 gallons), allowing me to spray 10 hectares at a time. I buy certified organic manure for compost, and get the biodynamic compost preparations onto the soil via Maria Thun's barrel compost spray.

François buys this from his neighbour, Cédric Guillaume-Corbin, whose Domaine La Péquélette consists of 8 hectares (20 acres) of Côtes du Rhône vines, 5 hectares (12 acres) of truffle oaks and 800 olive trees (biodynamically farmed but certified organic). François's wine is deep but smooth textured and uplifting, and the grape flavours are quite precisely defined. Domaine du Coriançon's signature 'Vinsobres' red bottling is made from from 75 per cent grenache noir (for redcurrant flavour), 24 per cent syrah (for mint) and a dash of mourvèdre (for damson). Around 18,000 bottles of it are made each year. If you like reds with a touch of oak flavour from barrel ageing, try the 'Claude Vallot' bottling, which François named after his late father. It comes from 60 per cent grenache noir and 40 per cent syrah and ages in new barrels (5,000 bottles).

Domaine Montirius, Le Clos Rouge, Vacqueyras (Côtes du Rhône, France)

Le Devès, F-84260 Sarrians (Vaucluse), France
T:+33 (0).4.90.65.38.28 www.montirius.com

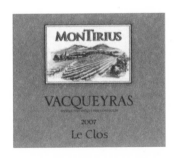

One day in 1990 Eric Saurel asked his wife Christine to get the washing and kids inside because he was about to spray a pesticide. Christine asked Eric whether he had told the neighbours to do the same as well. When Eric admitted he hadn't, the family converted their 58-hectare (143-acre) Vacqueyras and Gigondas vineyard in the southern Rhône to organics and then biodynamics (Demeter and Biodyvin certified). They even built a gravity-fed winery to minimise pumping the wines, and from lime mortar rather than cement. The winery's waste water is purified in gravity-fed sand-and-gravel beds that Eric designed.

The name of the estate, Montirius, is a contraction of the name of the Saurel's three children and is used for the domaine's red Gigondas wines (syrah and grenache blends) and for its Vacqueyras range. The top Vacqueyras red wine, called Clos Montirius or 'Le Clos' for short, is made from roughly equal amounts of syrah and grenache with a little mourvèdre. Eric sprays chamomile tea to stop the vines, some of which date from 1930, heat-stressing in summer. He follows this through in the winery by soaking the red grapeskins cool on their juice for a few days before warming the tanks up to get fermentation going proper. This gives what is a rich, inky-coloured red wine its lift and elegance. Give it plenty of air, decant it, and drink it *al fresco* during a barbecue, keeping it away from hot ovens or grills to stop it becoming over-warm.

> **ANOTHER PRODUCER OF BIODYNAMIC VACQUEYRAS**
>
> ...is Serge Férigoule of Domaine Sang des Cailloux (www.sangdescailloux.com). His best wine is an old vine bottling called Cuvée Lopy (Biodyvin certified).

Domaine Duseigneur, Antarès Rouge, Lirac (Côtes du Rhône, France)

Rue Nostradamus, Route de St Victor, F-30126 St Laurent des Arbres (Gard), France
T:+33 (0)4.66.50.02.57   www.domaineduseigneur.com

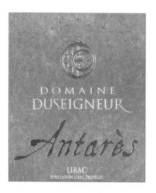

In the 1960s, Frédéric Duseigneur's parents returned to their native France from Algeria and planted a vineyard out of the scrubland around the villages of Laudun and Lirac in the southern Côtes du Rhône. 'My father had seen in Africa how important it is to have life in your soil, especially if you are farming in a hot climate,' says Frédéric, who took over here in 1992. A key part of the biodynamic approach is using plants that grow wild on the estate to keep the vines healthy, like thyme, rosemary, yarrow, chamomile, blackberry and lavendar. Frédéric says,

> *Thyme is a pointy, vertical plant, so in love with the sun's heat it really teaches your vines to express themselves upwards to the sun, helping to produce healthier flowers and stronger grapes. Wild blackberry buds help boost the vine's immune system by activating iron and stopping vines becoming anaemic.*

Domaine Duseigneur produces mainly red wines from 30 hectares (75 acres) of grenache noir, syrah and mourvèdre (Biodyvin certified). The Antarès bottling from vines in Lirac comes from mainly grenache noir on deep, sandy clay-limestone soils. This gives the wine its brightness and almost overpowering floral lift. The tannins have the dark, savoury-sweet ripeness of ripe black olives. Around 15,000 bottles are made each year.

OTHER PRODUCERS OF BIODYNAMIC SOUTHERN RHÔNE WINES ...include Fabrice Monod of Domaine de Fontvert (www.fontvert.com), Vincent Rochette of Domaine Roche Audran (www.roche-audran.com) in Visan whose oldest grenache noir vines date from 1962, Pascal Chalon of La Grande Ourse in Tulette, and Jérôme Bressy at Domaine Gourt de Mautens (www.gourtdemautens.com) for benchmark both normal and port-style red wines in Rasteau (all Demeter certified). The Boulle family of the excellent Domaine Les Aphillanthes in Travaillan switched to biodynamics having successfully treated their son's eczema with herbal remedies (Biodyvin certified).

Laurent Clapier at Mas Théo (www.mas-theo.fr), and Domaine des Estubiers, which is owned by Michel Chapoutier (see p. 174), are the two biodynamic producers of Grignan-lès-Adhémar (known as Coteaux du Tricastin until 2008), a fresher style of Rhône red (both Demeter certified).

In the Coteaux des Baronnies, Valéry Liotaud's Domaine La Rosière (www.domaine-la-rosiere.com), Jean Beaumont's Domaine du Faucon Dorée (www.faucon.doree.free.fr), and Michel Faure's Domaine du Vialard are all biodynamic and also grow apricots and olives (Demeter certified).

Domaine de Villeneuve, Châteauneuf-du-Pape Rouge (Southern Rhône, France)

Route de Courthézon, F-84840 Orange (Vaucluse), France
T:+33 (0).4.90.34.57.55 www.domainedevilleneuve.com

Domaine de Villeneuve, in the heart of the southern Rhône's Châteauneuf-du-Pape region, is a story of resurrection. Until the early 1990s its 9-hectare (21-acre) vineyard belonged to an ageing widow who sold her grapes to a local co-operative. The mourvèdre, grenache noir and syrah vines, many dating from the 1960s, others even older, were alive but struggling in arid soils made up of large puddingstones or *galets*. These stones act like storage heaters,

> BIODYNAMIC
> CHÂTEAUNEUF-DU-PAPE
> ...is also made by Michel Chapoutier (see p.174), the Coulon brothers at Domaine de Beaurenard (www.beaurenard. fr), and Jean-Claude Daumen's Domaine de la Vieille Julienne (vieillejulienne.com) (all Demeter certified).

reflecting light during the day and keeping the air around the vines warm at night. These *galets* help make Châteauneuf-du-Pape's red and white wines some of the world's most intensely ripe-tasting, with notably high alcohol levels (15 per cent by volume is normal).

Domaine de Villeneuve's new owner, Stanislas Wallut, coverted to biodynamics and began applying biodynamic compost to the soil, cooling the vineyard down, making it more earthy, allowing the old vines to refresh themselves and produce grapes that held more flavour and not quite so much sugar – thus reducing the potential alcohol in the finished wine (Biodyvin certified). Above ground, the vine leaves and shoots were sprayed with a biodynamic tea called Urticae 500. This is made from stinging nettle (with the Latin name *Urtica*) and weeping willow, mixed with biodynamic horn manure 500. Stanilas sprays Urticae 500 when the vine shoots begin growing in early spring, then again after the vine blossoms have become fertilised to produce the grapes. The Urticae 500 helps vines weakened by disease or heat stress to produce shoots and leaves robust enough to withstand the heat. Vines need green shoots and leaves to trap the solar energy needed for the grapes to get their flavours ripe. I often find drinking more than a glass or two of Châteauneuf-du-Pape really hard work, such is the heavy nature of the wines – their hot, baked flavours of game and leather are laced with so much alcohol I feel as if I am drinking port or a fruit liqueur rather than a table wine. What strikes me about Domaine de Villeneuve's Châteauneuf-du-Pape red wines is not just their depth of flavour (blueberry, red cherry, dark plum, aniseed) and purity, but their levity. This is one Châteauneuf-du-Pape red wine that will blow you away but won't knock you over.

Château Romanin, Côteaux d'Aix en Provence Les Baux Rouge (Provence, France)

Route de Cavaillon, F-13210 St Rémy de Provence (Bouches du Rhône), France
T:+33 (0)4.90.92.45.87 www.romanin.com

Wine was first made at Château Romanin in Provence in the fourth century BC. Greek traders shipped Romanin's wine in clay amphoras stamped 'Romania', hence the name. At 250 hectares (620 acres), this is one of France's biggest biodynamic estates, although Romanin mostly comprises biodiverse forests of oak, pine and herb-strewn scrub (*maquis*). There are several hectares of olives for oil and almonds, a herd of sheep, and 55 hectares (136 acres) of vines, all sheltered on the warm foothills of a mountain range called Les Alpilles ('The Little Alps'). For wine, Romanin's vineyards are designated part of Les Baux de Provence, which is Provence's most renowned wine sub-zone and a designated environmental protection area.

Over 80 per cent of Les Baux vineyards are organic or biodynamic. Château Romanin was the first to convert to biodynamics in 1989 (Demeter and Biodyvin certified). However its red, pink and white wines were somewhat flat until 2006 when it was sold to new owners: a famous wine family called Charmolüe. They had recently sold Château Montrose, a top Bordeaux estate. They gave Romanin's winery a scrub down, and made sure its grapes were hand-picked fresher and riper than before. This gave Romanin's Les Baux red wine

Mountains shelter the vines at Château Romanin in Provence, France.
Château Romanin

227

the kind of sturdy roundness of fruit, zip and focus one would expect from syrah, grenache, mourvèdre and cabernet sauvignon grapes grown on the warm limestone shards that dominate the vineyard soils here. Around 50,000 bottles are made each year.

> ANOTHER BIODYNAMIC PROVENCE VINEYARD
> ...making ripely generous reds is Paul Weindel's Tour des Vidaux (www.tourdesvidaux.com) (Biodyvin certified).

Domaine Comte Abbatucci, Ministre Impérial, Cuvée Collection, Vin de Table Rouge (Corsica, France)

Lieu-dit Chiesale, F-20140 Casalabriva (Corse), France
T:+33 (0)4.95.74.04.55 www.domaine-comte-abbatucci.com

Corsica's vineyards used to contain many ancient and genetically unique 'heirloom' grape varieties. In the 1960s these were largely ripped out and replaced with higher yielding, genetically standardised grapes by French colonialists fleeing Algeria during its 1954–62 war of independence from France. Antoine Abbatucci managed to save many of these heirloom grape varieties, some of which have grown on Corsica for 2,500 years, in his 24-hectare (60-acre) vineyard at Ajaccio on Corsica's western coast. His son, Jean-Charles took over in 1990 and converted the vines to organics and then, in 1999, to biodynamics (Demeter certified). 'I attended a seminar on biodynamics and within an hour I knew that this was what I had been looking for,' he says.

If what you are looking for is wine with layer upon layer of diverse flavours you have never come across before, then you should try to find some of Jean-Charles' wines (they are labelled as Vin de France rather than under the regional Ajaccio denomination). Dry white wines from vermentino ('Cuvée Faustine'), or from vermentino plus Mediterranean grapes like barbarossa, biancu gentile, brustiano, geneovese, rossala bianca, biancone, carcajolo bianca, paga debiti, riuminese and rossola brandica ('Général de la Revolution', 'Il Cavaliere Diplomate d'Empire') have such depth, artisan texture and freshness, you'd think you were drinking a wine made from alpine apples and orchard flowers rather than from grapes grown on parched Mediterranean scrub. The 'Faustine' rosé made from sciacarello is as refreshing as a pink champagne, despite not having any bubbles. Reds from sciacarello, nielluccio, carignan ('Faustine') are creamy with a

lovely twist of red and dark fruit. The 'Ministre Impérial Cuvée Collection' red, named after an Abbatucci ancestor, is made from morescola, morescono, aleatico, carcajolo nero, montanaccia, sciaccarello and nielluccio grapes. This red has fantastic freshness and delicacy, savoury tannins and juicy flavours of violets, liquorice, briary hawthorns and sage. Try with stewed rabbit or lamb. Only 2,000 bottles are made each year.

Hegarty Chamans, Cuvée No.2 Rouge, Minervois (Languedoc, France)
F-11160 Trausse (Aude), France
T:+33 (0)4.68.78.61.51   www.hegartychamans.com

Advertising guru Sir John Hegarty and his partner, Philippa Crane, began transforming Domaine de Chamans, a 17-hectare (42-acre) Minervois vineyard, after they bought it in 2002. They ripped out poorly planted plots of vines and returned

it to wild habitat. They retired the machine harvester in favour of hand-picking. And they adopted biodynamics (Demeter certified). For biodynamic compost, they use manure from beef cows that graze in the nearby Ariège mountains. Sir John says,

> *The compost brings a cool mountain influence into our hot Minervois soils, which seems to have calmed the vines down. When we bought Chamans we noticed grenache noir vines with both unripe green berries and ripe black ones on the same bunch. If you waited for the green ones to ripen then*

the already ripe ones would have become overripe and too alcoholic in the meantime. You had the choice of making either an unripe-tasting red if you picked early, or an overripe jammy one if you picked late. There was no in-between. Biodynamic compost seems to have been key in curing the vines of this potential problem because our grenache noir flowers much more homogeneously now. If each flower on every grape bunch is ready to be pollinated at the same time in spring it means that when you pick that bunch in autumn, every grape on that bunch will be ripe at the same time too.

Around 15,000 bottles of Hegarty Chamans Minervois Rouge 'No.2' are made each year from mainly grenache with light seasonings of mourvedre and cinsault. It shows concentrated warm blackcurrant fruit with minty mountain freshness and can age for up to a decade.

OTHER BIODYNAMIC VINEYARDS IN MINERVOIS AND ITS ENVIRONS
...include Domaine St Julien (www.lezaparel.com) which Stéphanie Minder and Ernest Aeschlimann have carefully turned into a self-sufficient biodynamic farm and vineyard (Demeter certified), Mireille and Pierre Mann's Mas des Caprices for Fitou and Corbières (Biodyvin certified), Jean-François Izarn's Borie La Vitarèle (www.borielavitarele.fr) for really terroir-driven St Chinian reds (Demeter certified), and Hugo Stewart and Paul Old's Les Clos Perdus (www.lesclosperdus.com) for rich, beautifully balanced Corbières (organic certification).
For a Minervois red made from 100 per cent syrah see p. 176

La Réserve d'O, SansSoo Rouge, St-Saturnin (Languedoc, France)
Rue du Château, F-34150 Arboras (Hérault), France
www.lareservedo.fr

Frédéric and Marie Chauffray sold wine in the Paris region before deciding to acquire their own 10-hectare (25-acre) vineyard in the high hilly Languedoc sub-regions of Terrasses de Larzac and St

Saturnin in 2004. Frédéric immediately began renovating the old vines by increasing the height of the wooden support posts and wires so the vines could produce longer shoots and more leaves with which to capture the heat and light of the sun for the grapes. They adopted biodynamic methods (Demeter certified), with compost made from local goat manure.

Around 15,000 bottles of a sumptuous red Terrasses du Larzac are made (from mainly syrah and grenache with 10 per cent cinsault). But it is Frédéric and Marie's smallest production wine, a St-Saturnin called 'SansSoo', which is most notable. SansSoo is made from roughly half syrah and half cinsault. The grapes are hand-picked early in the cool of the morning, crushed by foot, then fermented completely wild, with no addition of either yeast or sulphur dioxide preservative (E220). Around 2,000 bottles are made. The name 'SansSoo' is a play on words in French meaning 'no added sulphites'. You absolutely have to decant this (unfiltered) wine, preferably a day or two before you drink it, to get the most vibrant sensations from its bold, milky blackberry fruit.

Mas Foulaquier, Les Calades Rouge, Pic St Loup (Languedoc, France)

Route des Embruscalles, F-34270 Claret (Hérault), France
T:+33 (0)4.67.59.96.94   www.masfoulaquier.fr

Blandine Chauchat and Pierre Jéquier produce a cracking range of mainly red wines from Pic St Loup, one of the most renowned sub-regions of the Languedoc's coastal hills (Coteaux du Languedoc). There are 11 hectares (27 acres) of biodynamic vines (Demeter certified) on sometimes scorching pebbly topsoils cooled by red clay subsoils that hold rain and release it slowly to the vines like a damp but not dripping sponge. Syrah (red fruit) and grenache noir (black fruit) combine in wines like 'Orphée' and 'Le Rollier'; grenache is used on its own in 'Le Petit Duc', while the spikey carignan is used in 'Les Tonnillières'. My choice is 'Les Calades', a single vineyard planted with syrah and grenache surrounded by stone walls made from the limestone shards that the vines root in. The grapes are hand-picked and fermented in cement tanks, which are perfect for red wines because they insulate the fermentation and keep its speed nice and steady. The wine then ages in a mix of cement tanks and large wooden barrels. Les Calades shows really punchy soft red fruit in youth but gradually goes more animal and leathery with age. The locals drink it with wild boar stew.

Zélige Caravent, Le Jardin des Simples Rouge (Languedoc, France)

Chemin de la Gravette, F-30260 Corconne (Gard), France
T:+33 (0)4.66.77.10.98   www.zelige-caravent.fr

Luc Michel and his wife Marie Baldet make mainly red wines from 15 hectares (37 acres) of biodynamic vines around Pic St Loup (Demeter certified). This triangular-shaped rocky outcrop 16 miles (20 km) north of Montpellier in France's Languedoc is as old as the Pyrenees. Although Pic St Loup is cooled at night by Mediterranean breezes, summer days are blistering. Vines struggle to find water on bright, pebbly soils, which mercilessly reflect sunlight and heat. Luc says,

> We stop our vines overheating with mint, stinging nettle, and comfrey teas. We pick the leaves ourselves while hiking. We stop our red wines from being too heavy by blending in some wine from the cinsault grapes. Although cinsault is a fantastic grape for pink wines, some critics say it's far too light for serious reds. But we find cinsault's perfumed fluidity allows heavier red wine grapes like syrah and grenache noir to ease up, making a smoother red overall.

Luc and Marie's 'Jardin des Simples' is a classy, vibrant, blackberry- and apple-scented red wine made from 70 per cent cinsault. The remaining 30 per cent comes from different balances of syrah and grenache noir blended in. The oldest vines date from the 1940s.

Domaine de Fontedicto, Promise Rouge (Languedoc, France)

Fontarèche, F-34720 Caux (Hérault), France
T:+33 (0)4.67.98.40.22

Bernard Bellahsen was born in 1950 in Tunisia, where his father worked in the oil business. Bernard and his wife Cécile have 4 hectares (10 acres) of vines, olives, almonds and cherries in the arid hills near Béziers in France's Languedoc. They farm it using horses, rather than petrol-powered machinery. Bernard says,

> *This wasn't to rebel against my father. As a child in Tunisia I remember the baker delivering bread by horse. It made more sense than delivering it using fuel-burning trucks. Horses are slower than tractors but let you remain more in contact with the soil's natural rhythms. Horses are a practical rather than intellectual choice for me.*

Bernard grows his own wheat for bread he bakes in a wood-fired oven next to his winery. He taught himself biodynamics. His farm, self-contained and surrounded by woodland, is largely self-sufficient. It is a shining example of the biodynamic idea that each farm becomes a self-sustaining living organism, although Bernard has let his long-held Demeter biodynamic certification lapse for personal reasons.

He foot-treads the carignan, syrah, grenache noir, and aramon grapes for his red wine 'Promise'. He then ages the wine in old barrels for one year and it is bottled unfiltered and with no additives. Around 15,000 bottles are made each year. It has a rich scarlet colour, breathtakingly authentic red fruit flavours, with the characteristic deep, wild meatiness of the best Languedoc red wines underneath.

Vines grow beside the forest at Quivira Vineyards in California, USA.
Quivira Vineyards

Mas Gabriel, Les Trois Terrasses Hérault Rouge (Languedoc, France)

9 avenue de Mougères, F-34720 Caux (Hérault), France
T:+33 (0)4.67.31.20.95 www.mas-gabriel.com

Peter and Deborah Core left their comfortable, UK-based corporate life of financial management and commercial property law in 2003 to study winemaking in New Zealand. 'We thought it made sense to learn winemaking in English rather than in French,' says Peter. They attended the polytechnic in Gisborne, and soon came into contact with biodynamic winemaker James Millton (see p. 55). Once their winemaking studies finished, both Peter and Deborah learnt more about biodynamics via short courses at Hohepa Farm (www.hohepa.com) in Hawke's Bay. This charitable trust uses many of Rudolf Steiner's theories regarding therapy, spirituality, education and gardening as part of its curative care to the intellectually disabled. Local biodynamic expert Peter Proctor (see p. 237), who led the Core's courses, first came across biodynamics at Hohepa in the 1960s. 'When I saw the quality of the biodynamic crops there, that was that,' he said. He became Hohepa's farm manager while educating farmers in the non-developed world in general and in India in particular about how cow manure, compost and the biodynamic preparations could revitalise soils, crops and farmers.

When Peter and Deborah acquired their 6-hectare (15-acre) vineyard in France's Languedoc, they used biodynamic compost, which they made and spread by hand to re-energise the soils. Peter had the vineyard officially certified as organic. He says,

'The vineyard we bought was organic by neglect, and it gave very low yields. The compost, which we make from organic cow manure and the biodynamic compost preparations, has helped the vines produce slightly higher yields. But we still only produce 3,000 bottles per hectare [1,200 bottles per acre], when by law we could produce four times as much.

These low yields mean Mas Gabriel's wines are nothing if not concentrated, but they are also elegant with it, perhaps a result of the vines being given regular refreshing doses of stinging nettle extract made by soaking the nettle in cold rather than boiling water (unlike when making tea).

Peter Proctor talking about biodynamic preparations. Peter teaches biodynamics at Hohepa Farm in New Zealand, where the Cores, of Mas Gabriel vineyard in France, studied.

Clos Gabriel produces 800 bottles of a rich, quince-flavoured dry white called 'Clos des Papillon' from the rare carignan blanc; 2,000 bottles of dry, seductive rosé from 1950s carignan and cinsault called 'Fleurs Sauvages'; and two reds, one exuberantly currant-like and based on syrah called 'Clos des Lièvres', and another whose stewed blackberry, apple and cinnamon flavours are subtler, more savoury and based on carignan (85 per cent) and syrah or grenache called 'Les Trois Terrasses'. Around 8,000 bottles of it are made each year.

OTHER BIODYNAMIC VINEYARDS IN THE LANGUEDOC
...include the Bertrand family's Domaine de Malaveille (www.domainemalavieille.com), Turner Pageot (www.turnerpageot.com), Domaine Beau-Thorey (www.beauthorey.net) and Patrick Maurel's Terres du Pic, Olivier Binet and Pierre Jacquet's Domaine Binet-Jacquet (www.binet-jacquet.com) for bright red wines from dark schist in Faugères, Agnès and Denys Armand of Mas d'Espanet (www.masdespanet.com), Henri Gayzard of Domaine Ste Marie des Pins (www.domaine-sainte-marie.com) between Toulouse and Limoux (all Demeter certified); and Laurent Vidal's Mas Conscience and Thierry Hasard's Domaine de la Marfée (www.la-marfee.com) in St Georges d'Orques (both Biodyvin certified).

Domaine Cazes, Le Canon du Maréchal Rouge, Côtes Catalanes (Roussillon, France)

4 rue Francisco-Ferrer, F-66602 Rivesaltes (Pyrénées-Orientales), France
T:+33 (0)4.68.64.08.26 www.cazes-rivesaltes.com

The Cazes family have been making wine near Perpignan in France's Roussillon region since the early 1900s. They have a massive 165 hectares (407 acres) of vines, almost all of which are in a single block (all certified Demeter biodynamic). 'Being self-contained makes biodynamic farming much easier,' says production manager Emmanuel Cazes. The winery has to be pretty high-tech to deal with so much wine – 800,000 bottles are made each year – but low-tech solutions are used here too. 'We bought heating pots from a chef's kitchen to warm water for our herb teas and biodynamic spray preparations,' says Emmanuel. 'It takes a couple of days to spray all of our vines.'

The Cazes family's top brand is called 'Canon du Maréchal', honouring France's First World War general, Joffre, whose small, personal vineyard was the first vineyard the Cazes family ever bought. The Canon du Maréchal red wine is made from Mediterranean and Bordeaux grapes, mainly merlot and syrah with splashes of grenache and cabernet. Cool fermented, this is a juicy, everyday red with bright bubblegum and cherry-soda flavours.

Domaine Nivet-Galinier, Côtes du Roussillon Les Aspres (Roussillon, France)

Lou Jassal, Route du Soler, F-66300 Ponteilla (Pyrénées-Orientales), France
T:+33 (0)4.68.56.51.20

For sixteen years David Nivet produced two million bottles annually as head of co-operative in his native Roussillon. When he had had enough of the politics and in-fighting that goes with such a job, he and his partner, Lydie Galinier, decided it would be more fun to ferment the family's grapes independently in their own winery.

Nivet-Galinier comprises 9 hectares (20 acres) of mainly red vines in Les Aspres, an up-and-coming sub-region of Roussillon in the lee of the Mediterranean Pyrenees. The vines are biodynamic (Demeter certified) and lie in a single block. This makes it easier for David to apply biodynamic sprays and teas using a back sprayer. His preferred plant-based sprays are decoctions of willow and common horsetail 508 to stimulate the vine's self-defence mechanisms against rot and other fungal diseases. David makes biodynamic compost by mixing used grapeskins from the winery with a mixture of horse and cow manure. The soils in Les Aspres are very stony, although the red grapes have been planted where the ground is at its most clayey, because, as David explains, 'the clay retains enough water for the vines not to suffer heat stress in high summer.' Grenache noir, syrah and carignan are grown for red wines, with the oldest vines dating from the 1960s. David's top red wine, the Côtes du Roussillon Les Aspres, has bright, almost medicinal fruit flavours, with such firm, grippy tannins underneath that you'd best drink it with a filling, spicy local dish like Catalan meatballs (Boles de Picoulat), made from diced red meat seasoned with garlic and olives.

Le Clos du Rouge Gorge, Vieilles Vignes Rouge, Côtes Catalanes (Rousillon, France)

6 place Marcel Vié, F-66720 Latour de France (Pyrénées-Orientales), France
T:+33 (0)4.68.29.16.37

Cyril Fhal walks you around his 10-hectare (25-acre) biodynamic vineyard (organic certification) in Latour de France, one of the warmest villages in Rousillon, which is France's sunniest region. The vines grow on soils bursting with pebbles you could fry ostrich eggs on. The surrounding stone walls and Mars-like mountains radiate the heat. Fhal shows you his biodynamic compost pile. It is as diminutive as he is. You feel it stands zero chance of retaining its humidity or its worms in these temperatures. He leads you to his winery at the back of a tumbledown house in a mercifully shaded side street. You prepare yourself for his red wines, believing they will be as hot and alcoholic as a newly aflame, brandy-soaked Christmas pudding with stewed fruit flavours to match. You taste the first wine, relax and then swallow it, and the second. The wines bring you back to life, lifting you up, away from the heat haze into a hinterland cool enough for you to digest what Cyril is telling you: that his uncle was a founder member of France's biodynamic movement in the late 1950s, but that to gain as wide a perspective as possible about how wine should or *could* be grown, Cyril worked in Bordeaux and the Loire but in conventional rather than organic or biodynamic vineyards.

His compost is made from both cow manure and The Great Satan, chicken manure, which wine-growers feel is too much like a nuclear bomb for vines. Cyril says a tiny bit of chicken manure is the 'match' that lights the fuse to start all the microbiological transformations he needs in his compost. Then he will have what he desires, unavoidably hot topsoils but cool, living subsoils beneath. 'Such soils give you

The view from Bonterra Vineyard, California, USA.
Alan Campbell Photography

the most options at harvest as a winemaker,' Cyril says, meaning the grapes won't fall from perfect ripeness into overripe and unusable jamminess from one day to the next. He tips his red grapes into the vats as whole, not split, berries so that the juice is gently infused with the colours and flavours in the skins. His 'Vieilles Vignes' or 'old vines' red comes from carignan planted around 1910 and in the 1940s. Carignan is a grape derided for its clumsy, tannic-as-leather-shoes brutality, but Cyril's wine is like a velvet slipper. You'd willingly wear it home, even as the heat greets you again on the other side of the winery door when Cyril bids you farewell.

Bonterra Vineyards, The Butler, Mendocino County (California, USA)

13601 East Side Road, Hopland, CA 95449, USA www.bonterra.com

The Butler Ranch in northern California's Mendocino County was a sheep farm in the nineteenth century, a cherry orchard in the twentieth century, and became a vineyard at the start of the twenty-first. The vines were planted by Bonterra, the certified organic and increasingly certified biodynamic arm of Fetzer Vineyards (see p.97). Bonterra buys in certified organic grapes but also grows its own organic grapes on 270 hectares (670 acres). In addition, Bonterra has three biodynamic ranches called McNab (which was founded by Jimmy Fetzer), Blue Heron and Butler, with a total of 114 hectares (283 acres) of red and white wine grapes combined (Demeter certified).

Butler Ranch overlooks the town of Ukiah from steep slopes. Planting these with vines in 2001–2 (going biodynamic from scratch), risked causing erosion because of the machinery involved. To prevent this, Bonterra's vineyard chief, Dave Koball, sowed clovers and grasses in spring.

These bind the soil over summer to stop it from drying out and blowing away. We layed down hay as a mulch over

241

winter. Hay mulching is very time-consuming but worth it. We had really heavy rain here in autumn 2003 but the clarity of the water running into our drainage channels showed that our topsoil, which has taken hundreds of years to form, was staying on the ranch and not ending up on the valley floor and in the local river.

Butler is planted with red grapes from both Bordeaux and the Mediterranean. Koball aligned the vine rows 208–218 degrees to true north. He says,

This is about optimal for us in Mendocino. We look for the angle of the sun at two-thirty to four-thirty in the afternoon in July–August, when the heat is at its most intense. If your rows are oriented wrongly then grapes on one side of the row won't get ripe while those on the other side will be shrivelled and raisining.

For 'The Butler' single vineyard bottling, mainly syrah is used, with 20 per cent grenache, mourvèdre and petite sirah. The blend ages for 24 months in a mix of new and used French oak barrels, which are minimally toasted to avoid a disconnect between the oak flavours and the wine flavours: blackberry, black cherry, black pepper and cloves. Try with grilled mushrooms or a lamb chop with rosemary and garlic.

Paul Dolan Vineyards, Deep Red, Mendocino County (California, USA)

Mendocino Wine Co, 501 Parducci Road, Ukiah, CA 95482, USA
www.pauldolanwine.com

Paul Dolan's Italian winemaking ancestors arrived in northern California in the late nineteenth century. Dolan studied business, did a spell in the military, then studied winemaking. He managed Fetzer Vineyards when it was still family owned, becoming its first working non-family member. Fetzer launched its organic and biodynamic 'Bonterra' range under Dolan (see immediately above), making him a figurehead for a generation of northern Californian wine-growers wanting to adopt greener farming practices. While at Fetzer, Paul married Diana, one of the eleven Fetzer siblings (see p. 97 Ceàgo

Vinegarden, Sauvignon Blanc for a white wine made by another of the Fetzer siblings).

Together, Paul and Diana now have their own biodynamic vineyard in Mendocino called Dark Horse (Demeter certified). They call their top wine 'Deep Red'. This is an oak-aged Rhône-style wine blended mainly from syrah and petite sirah grapes, with smaller amounts of grenache noir and zinfandel. When Paul and Diana bought the vineyard, they ripped out its existing diseased vines and replanted using cuttings from wine-grower friends whose own vines were among the healthiest and best quality in

OTHER RHÔNE-STYLE RED WINES ARE MADE IN CALIFORNIA

...by brothers Tom and Steve Beckmen at their Purisima Mountain Vineyard in the Santa Ynez Valley; Frank and Teena Hillebrand of Narrow Gate (narrowgatevineyards. com) in Sierra Foothills; and Randall Grahm of Bonny Doon in Santa Cruz (www. bonnydoonvineyard.com), who buys in biodynamic grapes and was an early and leading exponent of Rhône-style wines in California (all Demeter certified).

Mendocino. This explains why Deep Red's flavours are so clear and pure (grapes from unhealthy cuttings produce wine with muddled, sweet-and-sour flavours). The Dolans deliberately planted the new vines on deep, nutrient-rich soils, which contained red clay – hence the name 'Deep Red'. The clay helps keep the vines from stressing when it gets too hot, making for wine with smooth rather than bitter textures. And the Dolans planted their vines in a cool site with an ideal southwest aspect, high in the Mendocino hills, at 300–365 metres (1,000–1,200 feet). Cool sites in warm climates help red wine blends like Deep Red keep their uplifting briary freshness, and not turn jammy, baked or heavy. As Paul Dolan says,

Life was hard for my grape-growing ancestors. What I learnt from them is the less you need to put into a vineyard, the more you're going to get out of it. If you set your vineyard up right, you'll waste less money on needless sprays while allowing the soil and the vines to speak clearly. From a deep red soil you should end up with a deep red wine. If you don't, it means you, not the soil or the vines, have messed up.

CHAMPAGNE
&OTHER SPARKLING WINES

Sparkling wine is the drink of celebration rather than of tree hugging. Perhaps this explains why champagne, the most famous fizz of all, is statistically the world's least 'green' wine region. Top champagne houses are part of luxury conglomerates incorporating *haute couture*, jewellery and perfume. They say a poor winemaker in Champagne is one who has to wash his own Mercedes. Booming champagne sales (roughly one million bottles are sold every day) have meant that until recently there has been little interest in biodynamics or organics, which seem like more work, more expense and more risk, and all for fewer bottles. Being green, or being seen to be green, is nice but not essential.

Yet far from being tree huggers, all the champagne growers whose wines are highlighted below say switching from conventional chemical farming to organics or biodynamics has given them more consistent yields of better quality grapes, which are easier to ferment. The champagne industry is becoming more aware of its heavier-than-average environmental impact. In recent years some of the bigger houses have made excellent champagnes from purchased biodynamic and organic grapes, and when some biodynamic vines of the family-owned Champagne Leclerc-Briant came up for sale recently, after its brilliant owner died prematurely, there was a scramble among the big houses for his vines (Demeter certified).

Sparkling wines like champagne can be made from either red or white grapes. After the grapes are crushed only the clear juice is used; the skins, which could turn the juice red, are discarded. This clear juice is fermented in a tank or (increasingly) in a barrel into a dry white wine. This is then put into a sealed bottled with some yeast and sugar, which sets off a second fermentation, creating the fizz. The fizzy wine is cloudy with yeast at this point, so the yeast is allowed to settle in the neck of the bottle by turning it upside down and freezing it. When the cork or cap on the bottle is removed the frozen plug of yeast flies out and the bottle can be topped-up and resealed ready for sale. Topping-up can see the addition of a *dosage*, or sweetener, to make the fizz taste a bit fruitier, but as you can see from the profiles below, not all producers choose to add this sweetener.

The Champagne way of making fizz, whereby the wine you drink actually fermented in the same bottle it is sold in, is now called the traditional method (*méthode traditionelle*). French wines made outside the Champagne region using the traditional method are called Crémant. All the wines featured below use the traditional method apart from Domaine Cousin-Leduc and Domaine Achard-Vincent. The way they make their fizz is explained in their individual profiles below.

Champagne Fleury, Fleur de l'Europe Brut NV (Non-Vintage) (Champagne, France)

43 Grande Rue, F-10250 Courteron (Aube), France
T:+33 (0)3.25.38.20.28 www.champagne-fleury.fr

When Jean-Pierre Fleury took over his family's Champagne vineyard in the early 1970s he became one of the first champagne growers to convert to organics. Organic growing was frowned upon at the time, but Jean-Pierre stuck with it, then converted to biodynamics in 1989. 'I am a keen astronomer,' he says, 'and I feel the best wines come from vines which are connected as much to the earth in which they grow as to the moon and stars above.' If this makes Jean-Pierre sound a bit of a 'new age' theorist he is nonetheless peerless on practicalities. For biodynamics he created a composting area in woodland around his main vine plots, taught some of his neighbours (Alain Réaut, Erick Schreiber, Thierry Hubschwerlin) the art of biodynamic composting and agreed to buy their biodynamic champagne grapes to supplement his own. Fleury now works with 25 hectares (62 acres) of biody-

Jean-Pierre Fleury between the vine rows at Champagne Fleury.

namic grapes, half of which he owns and half of which he buys (all Demeter certified).

Fleury is located in the Aube, the warmest and most southerly Champagne region where the pinot noir grape dominates. Pinot noir renders the Aube's champagnes richly textured enough to be drunk with a main course, or even tricky-to-match-with-wine starters, like smoked salmon. Fleury's Fleur de l'Europe is a classically bold, mouthfilling Aube champagne, with large, lively bubbles and opulently forthright flavours of Bramley apple and pear crumble.

Champagne Vouette et Sorbée, Fidèle Blanc de Noirs Extra Brut NV (Non-Vintage) (Champagne, France)

8 Rue de Vaux, F-10110 Buxières sur Arce (Aube), France
T:+33 (0)3.25.38.79.73 www.vouette-et-sorbee.com

Betrand Gautherot's parents were sheep farmers with a few vines in Champagne's southerly Aube sub-region. The grapes were sold to a local wine co-operative until 1997 when Bertrand took over and began making his own wine. Betrand lost his first crop to mildew. He says,

I'd seen how healthy my neighbour Jean-Pierre Fleury's vines [see p.247] had stayed. So in 1998 I converted to biodynamics [with Demeter certification]. The subsoils had become so compacted we had mudslides when it rained hard. My father, who supervises our local drinking water, says our vineyards drain better than when he was wine-growing. The soils have more life and the vines are better balanced. In the old days fresh sheep manure would be thrown on the vineyards. This had not been composted properly, so was too rich for the vines. We got high yields but of diseased grapes. Now I make biodynamic compost from properly fermented cow manure from my own cows. This feeds the soil and allows the vine roots to go deeper down. We get lower yields but healthier grapes.

As you might expect from someone now so intimately connected with his land, Bertrand makes his champagne in his parents' old sheep shed. The sheep have been replaced by the barrels in which Betrand ferments juice from his pinot noir (90 per cent) and chardonnay (10 per cent) grapes into still wines before running them by gravity into champagne bottles where they ferment a second time and acquire their bubbles. Bertrand's champagnes are made with no additions of sulphur dioxide preservative and have a cult following. His 'Blanc d'Argile' from 100 per cent chardonnay grown on clay (*argile*) is mouthwateringly taut champagne. His 'Fidèle Blanc de Noirs' is softer and denser and made from 100 per cent pinot noir. Walnut-skin in colour, it has soft, cidery flavours and such strong mouthfeel that – despite the bubbles – you should try decanting it very slowly into a large jug first. Decanting is unusual for fizz, but really pays off for oaky champagnes like this one (and David Léclapart's p.251), so that the deeply embedded fruit and earth flavours can express themselves.

Champagne Françoise Bedel, Entre Ciel et Terre Brut NV (Non-Vintage) (Champagne, France)

71 Grande Rue, F-02310 Crouttes sur Marne (Aisne), France
T:+33 (0)3.23.82.15.80   www.champagne-bedel.fr

Françoise Bedel took over her family's Champagne vineyards in 1977, but admits,

> I progressively reached a stage where I no longer felt in harmony with champagne. My champagnes seemed to taste exactly like other champagnes made many miles away and on completely different soil type, when they should have tasted very different. In 1996 I organised a tasting of champagnes produced by organic growers, including Jean-Pierre Fleury's biodynamic champagnes [see p.247], which impressed me. By 1999 my entire vineyard was under biodynamic management. We sowed barley, oats and wheat between the vine rows in winter to keep the soil loose and help our grapes be as expressive as possible. Now I feel my vines are alive, and produce wines unique to this site. I feel much closer to them.

Françoise has 9 hectares (21 acres) of which 90 per cent are red grapes, mainly pinot meunier and pinot noir (Biodyvin certified). The early ripening pinot meunier gives very musky, hawthorn-scented champagnes, as shown by Françoise's Entre Ciel et Terre ('Between Sky and Earth') bottling. This comes from clay-limestone soils, which give very tightly woven, forcefully textured, invigorating champagnes.

Champagne Larmandier-Bernier, Vieilles Vignes de Cramant Extra Brut Blanc de Blancs Grand Cru Millésimé (Champagne, France)

19 avenue du Général de Gaulle, F-51130 Vertus (Marne), France
T:+33 (0)3.26.52.13.24 www.larmandier.fr

After Pierre Larmandier-Bernier took over his family's 15-hectare (37-acre) Champagne vineyard when his father died young, he went straight to business school. There he learnt his champagnes needed to stand out from the crowd. Pierre also started tasting wines from biodynamic Alsace producers like Marc Kreydenweiss (see p. 83) and Olivier Humbrecht (see p. 86). Pierre says,

I could immediately see these domaines were farmed to allow a fuller terroir expression [wines with a unique sense of place], providing a point of difference from the mainstream.

Pierre worked with biodynamic wine-growers first-hand before converting his own vines to biodynamics (with organic certification). 'My soils were already rich in nutrients; the problem was the vines couldn't get to these nutrients,' he says, because the worms, and other soil organisms that help vine roots feed, had disappeared due to the use of weedkillers and soluble fertilizers.

We make a good living here in Champagne. I can go to the beach or go ski-ing every weekend and carry on using the same vineyard products as my father. But if we can farm better by changing, then why not?

Pierre's vines are mostly chardonnay and located in the best Champagne villages for chardonnay, namely Avize, Chouilly, Cramant, Oger and Vertus on the Côte des Blancs. Pierre presses his grapes, letting their juice look quite murky before it is allowed to ferment. Pierre says murky juice, 'contains more food for the natural yeasts, which give more complex flavours and textures than using yeast out of a packet.' His Vieilles Vignes ('old vines') champagne comes from chardonnay planted in the village of Cramant in the 1930s and 1960s. This is a multi-layered champagne: when young it has dense, clear flavours of yellow fruits and white flowers. If you can leave the wine six years or so in bottle, these flavours become breadier, broader, and more rewardingly savoury and intense, and show just how good a job Pierre Larmandier is doing at making champagne that is both classically representative of the region and reassuringly different from the mainstream.

Champagne David Léclapart, Blanc de Blancs L'Apôtre Brut NV (Non-Vintage) (Champagne, France)

8 rue St Vincent, F-51380 Trépail (Marne), France
T:+33 (0)3.26.57.07.01 david.leclapart@wanadoo.fr

David Léclapart is a very unusual champagne grower, partly because he told his mother he'd take over his late father's vines only if she allowed him to go biodynamic. This kind of ultimatum is both risky and rare in a region as socially regimented as Champagne. David is also unusual because his entire 3-hectare (7-acre) vineyard lies in a single village, Trépail. Virtually all other champagne is made from grapes blended from several villages. For all his champagnes, David ferments the grape juice into a bone-dry still white wine in 228-litre (60-gallon) wooden barrels (bought secondhand from Domaine Leflaive, see p. 39), rather than in steel tanks (barrel fermentation is still very rare in Champagne, but is becoming fashionable among biodynamic growers, Betrand Gautherot of Vouette et Sorbée, p.248, being another example). The still white wines are then bottled, where they ferment a second time to give them their fizz.

L'Apôtre is made from chardonnay planted in 1946 by David's grandfather. Only 3,000 bottles (10 barrels) are made each year. It is a Blanc de Blancs, champagne-speak for a 100 per cent chardonnay wine (most champagne is made from a blend of both red and white grapes). L'Apôtre ('the apostle') has a freshly baked breadcrust and oatmeal smell, and tastes of smooth wet stones. It is best drunk with food and decanted (see Vouette et Sorbée p.249, for why). David's other champagnes, L'Artiste and L'Amateur are also 100 per cent chardonnay, barrel-fermented wines, but from different vine plots to L'Apôtre.

Champagne Franck Pascal, Rosé Tolérance NV (Non-Vintage) (Champagne, France)

1 bis rue Valentine Regnier, 51700 Baslieux sous Châtillon (Marne), France
T:+33 (0)3.26.51.89.80

Franck and Isabelle Pascal began converting their 4-hectare (9-acre) Champagne vineyard to organics in 2000 and to biodynamics a couple of years later (with organic certification). Franck has a science background but says 'science can be a double-edged sword. It can save your life, but can also destroy it,' referring to the soldiers he saw affected by chemical warfare while working with the French army. Franck feels his vines need two things to attain balance. First, that the quite heavy limey-clay soils his vines grow in needed a kick-start with biodynamic compost made from horse and cow manure, plus grape residues left over from winemaking. 'Compost brings worms and other organisms to the soil. They soften and open the soil and allow vine roots to feed and breathe more easily.' Franck even adds whey to his compost to help it ferment as healthily as possible. The second major focus here is spraying the vines with plant and other teas. Franck says,

> These teas improve the vines' resistance to our climate and help keep them strong enough to stay disease-free. If you start drinking water only once you have arrived in the desert it is already too late. You will dehydrate and get ill. You need to prepare for the worst, and that's what we try to do in our vines.

Franck and Isabelle made a richly yeasty but tight-grained NV (non-vintage) champagne called Sagesse ('wisdom') and a more obviously exuberant pink champagne called Tolérance ('tolerance'). This is made from pinot meunier grapes, which give tulip scents, and pinot noir which gives the cool, raspberry-ripple tang.

A **non-vintage** (NV) wine blends the produce of two or more years. This is a common practice allowing winemakers to create more consistent sparkling wines, year on year.

Domaine Tripoz, Crémant de Bourgogne Blanc Nature (Burgundy, France)

Place de la Mairie, F-71000 Loché (Saône et Loire), France
T:+33 (0)3.85.35.66.09 www.tripoz.fr

It was because Céline Tripoz's Parisien family had land in the village of Loché in southern Burgundy that she met and married Laurent, a local farmer's son. Laurent was set to become a cabinet-maker, but in 1986 he turned to growing wine grapes and rootstocks instead. By 1990 he and Céline had started fermenting their own grapes, rather than sending them to the local co-operative. They expanded their vineyards at breakneck pace for the next decade. Then, in 2001, they converted their by now 11-hectare (27-acre) vineyard to biodynamics (Demeter certified).

Céline and Laurent make dry, still, effortless, creamy-crisp white wines from chardonnay planted in Mâcon-Loché, Mâcon-Vinzelles and Pouilly-Loché. Their Crémant de Bourgone Blanc (sparkling white Burgundy) is also 100 per cent chardonnay. It is labelled 'Nature' because no sugar is added – either to help the juice make a strong enough still base wine or to make this still base wine turn fizzy. Nature is a chewily authentic fizz, ideally drunk with only perfunctory ceremony, as chilled as a polar bear's paws, after you have spent a blisteringly hot day working in your vegetable garden. 20,000 bottles are made each year.

Champ Divin, Crémant du Jura Cuvée Chanson Zero Dosage (Jura, France)

39 rue du Château, F-39570 Gevingey (Jura)
T:+33 (0)3.84.24.93.41 www.champdivin.com

Both Fabrice Closset and Valérie Gaziaux had parents who practised apiculture and biodynamic gardening. Fabrice and Valérie themselves studied soil science, worked in Africa, then returned to consult to organic wine-growers in the Loire. In January 2008 the couple took over a 5-hectare (12-acre) organic vineyard in the Jura region of eastern France and converted it to biodynamics (Demeter certified). The most important plant teas used here include one made from

253

willow branches and leaves, which helps vines stay disease-free on the Jura's rich but often chilly soils, and one from valerian flowers. Fabrice says,

> We spray valerian to de-stress our vines. For example, after we prune the dormant, woody shoots in winter or trim the green sap-rich shoots in spring. Vines which have been cut really do seem to get back into their stride a bit quicker with the valerian. This is why we also spray our vines with valerian if the weather gets really hot and they suffer heat stress, or when their shoots and leaves get damaged by hail.

Fabrice and Valérie make still white wines from chardonnay and a local grape called savagnin, plus reds from pinot noir. They also make around 7,000 bottles of a sparkling Crémant du Jura each year. Called Cuvée Chanson this is blended from around one third pinot noir, which gives doughnut softness, and two thirds chardonnay, which provides a more steely roundness. Perhaps the efforts Valérie and Fabrice are making to keep their vines stress-free allows them to bottle their Cuvée Chanson without using a *'dosage'*, which is a small

amount of sweetened wine used as a top-up. A *dosage* is often used (quite legally) to give a bit of sex appeal to champagne and other sparkling wines that would otherwise taste raspingly green. 'Sparkling wines are best made from grapes picked early,' says Fabrice. 'The key thing is to be able to pick early but ripe enough in flavour so there is no need to hide any green or unripe flavours with a *dosage*.'

Domaine Cousin Leduc, Grolleau Rosé (Loire Valley, France)

7 rue du Colonel Panaget, F-49540 Martigné Briand (Maine et Loire), France
T:+33 (0)2.41.59.49.09

Joseph Cousin (born 1903) worked his 12-hectare (30-acre) Loire vineyard with horses until 1978, adopting tractors only for the final seven years of his life. His grandson Olivier, a horny-handed man of the soil if ever there was one, then took over, but took another thirteen years to fulfil his dream of ditching tractors once and for all in favour of a return to horses. Why? Olivier says,

> *Horses are cheaper. If I get a flat tyre I can fix it cheaply enough by plugging the puncture or getting a new inner tube. But if I completely shred a tyre on rocky ground it costs me time to tow the damaged tractor back from the vineyard, and money. A new tyre costs nearly the same as feeding one of my horses for an entire year. Horses are more practical because you can work with them even if the soil is too wet for a machine. Horses compact the soil less. Vines get ill in compact soils. They can't breathe or find the nutrients and water they need. Horses force you to look at your vineyard in a much more connected way because the connection they have to the soil is something a tractor never has. As a wine-grower you must sense what is going on in your vines. When you walk your vines with a horse you can hear if the right insects or bees are making the right noises, or whether the vine leaves look too shiny or too deydrated as they are ruffled by the breeze. You can't hear this from a sealed, air-conditioned cab with music from your favourite CD blasting out.*

Olivier has set aside three hectares of prairies so his equine workers can graze homegrown grasses.

He makes his wines from fermented grape juice and nothing more: no yeasts, no additives, no preservatives – just juice (Demeter certified). His Grolleau Rosé is an off-dry sparkling pink made by bottling semi-fermenting grape juice from grolleau gris and cabernet franc, then sealing this with a cork. When you pull the cork you are greeted with a cloudy, frothy wine that radiates naturalness and joy.

Domaine Huet, Vouvray Pétillant Brut (Loire Valley, France)

11–13 rue de la Croix Buisée, F-37210 Vouvray (Indre et Loire), France
T:+33 (0)2.47.52.78.87   www.huet-echansonne.com

As well as making still wines, Vouvray producer Noël Pinguet of Domaine Huet (see p. 51) also makes ridiculously underrated sparkling wines. Produced from the grapes of his younger chenin blanc vines, these bright, golden-coloured wines come in two styles: *mousseux*, which is fully sparkling as champagne, and *pétillant*, which is less fizzy, more foamy in fact, but much easier to drink with food.

The *pétillant* wines can be dry (*brut*) or off-dry (*sec*). I prefer the *sec*, partly because I have a sweet tooth, but also because I prefer its soft honey flavours to the more bready ones in the *brut*. Although either style can be drunk with food, their lightness means that they perhaps work best as aperitifs.

Domaine Achard-Vincent, Clairette de Die Méthode Dioise Ancestrale (Rhône Valley, France)

Le Village, F-26150 Sainte-Croix (Drôme), France
T:+33 (0)4.75.21.20.73   www.domaine-achard-vincent.com

The town of Die in the southern Rhône Valley seems an unlikely source of sparkling wine, but the tradition of bottling fizzy wines here is possibly older than in Champagne to the north. Cool climates produce the best sparkling wines and Die benefits from being on the high Alpine foothills at 400 metres (1,300 feet), between Valence and Montélimar. Jean-Pierre and Claudie Achard were among France's first organic wine-growers, converting in 1978. Then in 2008 their son Thomas converted the family's 12-hectare (30-acre) vineyard to biodynamics (Demeter certified). Thomas makes biodynamic compost using manure from a local herd of organic milk cows, plus the grape pips and stems left over from the 100,000 bottles of sparkling wine produced here each year.

Thomas's Clairette de Die Méthode Ancestrale is a blend of 80 per cent muscat blanc à petit grains and 20 per cent clairette. The *méthode ancestrale* means the grapes are pressed and their juice starts fermenting in open tanks. While still bubbling away it is transferred to sealed bottles where it continues fermenting, but more slowly than before, as the wine yeast struggles to cope with the carbon dioxide gas produced, which gives the wine its fizz. Once the yeast gives up, the wine is run back to a clean tank, filtered clear and re-bottled. The resulting wine has the heady, grapey sweetness of muscat, a crisp backbone from the clairette and a warm, bready yeast character from the fermentation in bottle. With a gentle fizz and only around 7 per cent alcohol, this is an incredibly refreshing summer quaffer.

Domaine Martin Schaetzel, Crémant d'Alsace Blanc (Alsace, France)

3 rue de la 5ème Division Blindée, 68770 Ammerschwihr (Haut-Rhin), France
T:+33 (0)3.89.47.11.39   www.martin-schaetzel.com

Martin Schaetzel bottled his first wines in 1930. His nephew Jean and Jean's wife, Béatrice, took over here in 1986. Jean's day job is teaching wine-growing and winemaking. From 1997 he began converting his own 13-hectare (32-acre) vineyard to biodynamics (Demeter certified). He argued locally that biodynamics was a good way of improving wine quality because it forces growers to be less greedy, as they must ask lower grape yields from their vines (Alsace has the highest wine grape yields in France). Although some of his neighbours told Jean he should stick to his day job and not be such a busybody telling everyone else what to do, plenty more felt he had a point. Realising talk was good but practical action was better, Jean played a central role in organising a communal composting programme in Alsace's key wine villages. This allowed wine-growers to compost the grapeskins, pips and stems left over from winemaking with locally sourced animal manure. The composting programme, called 'Vignes Vivantes' or 'living vines', is a key reason why Alsace is now one of the greenest wine regions in the world: over 10 per cent of its nearly 16,000 hectares (40,000 acres) of vines are certified organic or biodynamic.

Schaetzel specialises in still, often medium-dry white wines from riesling, gewürztraminer and pinot gris from his top grand cru site, Kaefferkopf. For everyday drinking, try his sparkling Alsace white, made from hand-picked bunches of pinot blanc pressed super-slowly (up to fifteen hours) for the clearest tasting juice, producing an incisive, take-your-breath-away fizz.

Cavas Recaredo, Cava Brut Nature Vintage (Penedes, Spain)

C/ Tamarit nº 10, 08770 Sant Sadurní d'Anoia (Barcelona), Spain
T:+34 (0)938.910214 www.recaredo.es

Spain's sparkling wine or 'cava' production centres on the town of Sant Sadurní d'Anoia near Barcelona on the Mediterranean coast. The high hills inland from here, in the Penedès sub-region, get the kind of night cooling that grapes used in sparkling wines need. Brothers Josep and Antoni Mata Casanovas took over the winery from their father, who founded it in the 1920s. Josep says,

We heard about biodynamics while on sales trips to France and Germany. Then we attended seminars hosted by well-known biodynamic consultants. We converted to organics, which was straightforward in our sunny climate. We trialled biodynamics, but with no consultant. Just our own curiosity carried us through. We found organics worked very well but biodynamics worked even better. We became the first Spanish vineyard for [still] white and sparkling wines to be awarded full Demeter biodynamic certification.

Recaredo has 50 hectares (120 acres) of vines and makes its Brut Nature Vintage from the three classic cava grapes: xarel-lo for braeburn-apple roundness, macabeu for buttery texture, and parellada for floral flavours. The classic bread-and-oatmeal character the cava picks up while ageing in the bottle on its spent fermentation yeast is protected by Cavas Recaredo who choose not to add extra sugar to make the fizz taste fruiter, even though that would be permitted under cava's rules. This is a fizz to savour with a couple of friends rather than with food.

Avondale, Armilla Brut (Paarl, South Africa)

Klein Drakenstein, Paarl 7624, South Africa
T: +27 (0)21.8631976 www.avondalewine.co.za

Johnathan Grieve's family produced a successful range of natural health foods before getting into wine by buying Avondale in 1996. This 100-hectare (250-acre) vineyard is located in Paarl, one of South Africa's hottest sub-regions. Its soils and vines, however, show few obvious signs of heat stress. Johnathan has made great efforts to align the energy flows in the soil so that the vines (which have organic certification) can grow in the most healthy way. The biodynamic preparations are transmitted to the vines using radionics or energy waves, rather than by spraying or spreading them using a tractor. Tractors are used, but to spray herb teas and microbe-rich compost teas on the vines to increase their disease resistance. Ducks patrol the vines to eat any snails trying to make grape bunches

Johnathan Grieve of Avondale, South Africa

their home. And worried about cross-contamination from GM crops (which are allowed in South Africa), Jonathan has even entertained the idea of infusing his land with minute particles of gold because 'gold is uncorruptible'.

From Johnathan's smart gravity-fed winery emerge full-throated Bordeaux- and Rhône-style red wines and textured, subtle dry whites from chardonnay, chenin blanc and white Rhône grapes. His top wine for me, however, is his sparkling white 'Armilla'. Johnathan ferments its chardonnay juice into a very crisp, dry still white wine, which (unusually) he then leaves in tank for two years to soften. This still wine is then bottled with added sugar and yeast for the bubbles to form. The result is a mouthfilling sparkler with juicy peach flavours and an irresistibly creamy mouth-feel. 10,000 bottles are made each year.

Duck patrol: Avondale Wines in South Africa uses ducks to control snails and slugs.

Quartz Reef, Methode Traditionelle Non-Vintage, Bendigo (Central Otago, New Zealand)

6–8 Hughes Crescent, Cromwell 9342, Central Otago, New Zealand
T:+64 (0)3.445.30844 www.quartzreef.co.nz

Rudi Bauer got into biodynamics as a youngster, 'perhaps because of my Austrian blood,' he jokes (Rudolf Steiner, who created biodynamics in 1924, was also Austrian). During his first job, Rudi persuaded his boss to stop using weedkillers on prime vineyards in New Zealand's southerly Central Otago region. Rudi then developed his own 25-hectare (61-acre) vineyard nearby, at Quartz Reef, but only went biodynamic in 2008 (Demeter certified) after years of conventional farming. He says,

The soils are so rocky they look like Mars. Weedkillers got the weeding done cheaply but they left the soil harder and rockier than it was before. To avoid weedkillers, we bought a tractor-mounted weeding machine, but it kept smashing on the rocks and ripping irrigation lines because the ground is so uneven. We lifted the irrigation lines up to knee-height and removed tonnes of rocks from the vineyards by hand. Then we made concerted efforts to spread our homemade biodynamic compost and manure-based sprays, reversing the soil hardening the weedkillers caused. There is no doubt that our vineyard, from the soil up to the people working in it, is a happier place since we began converting to biodynamics.

Although Rudi makes lovely still pinot gris white wines with crunchy apple flavour, and also really diverting pinot noir reds, he is best known for some of New Zealand's top sparkling wines. His Methode Traditionelle Non-Vintage is benchmark New Zealand fizz. It is made from 70 per cent pinot noir and 30 per cent chardonnay, and Rudi says he styles it to be 'soft rather than acidic, dry tasting but ripe. New Zealand grapes have bold fruit flavours, and while we are not trying to hide that sense of fruit we don't want to load the wine with too much overt sweetness.' The result is an unashamedly moreish fizz you want to drink heartily rather than sip nervously: a party wine with abundant class.

OTHER BIODYNAMIC CHAMPAGNE PRODUCERS OF NOTE
...include Yves Dufour (Demeter certified); Hughes Godmé (www. champagne-godme.fr), who has some vines dating from before World War One (Biodyvin certified); and Benoît Lahaye, who is now ploughing his vines by horse (Biodyvin certified). Outside the Champagne region in France, sparkling wines are made by Pierre Martin's Domaine de la Pinte (www.lapinte.fr) in the Jura (Demeter certified).

SPARKLING WINES FROM BIODYNAMIC ESTATES OUTSIDE FRANCE
...include Daniela and Thomas Harteneck (www.weingut-harteneck.de) in Germany's Baden Markgräflerland where the wines are labelled as 'sekt'; Antonella and Marco Folicello (www. folicello.it) for lambrusco with no added sulphites from Italy's Emilia-Romagna; the I Tre Poggi (www.itrepoggi) estate in Italy's Piedmont for the grapey-sweet moscato d'asti, Summerhill Pyramid Winery (summerhill.bc.ca) in Okanagan, Canada; and Laverstoke Park Farm (www.laverstoke.co.uk) and Springfields in England. (These are all Demeter certified.)

Listing of Wines by Place

CHAMPAGNE

CORSICA

JURA AND SAVOY

HUNGARY
Pendits, Dialog, Tokaji 116

ITALY
Amerighi Stefano, Syrah, Tuscany 177
Cantine del Notaio, La Firma Aglianico del Vulture, Basilicata 133
Cascina degli Ulivi, Filagnotti, Gavi, Piedmont 61
Cascina Zerbetta, Barbera del Monferrato, Piedmont 134
Cefalicchio, Ponte della Lama Rosato, Puglia 126
Cooperative Olearia Vinicola Orsogna, Coste di More Montepulciano
  d'Abruzzo, Abruzzo 146
Fattoria Caiarossa, Toscana Rosso, Tuscany 213
Fattoria La Vialla, Casa Conforto Chianti Superiore, Tuscany 209
Foradori, Granato Vigneti delle Dolomiti, Trentino-Alto Adige 186
La Raia, Gavi, Piedmont 61
Loacker Schwarhof, Sauvignon Blanc Tasnim, South Tyrol 96
Nuova Cappelletta, Barbera del Monferrato, Piedmont 135
Pian dell'Orino, Rosso di Montalcino, Tuscany 173
Pievalta, Verdicchio dei Castelli di Jesi Dominè, Marche 108
San Giuseppe, Brunello di Montalcino, Tuscany 172
Tenuta di Valgiano, Colline Lucchesi Rosso, Tuscany 212

NEW ZEALAND
Burn Cottage Vineyard, Pinot Noir, Central Otago 168
Felton Road, Pinot Noir, Bannockburn, Central Ontago 167
The Millton Vineyard, Chenin Blanc Te Arai, Gisborne 55
Quartz Reef, Methode Traditionnelle Non Vintage, Bendigo,
  Central Otago 262
Richmond Plains, Sauvignon Blanc, Nelson 101
Seresin Estate, Sauvignon Blanc, Marlborough 101

PORTUGAL
Aphros, Branco Vinho Verde 71

SOUTH AFRICA
Avondale, Armilla Brut, Paarl 259
Reyneke, Cornerstone Red, Stellenbosch 206
Reyneke, Sauvignon Blanc Reserve, Stellenbosch 105